Information Technology and Global Governance

Series Editor

Derrick L. Cogburn, American University, Bethesda, MD, USA

Information Technology and Global Governance focuses on the complex interrelationships between the social, political, and economic processes of global governance that occur at national, regional, and international levels. These processes are influenced by the rapid and ongoing developments in information and communication technologies. At the same time, they affect numerous areas, create new opportunities and mechanisms for participation in global governance processes, and influence how governance is studied. Books in this series examine these relationships and influences.

More information about this series at
https://link.springer.com/bookseries/14855

Rebekah Dowd

The Birth of Digital Human Rights

Digitized Data Governance as a Human Rights Issue in the EU

palgrave
macmillan

Rebekah Dowd
Department of Political Science
Midwestern State University
Wichita Falls, TX, USA

Information Technology and Global Governance
ISBN 978-3-030-82968-1 ISBN 978-3-030-82969-8 (eBook)
https://doi.org/10.1007/978-3-030-82969-8

Cover illustration: MR.Cole_Photographer/Moment/Getty Images

This Palgrave Macmillan imprint is published by the registered company Springer Nature Switzerland AG
The registered company address is: Gewerbestrasse 11, 6330 Cham, Switzerland

To the one who always remains, is ever faithful, and continually surprises me.

Acknowledgments

Books do not write themselves; they are written by people. While this book was written entirely by me, and therefore any credit or blame for the content should lay at my door, I would be woefully remiss if I didn't acknowledge the people without whom I could not have finished this project. Each person listed here has my deepest gratitude.

To Those At Home

Jenson, Sydney, Ethan, and Lily-Kat: you are my sources of inspiration and encouragement. Thanks for the love, laughter, and patience! To my parents: you've always supported me, in places near and far; thanks for giving your love in this way. To Dr. Adnan Rasool and Jia Rasool: your individual wisdoms and our friendship make me want to be worthy of your support. To IM: Your contribution lay in our future, but I'm holding you to that promise.

To My GSU Family

Dr. Charles Hankla, Professor Jelena Subotic, and Dr. Toby Bolsen: I could not have chosen a better dissertation committee. You've repeatedly reminded me of how fortunate I have been to enjoy your mentorship. To Professor Bill Long—thank you for showing me kindness, giving advice, and teaching me how to follow my own path. To my colleagues—Recha

Reid, Dr. Alexandra Pauley, and Christopher Jackson—you guys are great reviewers and even better friends.

To My Oxford Community

Dr. Lynn Robson: you opened my eyes to what scholarship could be for a non-traditional student. Dr. Ian Finlay: you taught me to be a better writer, to eat some chocolate along the way, and to keep seeing myself as an Oxford woman. Dr. Lucas Kello: thank you for giving space to a visitor, who learned more than you know from being an observer of your scholarship and leadership at work. Much thanks also to Dr. Viktor Mayer-Schönberger, for giving time and words of encouragement; many people publish, but few invest in others.

To My MSU Community

Dr. Linda Veazey: thank you for giving me a chance and for supporting me time and again. To the amazing Mary Gant: your positive spirit is so beautiful. Thanks to Dr. Lee Gagum for help with German translations. To Emily Beaman and Brendon Miller: your outstanding research assistance is but a sign of great things to come for both of you. Zetta Cannedy: thanks for the attention to detail on even the most tedious of tasks! Caroline Gomez: you are one of the rare humans walking the planet, whose spirit lights a candle for all around her; I will be following your future successes.

To Those Who Provided a Word, Or a Space, in Due Season

So much could be said about the research communities created by Dr. Amanda Bittner and Dr. Mirya Holman; thank you both for crafting connections literally across the planet, and spaces in which academic writers can meet, be held accountable, and share some humor. Thanks to Dr. Leanna Powners, for offering timely publishing advice. To the Collective and Frank & Joe's cafes: thank you for providing friendly baristas, great coffee, and peaceful ambience, without which this caffeinated writer could not have produced text. Thanks to Rebecca Roberts, Madison Allum, and Punitha Balasubramaniam at Palgrave Macmillan, who read, reviewed, emailed, and reminded, so that this book would become reality.

A huge word of thanks to Professor Derrick Cogburn, the editor of the Information and Technology Governance series: you opened the door to me to become a published book author.

Contents

List of Figures

List of Tables

PART I

The Origin of Digital Human Rights

Digital human rights are an extension of human rights protections over personal, digitized data. Anyone using the internet in the West today is aware, though they may not realize it, of the presence of digital human rights. Most of us are much less aware of what these rights entail, how they originated in Europe, and why. This book offers an explanation for this outcome.

In the first chapter of the book, I provide an overview of my claims. Personal, digitized data is important for all of us today, given the internet-based world in which we live, and making this issue very important to governments who must decide how to regulate data. However, in addition to governments, certain interest groups are particularly focused on data use. These include firms within the digital economy, national security actors seeking to ensure social order, and human rights advocates who highlight the links between personal data and individual identity. This chapter outlines a two-phase process, whereby these three groups moved to impact data policy within the European Union. The EU has since become not only the point of origin for digital human rights in Europe, but also exports these rights globally.

Chapter 2 digs deeper into the history of digital human rights. Using the international relations theories of realism, liberal institutionalism, and constructivism, I map out how digital human rights first emerged within the European Union. Then, I ask, *under what conditions did EU states create their national policy preferences*? To answer this question, it's necessary to look more carefully at data brokering, security threats, and the power of epistemic community norms. Next, using another international relations (IR) tool, regime theory, I describe how the entire group of EU countries were able to cooperate and indeed prioritize a convergence point for high levels of digitized data protection in the EU. By the time you have finished both chapters in Part I, you will have a clearer understanding of the key variables at stake, and therefore be able to interpret the data presented in Part II.

CHAPTER 1

Digitized Data as a Political Object

In mid-March 2018, the Cambridge Analytica data scandal broke onto the international news cycle. Over 50 million social media users in the United States and Europe had information about their internet behavior collected, analyzed, and catalogued for political use by candidates during elections, via the meta-data people generated while online with Facebook.[1] Facebook executive Mark Zuckerberg was reprimanded during subsequent hearings held by Congress and the European Parliament. In contrast to the limited or lack of data protections in many regions, when Members of the European Parliament (MEPs) met with Zuckerberg, they cited violations of existing data protection laws that had been breached. Yet, one has to ask, why had Europe, and the European Union (EU) in particular, established a more aggressive policy stance toward protecting digitized data than had other regions?[2]

This book argues that protection of digitized personal data as a fundamental human right, or "digital human rights," emerged as a result of domestic and international pressures placed on EU policy-makers by

[1] Granville (2018).

[2] Fuster (2016); EU policies over data began in 1973 with the *Community policy on data processing*. US action began with the 1977 US Privacy Protection Study Commission, resulting in no legally binding legislation. As of this writing, there remains no single comprehensive U.S. federal law that constrains data collection and use (see Jolly and Loeb 2017).

R. Dowd, *The Birth of Digital Human Rights*, Information Technology and Global Governance,
https://doi.org/10.1007/978-3-030-82969-8_1

specific actors promoting data protection as a fundamental human right. I define digital human rights as the extension fundamental human rights protections for digital data tied to a person's identity and behavior in the physical or virtual realms. Digitized data refers to any data that is created, stored, used, transferred, and/or manipulated using computer technology, in this case, data of a personal nature. Digitized data can exist entirely on internal computer networks, or it can be cloud-based. At the domestic level, three key structural factors influenced EU member states' national data laws. At the international level, key international organizations pressured states to comply with policy recommendations that led to supranational data protection. In both scenarios, the strategic placement of legal and human rights scholars contributed to the expanding scope of digital human rights.[3]

Digital human rights protections concern data that has been stored in two ways. First, personal data began as information recorded in manual forms, such as in traditional paper records. Today, personal data is largely "cyber data." Cyber data describes information that is collected about individuals, including their personal internet preferences and habits, as well as private financial or personal information collected while they use devices or computers connected to the internet.[4] Second, digitized cyber data will often include personal information regarding individuals' demography, personal beliefs, political actions, and general behaviors. Within this book, the term "digital human rights," or DHR, refers to human rights surrounding digitized personal data, including cyber data. National data governance varied among EU states from the 1970s–1990s, including three main policy preferences: treating data as an economic commodity, seeing it as a surveillance tool to protect national security, and tying data to privacy and identity rights. However, after the mid-1990s, the EU passed supranational data policies resulting in convergence around a largely protective data regime based on human rights. The resulting complex institutional environment calls for uniformity of protection in

[3] Supranational legislation refers to policy mandates which were passed through a majority vote, and include a requirement for policy implementation even among states that did not vote to affirm the policy. It contrasts with intergovernmental policy, which passes into law via unanimous acceptance.

[4] For the remainder of this book, when I refer to "data", this refers to digitized personal and/or cyber data.

some areas, but leaves policy gaps open to state interpretation in other areas.

Political science research examining data has explained policy-making in some areas, such as governmental data use within cyber defensive practices, or as a part of national security surveillance of risky actors, but our understanding remains thin of the root causes for creating digital human rights around the personal data of the mass public. It's important to ask, what concerns arose in Europe that resulted in the European Union becoming the first area to create jurisdiction relating to protecting digital human rights? We do know that personal data was originally seen as a commodity with potential global economic impact, and has continued to remain as such.[5] Data access and distribution has been likened to a civil society tool, facilitating democratic discourse.[6] Other research has shown data and internet control as a byproduct of information management efforts by authoritarian states,[7] or has investigated data surveillance for national security purposes.[8] None of this literature addressed *why* digital human rights emerged as a supranational mandate for the EU, despite diverse national policy preferences.

This project seeks to explain *why* and *how* the European Union policy moved toward a rights-based stance on digitized data, the phenomenon of digital human rights (DHR). First mover states, such as Sweden and Germany, incorporated digital human rights into national legislation, due to pressure from human rights interests within these countries during the 1960s and 1970s. As data digitization and computer databanks grew in scope, national laws were often at conflict with one another. The EU Commission took the decision to create a supranational data legislation in order to harmonize member states' divergent policies. Initial EU data laws in the 1980s revolved around preserving the economic value of commodified data, particularly as a part of Single Market integration goals. In 1995, the EU created the first comprehensive digital human rights law applicable to both public and private sectors, allowing for multiple stakeholders' aims, such as data freedoms in business and security arenas, while also preserving data privacy.

[5] Mayer-Schönberger and Cukier (2013) and Mayer-Schönberger and Ramge (2018).

[6] Powers (2015) and Wischmeyer (2019).

[7] Mueller (2010).

[8] Choucri (2012).

While groundbreaking in nature, Directive 95/46/EC became increasingly obsolete as technological advances expanded the users of digitized data and the applications to which it might by applied. Working Party 29 (WP 29), a committee staffed with legal rights professionals and academics, was tasked by the EU Commission with data policy oversight. WP 29 suggested a series of expanded human rights protections from 1995 to 2016. One of the greatest areas of conflict arose over the obligation of third-party states to protect EU citizens' data in accordance with Directive 95. Over time, the utility of Directive 95 diminished to the point of requiring an updated piece of legislation to address a wide variety of gaps in specificity and the need for new protections: The General Data Protection Regulation (GDPR) replaced Directive 95 in 2016. At present, the EU not only enforces the digital human rights obligations upon EU member states, but it has increasingly shown itself willing to pressure other governments, such as the United States, and private actors, such as firms, to fully protect EU citizens' data according to GDPR standards. The GDPR contains the most stringent global standard for DHR, while still allowing for economic commodification and security use of digitized data. Understanding the process by which this policy originated is extremely valuable to our larger knowledge about EU policy policymaking involving multiple interest areas. Let's look at each of the main areas in order.

The Multiple Uses of Digitized Data

Internet Data as an Economic Commodity

As mentioned, researchers have linked data use to economic development and growth. In the early 1980s, the OECD (Organisation for Economic Co-operation and Development) promoted the idea that data commodification (treatment of data as an economic commodity) was crucial to future economic growth among its member states. Later, the organization, whose membership includes a number of European and North American states, would promote internet access diffusion as a crucial expansion of communication infrastructure, integral to business growth. This was emphasized particularly for low development states trying to catch up with early industrializing states.[9] Linking data

[9] OECD (2009); See also OECD Digital Economy Papers, multiple years.

commodification and internet access with the value of access to telephone, electricity, or banking services, economists emphasized the importance of allowing developing states to generate economic opportunities and facilitate growth via data processing and internet diffusion.[10] Other researchers disagreed with that notion, arguing that ICT (information and communications technology) expansion and internet connectivity did not *directly* contribute to larger economic growth, but indirectly improved trade.[11] Increased trade then led to expanded growth. Cast as facilitators of other business activity, internet diffusion and data use were viewed as highly important to economic growth.

In a slightly different look at the financial impact of data, newer work focused on the economic value of "big data" generated through internet use.[12] The successful business model of Facebook, Amazon, Apple, Netflix, Alphabet/Google (FAANG)[13] relies upon generation of big data as an economic commodity similar to labor or capital, during the process of surveillance capitalism.[14] Data-based service providers initially often hide the fact that their profits depend on the continued ability to collect data from consumers without restriction and then sell this data to other corporations. They promote the idea that internet interaction represents users having critical access to an information space, similar to that of press freedom, when in fact what these firms offer users is the right to access the internet marketplace.[15] The services provided by FAANG have generated enormous caches of data that have fueled the largest amount of growth in the ICT sector to date.[16] As states attempt to securitize or protect cyber data, including data managed by big-data firms like Microsoft and Amazon, these corporations pushed back to ensure

[10] Oyedemi (2015).

[11] Meijers (2014).

[12] Big data includes cyber data generated by mass volume of internet use on mobile and internet-ready devices. Big data contains front end-data (personal details that are divulged as text is typed) as well as meta-data (likes, content visited, internet use patterns, internet profiling of users).

[13] Facebook, Amazon, Apple, Netflix, and Alphabet (FAANG).

[14] Mayer-Schönberger and Cukier (2013) and Zuboff (2015).

[15] Powers (2015).

[16] Jorgensen (2017).

that their data profiteering business model remains protected.[17] As noted with the Cambridge Analytica scandal at the beginning of this chapter, the public and governments are now demanding more data use accountability during surveillance capitalism.

Looking forward, social scientists predict that data-rich markets will continue to evolve and impact the mechanisms of successful economies.[18] Viktor Mayer-Schönberger and Thomas Ramge hypothesize that the exponential power of the internet to facilitate communication will likely alter the value of money through an effect upon market coordination.[19] They argue that data-rich markets will disproportionately benefit big-data intermediaries (including major data brokers such as Google), who will transmit the latent wealth in data to the markets that need it most. If the financial services and banking sectors do not adapt to the commodification of meta-data and adjust their business practices accordingly, their ability to profit from data-rich markets will be minimized at best and non-existent at worse. Again, all of this activity is reliant upon personal and cyber data generated by billions of internet users.

Digitized Data Distribution as a Public Good

Internet accessible data distribution is often framed as a critical civil society mechanism for promoting healthy democracy.[20] Research shows that the internet has become an informational tool and a new public space for the exchange of free political debate.[21] Similar to traditional broadcast media such as television and radio, or traditional print media like newspapers, data about politicians and other governmental actors disseminated on websites and social media serve as government accountability tools.[22] As a result, individuals and groups are able to practice a virtual form of civic activism.[23] Online activism has occurred around many issue areas,

[17] Upcoming: F. Cheneval (2017) and Jorgensen and Desai (2017).

[18] Burton-Jones (1999), Mayer-Schönberger and Cukier (2013), Mayer-Schönberger and Ramge (2018) and Powers (2015).

[19] Mayer-Schönberger and Ramge (2018).

[20] Margetts et al. (2016) and Powers (2015).

[21] Bassini (2019), Papacharissi (2010) and Tolbert and McNeal (2003).

[22] Deibert et al. (2010) and Karpf (2016).

[23] Margetts et al. (2016).

including opposition to multilateral investment agreements,[24] support by NGOs for the international mine ban treaty,[25] and the Arab Spring protests promoting democratization.[26] In fact, political participation in the modern world will be handicapped if a population does not have access to key data about government misbehavior via the internet or have the ability to circulate such data via mobile means.[27] In addition, using the internet has opened political opportunities to communities whose voices have been previously disenfranchised, or amplified voices seeking an opportunity to disseminate their political views.[28] Lack of internet access or having government restrictions on how individuals distribute data using mobile networks or the internet is identified as limiting political human rights, similar to restrictions on public protests, or bans on secret ballot voting.[29]

While some Western states identify internet access as a public space ensuring political participation, a number of non-Western states fear the loss of government control over information disseminated to citizens. For these states, the internet and exchange of free information (data) is a political tool which could contribute to political or social disorder, something they seek to control outside of Western norms of free access.[30] For instance, China and Russia created the International Code of Conduct for Information Security inside their Shanghai Cooperation Organization in 2011, primarily as a challenge to US hegemony over this issue area. To date, China has the most aggressive protection against global internet exposure, by setting protocols programmed into routers or software at key choke points designed to block certain outside subject matter.[31] Needless to say, the lists of prohibited content include anything critical of state practices or the Communist party, in addition to Western entertainment deemed a threat to Chinese culture. China is not alone, as Russian

[24] Deibert (2000).

[25] Beier (2003).

[26] Eltantawy and Wiest (2011) and Wolfsfeld et al. (2013).

[27] Godberg (2011).

[28] Norris (2001) and Wischmeyer (2019).

[29] Joyce (2015) and Wicker and Santosa (2013).

[30] Choucri (2012).

[31] Deibert and Rohonzinski—Chapter 1, *Access Controlled*, volume edited by Deibert et al. (2010).

authorities have blocked access to Skype and Facebook, among other platforms, with access to such sights deemed "politically disruptive."[32] Notably, though prior research on this topic has grown our understanding of the norms of internet access and usage, it has focused less upon the implications of internet governance over personal, digitized data.

Data as Information Weaponry

Some states rely on data and data networks not only as a tool for surveillance, but also as offensive warfare. The underlying assumption is that the ever-present threats between states motivate creative development and deployment of "virtual weapons" used for national defense or offense.[33] Cyber-structural attacks can be perpetrated by states or private actors who use data in "deliberate actions to alter, disrupt, deceive, degrade, or destroy computer systems or networks or the information and/or programs resident in or transiting these systems or networks."[34] Utilization of cyber data and online data networks occurs during general surveillance, deployment of espionage software, and denial of service attacks on critical infrastructure like government or banking websites (purportedly used by Russia against Georgia and Estonia).[35]

In the pursuit of government interests, collection of the personal data of citizens or persons abroad becomes a byproduct of national security.[36] As such, states will utilize invasive data surveillance inside and outside state lines.[37] These practices directly and indirectly impact governments and politicians, but also impact non-state actors, be they private citizens or corporations. The Snowden leaks revealed how vastly invasive state surveillance led to mass acquisition of personal data, in violation of the privacy of global political leaders and the general public.[38] Politicians'

[32] Nocetti (2015).

[33] Kello (2017).

[34] Owens et al. (2009, p. 1) and National Research Council (2010, p. viii).

[35] Osnos et al. (2017) and R. J. Deibert (2013).

[36] Deibert (2013, 2020).

[37] Lyon (2014) and Friedewald et al (2017).

[38] Edgar (2017).

private emails and "fake news" stories have been released for geopolitical purposes on social media and on Wikileaks.[39] Confidentiality attacks and illegally obtained intellectual property have contributed to sticky trade relations between the United States and China, as the United States accuses China of unfair economic practices in violation of WTO (World Trade Organization) principles.[40] Clearly, non-authorized data acquisition and distribution has grown across time.

The Internet and Data Governance

Since the 1990s, when wider internet diffusion began in academia and governments, researchers predicted data policy convergence due to the expected outcry against invasion of privacy from networked databanks.[41] Mueller cited the commonality of sovereignty threats faced by all states, as their need to cope with transnational interconnectivity and increased communications between private actors should drive the desire for new transnational policy on internet governance, including data privacy.[42] Like Mueller, Newman expected global policy convergence favoring consumer data privacy given the pressure the EU placed upon MNCs (multinational corporations) to protect individuals' identity when using EU citizens' data.[43] Yet policy convergence has *not* occurred outside of the European Union. For instance, the US model relies upon corporate self-regulation of data privacy, while the EU has codified a more top-down regulatory model.[44] In addition, many hybrid regimes, or non-democracies expressly forbid free internet access, and/or offer alternative, government-created social media platforms imbedded with their own citizen surveillance tools.[45]

In general, much of the data governance literature has tried to explain legalization of the privacy aspect of data and how these laws effect

[39] Brooking and Singer (2016).

[40] Singer and Friedman (2014, p. 70).

[41] C. J. Bennett (1992), Blackmer (2019) and Dunleavy et al. (2006).

[42] Mueller (2010).

[43] Newman (2008).

[44] Newman (2008)

[45] Friedewald et al. (2017) and Deibert (2020).

states' behavior in terms of surveillance.[46] Other literature postulates that future internet use could result in governments setting behavior-based protections, attempt to control general functions of the internet, and/or allow for some "virtual forgetting" of digitized data when demanded by consumers.[47] Far less is known about the role of sub-state interests in shaping government policy preferences. There is worry that increased privacy protections could result in increasing information when accessing online platforms or social media sites. Internet users may be asked to compromise on data protections, in order to receive free online services.[48]

Problematically, governments can and do collect data on individuals, yet do not classify their practices in the same way as online consumer surveillance, but disconnect the data collection from the privacy of individuals on the other side of a screen somewhere.[49] In other words, if a computer program and not a human individual collects the data and sifts it for dangerous activity, governments may not define this activity as an invasion of personal privacy. Despite these practices by the United States and other states, at times the public has been willing to forego freedom of control over their data to shore up national security against domestic or international terrorists, or others seeking to harm the public.[50] Given these findings, where does this leave our understanding of the emergence of digital human rights in the EU?

This book reveals that domestic interests can and do have significant power, both pre- and post-legislation, to alter not only domestic legislation, but also regional policy preferences. In the case of the EU, individual states crafted national data legislation based on their domestic pressures: the United Kingdom chose data commodification priorities to achieve regional and global ICT competitiveness, while Germany and Sweden faced privacy and surveillance concerns which mandated a more human-rights based approach. Cross-border data mobility placed additional pressure on states, as divergent data policies generated conflicting data management practices. The EU chose a human rights foundation,

[46] Bamburger and Mulligan (2013), Bennett (1992), Flaherty (1989), Fuster (2016), Newman (2008), Petkova (2019), Pollicino and Susi (2019) and Soh et al. (2019).

[47] H. Z. Margetts (2009).

[48] Lenard and Rubin (2010).

[49] Gros et al. (2017) and Schneier (2015, p. 152).

[50] Schneier (2015, p. 268).

with provisions for business and security data utilization. The implied goal was to treat digitized data protection as a fundamental human right.

Theoretical Foundation

I identify two phases of the causal pathway toward EU digital human rights development. National policies were created from 1970 to 1999, during "Phase I." Key domestic structural factors, including security threats, contribution to the economy by ICT firms, and input by legal and human rights scholars contributed to national policy preferences during these decades. During "Phase II" (the mid-1990s to present), the European Union created EU Directives and Regulations signifying the emergence of digital human rights. It was during this second phase that EU member states determined which national preferences would prevail at the EU level, and which compromises would be accepted when national policies were at conflict with one other.[51]

Phase I: 1970-Mid 1990s

The origin of digital human rights in the EU began in the 1970s, as individual states set national policies. During Phase I, the public and private sector computerization of personal data expanded rapidly. States had to decide how to treat the automatic processing of data, data storage, and the rapid growth of networked databanks. Policies varied in three distinct directions. Some saw personal data as important to the flow of business in the Single Area Market; these states sought freedom of movement for data as an economic commodity. Some identified data as a law enforcement tool; these states legalized data access for various national security actors. Finally, some linked data protections to the larger human rights regime of individual privacy, thereby adding legal protections for digitized data. While these policies are not mutually exclusive, when these three interests came into conflict, states had to choose a primary preference, essentially generating a normative hierarchy.

[51] Voigt and von dem Bussche (2017).

Phase II: Mid-1990s to Present Day

At the beginning of Phase II (mid-1990s), the widespread diffusion of internet use forced advanced economies to acknowledge the need for cyber data policies. As noted, national level policies were created in Phase I, but little region-wide coherence existed. In some cases, existing national policies set conflicting expectations during cross-border data transfers for business use or security cooperation. Intergovernmental organizations (IGOs) such as the OECD and the Council of Europe (CoE) suggested a series of protective frameworks for member states that would reduce policy confusion and facilitate transnational data mobility. The European Commission responded to these suggestions by moving data governance onto the EU legislative agenda.

The EU Commission, Council, and Parliament faced policy convergence challenges related to competing national preferences among EU Member States. The mixed preferences of particularly influential states such as Germany (for rights-based protections) and the United Kingdom (for data commodification), prevailed at the supranational level. During the legislative process, the EU Commission and Council utilized advice from epistemic professionals, often from the legal field, to provide policy options for the Union. Specifically, a permanent advisory committee known as Working Party 29 had enormous impact upon the evolution of DHR from 1995 to 2016. Despite growing numbers of national laws since 1970 that included mechanisms for digital human rights, EU data protection continues to evolve, and the aggressive global stance for data protections taken by the EU warrants additional explanation, particularly given the international impact of EU policy-making.

The Research Puzzle

The recent Cambridge Analytica scandal exemplifies the core dilemma addressed in this book: *Why and How Did EU States Create Digitized Data Policies in Relation to Competing Domestic Interests for Data Commodification, Digitized Data Surveillance by Security Officials, or Digital Human Rights*? This book uncovers the ways in which states prioritized between the competing interests and in multiple governance spaces. First and foremost, it is important to recognize that data legislation in the European Union happened at two levels.[52] National

[52] Putnam (1988) and Milner (1997).

policy-makers were constrained by the wishes of domestic interest groups. The domestic policy environment contained multiple stakeholders that attempted to influence policy outcomes. These groups organized and advocated for laws that would be the most beneficial to them within their country. Second, data policy coordination between EU member states experienced the same competitive struggle for policy power that had occurred at the national level. Member states were expected to abide by the constraints of membership criteria; regional policy convergence was and is expected in certain issue areas. Finally, when EU member states are also members of additional IGOs, this compounds the policy convergence pressure in shared issue areas. The digital human rights laws in the EU today are a result of this competitive and complex space. Within international relations, we call this formal policy space a "regime." Only by researching the emergence of data regimes in their states of origin will we uncover the contributing factors to EU policies of digital human rights. I offer a new way of conceptualizing digital human rights, utilizing the tools of content analysis and historical case comparisons, as seen within the disciplines of international relations and comparative politics. Understanding the policy negotiation process is hugely beneficial to scholars and policy-makers alike, for a variety of reasons.

Digital Human Rights Research and Policy Coordination

Why did high levels of data protection first occur in Sweden and Germany, and not in other states, such as the United Kingdom and France? Why did the United Kingdom finally support EU data protections in the 1980s? The coordination needed to realize supranational data legislation has important implications not only for data policy research, it also exposes the compromises necessary when the national legislation of member states is at conflict with one another. How these differences were accommodated in the 1980s and 1990s when setting EU-level data policy is of crucial importance in an era of increasing political fragmentation within the EU on several other issue areas. In this book, I answer these questions by arguing that policy coordination is crucial to the way we assess the development of digital human rights regimes.

Divergences in states' preferences continue to matter in the long-run, even after EU policy is set. For instance, increased economic woes in several EU states led to conflicts over EU fiscal policy following the

2008 financial crisis. Member states such as Hungary or Poland have regressed on matters of judicial independence since 2015. The Brexit drama was largely motivated by disagreements over shared EU immigration and trade policy obligations. Given the fact that a regional convergence toward digital human rights has emerged in the Europe Union and nowhere else to date, explaining this case of policy compromise can increase our understanding of the EU policy-making process. This study also generates important contributions to the human rights and data governance literature, through examination of which actors are the most influential during policy coordination, and why certain human rights regimes emerge in a regional or global system. Finally, it also helps us better understand policy compliance post-legislation.

There are many factors that shaped the development of digital human rights legislation in the EU. The European Union was founded to ensure economic integration first and foremost, and the protection of the Single Market remains a priority. In the 1970s and 1980s, the EU Commission started multiple EU programs to increase growth in various industries of the ICT sectors. In 2014, the EU Commission added a strategy for a Digital Single Market to the Single Market programme, bringing data governance to center stage once again. The interaction between economic interests intersected with human rights issues has gone virtually unexplored. Furthermore, the change to data policy following the New York (09.11.01), Madrid (03.11.04), and London (07.07.05) bombings warrant additional research. Key questions remain:

Why did the national laws created by EU states follow three common pathways (data profiteering, data as a surveillance tool, digital human rights protection)?

Why did the EU settle primarily upon the digital human rights model, rather than continue to pursue data commodification (the first EU data policy)?

What role did key elites play in the adoption of or blocking of a comprehensive EU digital rights policy?

This book will answer these questions in the following chapters. Chapter 2 begins with an explanation of how new human rights emerge. I start by looking at creation patterns for other types of human rights. I explain the mechanisms of international human rights networking, followed by an introduction of key actors involved, and a discussion of the common strategies they employ. Then, I present the theoretical argument for how digital human rights emerged as a new regime at the national and international levels. The theory utilizes existing conceptual knowledge on regime creation and complexity. I then outline the hypotheses necessary to test the theoretical argument, relying upon actor agency and structural interest involvement.[53] Finally, I lay out the case study method of testing the associated hypotheses, and perform content analysis of official EU documents.

Chapter 3 begins the national case studies, where I map out the evolution of data policy outcomes that occurred in the early days of data proliferation. Descriptive statistics reveal how key structural factors shaped national laws; these factors include domestic terror incidents, economic dependence upon ICT sector growth, and the consultation of legal experts. In the Swedish study, I trace the origin of the cultural ideal of personal "*integritat*," and how it contributed to the Swedish approach to digital human rights. In Chapter 4, I turn to Germany. Despite significant domestic terror incidents in the 1970s and 1980s, the oppressive surveillance of the Stasi during the Cold War era left a lasting legacy of fear against government heavy-handed collection of personal data for the monitoring of public behavior. Chapter 5 explains the unique case of the United Kingdom, which was much more hesitant to adopt data protection legislation. The Thatcher government finally acquiesced to demands for a DHR-based law when the country's own ICT sector demanded such a law, fearful of business losses without such protections.

Chapter 6 examines supranational legislative efforts beginning in 1970s, with an intense focus upon the mid-1990s–2016, when the EU Commission sought to achieve data policy congruence among EU Member States. In this chapter, I apply structuralist interpretations of EU policy-making to explain why data policies could be shaped by three factors after the advent of computerized data: rights-based protections, security use of data, and data commodification. Extensive content analysis of over 82 policy documents reveals the hierarchy of priorities in EU for the three main preferences. I pay particular attention to the process of passing the landmark legislation in EU data protections, the General Data Protection Regulation (GDPR, 2016). The

[53] Geortz and Diehl (1992) and Hawkins and Llloyd (2003).

chapter concludes with a comparison of the findings to the policy-making arguments of functionalist theory.

Chapter 7 explores the ways that epistemic actors within the legal and academic community of human rights experts significantly and profoundly expanded the scope of DHR in the EU. I discuss the established knowledge regarding the policy influence of epistemic professionals, and apply this understanding to the members of Article 29 Working Party (WP 29), an advisory committee created by Directive 95/46/EC. Through their efforts as sole information providers on this topic for the Commission and Council, WP 29 successfully linked the need for expanded DHR protections to the normative identity of EU states as human rights protectors, bound in the Union's commitment to protect such rights. WP 29 had huge policy-shaping power due to their socially networked values as legal and human rights advocates from within the judicial, criminal justice, and academic professions.

Chapter 8 begins by looking at the role of identity in norm adoption, with a careful examination of the ways in which states and organizations leverage international relationships to promote global norm diffusion. Then, I compare this model of norm socialization to the behavior of the EU. I start with the important EU–US relationship, and trace the evolution of cross-Atlantic data exchanges through the Privacy Shield and Safe Harbour agreements, by which the EU required American firms to fulfill digital human rights protections. Next, I provide an overview of cases taken by the European judicial system, as it ruled on multiple cases of DHR abuses outside EU borders, including the landmark *Schrems I* and *II* cases against Facebook. Then, the chapter concludes with a look at enforcement mechanisms used to punish non-state actors, with fines levied against several MNCs including Google and H&M, for failing to meet the digital human rights standards of the GDPR.

The final chapter of the book, Chapter 9, discusses the broad implications of the book's findings for social science and the policy world. Historically-speaking, supranational EU data legislation occurred as a result of technological change interacted with human rights advocacy. During the process of creating supranational data legislation and subsequent oversight, epistemic professionals had a disproportionate amount of influence as information providers to EU lawmakers. Yet digital human rights are constantly being challenged.

Increased terrorism has redefined the security threat landscape. The Covid-19 pandemic revealed that data protection infringement could occur through tracking and tracing efforts, when public health is threatened on a wide scale. As governments react to these threats, new agents rise to the foreground who are attempting to push back against the EU's view of data governance. By example, states like China *oppose* a Western view of digital human rights, and social media firms such as Facebook and Twitter may *seek to redefine* the norm space for digitized personal data. There will likely be persistent tension between digital human rights provisions and states' political will to maintain policy sovereignty. Ultimately, the international system must determine if digitized personal data is a commodity of the commons, or a permanent and identity-based component of human rights, worthy of global protections.

Bibliography

Acharya, Amitav. 2011. "Norm Subsidiarity and Regional Orders: Sovereignty, Regionalism, and Rule-Making in the Third World." *International Studies Quarterly* 55: 95–123.

Alter, Karen J., and Sophie Meunier. 2009. "The Politics of International Regime Complexity." *Perspectives on Politics* 7 (1): 13–24.

Bamberger, Kenneth A., and Deirdre K. Mulligan. 2013. "Privacy in Europe: Initial Data on Governance Choices and Corporate Practices." *George Washington Law Review* 81 (5): 1529–1664.

Bassini, Marco. 2019. "Fundamental Rights and Private Enforcement in the Digital Age." *European Law Journal* 25 (2): 182–197.

Beier, J. Marshall. 2003. "Emailed Applications are Preferred: Ethical Practices in Mine Action and the Idea of Global Civil Society." *Third World Quarterly* 25: 795–808.

Bennett, Colin J. 1992. *Regulating Privacy: Data Protection and Public Policy in Europe and the United States.* Ithaca, NY: Cornell University Press.

Blackmer, W. Scott. 2019. "Data Protection in the Private Sector: Convergence or a Localisation of Rights and Expectations?" In *Human Rights, Digital Society and the Law: A Research Companion*, edited by Marti Susi, Chapter 19. Abingdon, Oxford: Routledge.

Brooking, Emerson T., and P. W. Singer. 2016. "War Goes Viral: How Social Media Is Being Weaponized." *The Atlantic*: 70–83.

Burton-Jones, Alan. 1999. *Knowledge Capitalism: Business, Work and Training in the New Economy.* Oxford: Oxford University Press.

Cavelty, Myriam Dunn. 2013. "From Cyber-Bombs to Political Fallout: Threat Representations with an Impact in the Cyber-Security Discource." *International Studies Review* 15: 105–122.

Cheneval, Francis. 2017. "Towards Property-Owning Democracy by Private Property of Personal Data." *Centre for Technology and Global Affairs.* Accessed January 1, 2017 . https://www.ctga.ox.ac.uk/event/towards-property-owning-democracy-private-property-personal-data.

Choucri, Nazli. 2012. *Cyberpolitics in International Relations.* Cambridge, MA: Massachusetts Institute of Technology.

Clarke, Richard A. 2016. "The Risk of Cyber War and Cyber Terrorism." *Journal of International Affairs* 70: 179–181.

Colarik, Andrew Michael. 2006. *Cyber Terrorism: Political and Economic Implications.* Hershey, PA: Idea Group.

Council of the European Communities, Commission of the European Communities. 1992. "Treaty on the European Union." Accessed April 6, 2019. https://europa.eu/european-union/sites/europaeu/files/docs/body/treaty_on_european_union_en.pdf.

Custers, Bart, Simone van der Hof, and Bart Schermer. 2014. "Privacy Expectations of Social Media Users: The Role of Informed Consent in Privacy Policies." *Policy & Internet* 6 (3): 268–295.

Deibert, Ronald J. 2000. "International Plug'n Play? Citizen Activism, the Internet, and Global Public Policy." *International Studies Quarterly* 1: 255–272.

———. 2013. *Black Code: Surveillance, Privacy, and the Dark Side of the Internet.* Toronto: McClelland & Stewart.

———. 2020. *Reset: Reclaiming the Internet for Civil Society.* Toronto, ON: House of Anansi Press.

Deibert, Robert, John Palfrey, Rafal Rohozinski, and Jonathan Zittrain. 2010. *Access Controlled: The Shaping of Power, Rights, and Rule in Cyberspace.* Cambridge, MA: MIT Press.

Drezner, Daniel W. 2007. *All Politics Is Global: Explaining International Regulatory Regimes.* Princeton, NJ: Princeton University Press.

Dunleavy, P., H. Margetts, S. Bastow, and J. Tinkler. 2006. *Digital Era Governance: IT Corporations, the State, and E-Government.* Oxford: Oxford University Press.

Edgar, Timothy H. 2017. *Beyond Snowden: Privacy, Mass Surveillance, and the Struggle to Reform the NSA.* Washington, DC: Brookings Institution Press.

Eltantawy, Nahed, and Julie B. Wiest. 2011. "Social Media in the Egyptian Revolution: Reconsidering Resource Mobilization Theory." *International Journal of Communications* 5: 1207–1224.

European Commission. n.d. "Data Protection: Legislation." Accessed December 7, 2017. http://ec.europa.eu/justice/data-protection/law/index_en.htm.

European Parliament, Office of the President. 2018. "Answers from Facebook to Questions Asked During Mark Zuckerberg Meeting." May 23. Accessed May 25, 2018. Why Did Europe, and the EU in Particular, Have a More

Aggressive Policy Stance Toward Protecting Cyber Data Than Did Other Regions?
European Union. 2014. "Communication from the Commission to the European Parliament, the Council, the European Economic and Social Committee and the Committee of the Regions A Digital Single Market Strategy for Europe." *EUR-Lex*, July 15. Accessed December 1, 2017. https://www.google.com/url?sa=t&rct=j&q=&esrc=s&source=web&cd=1&ved=0ahUKEwiyu_2NxOnXAhWDQiYKHRKUB48QFggpMAA&url=http%3A%2F%2Feur-lex.europa.eu%2Flegal-content%2FEN%2FTXT%2F%3Furi%3Dcelex%253A52015DC0192&usg=AOvVaw0r4zq-qZFhJD83xzd81Hpc.
———. 2016. "Regulation (EU) 2016/679 of the European Parliament and of the council of 27 April 2016." *EUR-Lex*, May 4. Accessed November 15, 2017. http://data.europa.eu/eli/reg/2016/679/oj.
Flaherty, David H. 1989. *Protecting Privacy in Surveillance Societies: The Federal Republic of Germany, Sweden, France, Canada, & the United States*. Chapel Hill, NC: The University of North Caroline Press.
Franda, Marcus. 2001. *Governing the Internet: The Emergence of an International Regime*. Boulder, CO: Lynne Reinner.
Friedewald, Michael, J. Peter Burgess, Johann Čas, Rocco Bellanova, and Walter Peissl, . 2017. *Surveillance, Privacy and Security: Citizens' Perspectives*. 1st edition. London: Routledge.
Fuster, Gloria González. 2016. *The Emergence of Personal Data Protection as a Fundamental Right of the EU*. Cham: Springer.
Godberg, G. 2011. "Rethinking the Public/Virtual Sphere: The Problem with Participation." *New Media & Society* 1: 1–11.
Goertz, Gary, and Paul F. Diehl. 1992. "Toward a Theory of International Norms: Some Conceptual and Measurement Issues." *Journal of Conflict Resolution* 36: 634–664.
Goldsmith, Jack L., and Tim Wu. 2006. *Who Controls the Internet?: Illusions of Control in a Borderless World*. New York, NY: Oxford University Press.
Goldstein, Judith, and Robert O. Keohane. n.d. *Ideas and Foreign Policy: Beliefs, Institutions, and Political Change*. Ithaca, NY: Cornell University Press.
Granville, Kevin. 2018. *Facebook and Cambridge Analytica: What You Need to Know As Fallout Widens*. March 19. Accessed March 27, 2018. https://www.nytimes.com/2018/03/19/technology/facebook-cambridge-analytica-explained.html.
Gros, Valentin, Marieke de Goede, and Beste Isleyen. 2017. "The Snowden Files Made Public: A Material Politics of Contesting Surveillance." *International Political Sociology* 11 (1): 73–89.
Hawkins, Darren, and Joshue Lloyd. 2003. "Questioning Comprehensive Sacntions: The Birth of a Norm." *Journal of Human Rights* 2: 441–454.

Jančiūtė, Laima. 2017. "EU Data Protection and 'Treaty-Base Games': When Fundamental Rights Are Wearing Market-making Clothes." In *Data Protection and Privacy: The Age of Intelligent Machines*, 1–31. Oxford: Hart Publishing.

Jolly, Leuan, and Loeb & Loeb. 2017. "Data Protection in the United States." July 1. Accessed April 20, 2018. https://uk.practicallaw.thomsonreuters.com/6-502-0467?transitionType=Default&contextData=(sc.Default)&firstPage=true&bhcp=1.

Jorgensen, Rikke Frank. 2017. "What Platforms Mean When They Talk About Human Rights." *Policy and Internet* 9 (3): 280–296.

Jorgensen, Rikke Frank, and Tariq Desai. 2017. "Right to Privacy Meets Online Platforms: Exploring Privacy Complains Against Facebook and Google." *Nordic Journal of Human Rights* 35 (2): 106–126.

Joyce, Daniel. 2015. "Internet Freedom and Human Rights." *The European Journal of International Law* 26 (2): 493–514.

Karpf, David. 2016. *Analytic Activism: Digital Listening and the New Political Strategy*. New York, NY: Oxford University Press.

Keck, Margaret E., and Kathryn Sikkink. 1998. *Activists Beyond Borders: Advocacy Networks in Transnational Politics*. Ithaca, NY: Cornell University Press.

Kello, Lucas. 2017. *The Virtual Weapon and International Order*. New Haven, CT: Yale University Press.

Krasner, Stephen D. 1982. "Structural Causes and Regime Consequences: Regimes as Intervening Variables." *International Organization* 36 (2): 185–205.

Lenard, Thomas M., and Paul H. Rubin. 2010. "In Defense of Data: Information and the Costs of Privacy." *Policy & Internet* 2 (1): 149–183.

Longo, Matthew. 2018. *The Politics of Borders: Sovereignty, Security, and the Citizen After 9/11*. Cambridge: Cambridge University Press.

Lynn III, William J. 2010. "Defending a New Domain: The Pentagon's Cyberstrategy." *Foreign Affairs* 89 (5): 97–108.

Lyon, David. 2014. "Surveillance, Snowden, and Big Data: Capacities, Consequences, Critique." *Big Data & Society* 1: 1–13.

Margetts, Helen Z. 2009. "The Internet and Public Policy." *Policy & Internet* 1 (1): 1–21.

Margetts, Helen Z., Peter, John, Scott Hale, and Taha Yasseri. 2016. *Political Turbulence: How Social Media Shape Collective Action*. Princeton, NJ: Princeton University Press.

Mayer-Schönberger, Viktor, and Kenneth Cukier. 2013. *Big Data: A Revolution That Will Transform How We Live, Work, and Think*. London: John Murray.

Mayer-Schönberger, Viktor, and Thomas Ramge. 2018. *Reinventing Capitalism in the Age of Big Data*. London: John Murray.

Mazanec, Brian M. 2015. *The Evolution of Cyber War: International Norms for Emerging-Technology Weapons.* Washington, DC: Potomac Books/University of Nebraska Press.

McAdam, D., J. D. McCarthy, and M. N. Zald. 1996. *Comparative Perspectives on Social Movements: Political Opportunities, Mobilizing Structures, and Cultural Framings.* New York, NY: Cambridge University Press.

Meijers, Huub. 2014. "Does the Internet Generate Economic Growth, International Trade, or Both?" *International Economics & Economic Policy* 11: 137–163.

Milner, Helen. 1997. *Interests, Institutions, and Information.* Princeton, NJ: Princeton University Press.

Moravcsik, Andrew. 2000. "The Origins of Human Rights Regimes: Democratic Delegation in Postwar Europe." *International Organization* 54 (2): 217–252.

Morgan, Patrick M. 2010. "Applicability of Traditional Deterrence Concepts and Theory to the Cyber Realm." In *Proceedings of a Workshop on Deterring Cyberattacks: Informing Strategies and Developing Options for U.S. Policy*, by National Research Council, 55–76. Washington, DC: National Academies Press.

Mueller, Milton L. 2010. *Networks and States: The Global Politics of Internet Governance.* Cambridge, MA: Massachusetts Institute of Technology Press.

National Research Council. 2010. *Proceedings of a Workshop on Deterring Cyberattacks: Informing Strategies and Developing Options for U.S. Policy.* Policy and Global Affairs Division, Computer Science and Telecommunications Board. Washington, DC: The National Academies.

Newman, Abraham L. 2008. *Protectors of Privacy: Regulating Personal Data in the Global Economy.* Ithaca, NY: Cornell University Press.

Nocetti, Julian. 2015. "Contest and Conquest: Russia and Global Internet Governance." *International Affairs* 91 (1): 111–130.

Norris, Pippa. 2001. *Digital Divide: Civic Engagement, Information Poverty, and the Internet Worldwide.* New York, NY: Cambridge University Press.

Nussbaum, Matthew. 2018. "Trump Campaign Sprints Away from Cambridge Analytica." *Politico.eu*, March 20. Accessed March 29, 2018. https://www.politico.eu/article/cambridge-analytica-trump-campaign-tries-to-distance-itself-from-scandal-ridden/.

Olson, Parmy. 2018. "EU Probes Facebook's Data Sharing with Cambridge Analytica, Raising Prospect of Fines." March 19. Accessed March 29, 2018. https://www.forbes.com/sites/parmyolson/2018/03/19/eu-probe-facebook-cambridge-analytica-fines/#6ebabb685fd6.

Organisation for Economic Cooperation and Development. 1985–2018. "OECD Digital Economy Papers." Accessed April 5, 2019. https://www.oecd-ilibrary.org/science-and-technology/oecd-digital-economy-papers_20716826?page=16.

———. 2009. *The Developmental Dimension: Internet Access for Development*. Paris: Organization for Economic Cooperation and Development.

———. 2011. "Terms of Reference for the Review of the OECD Guidelines Governing the Protection of Privacy and Transborder Data Flows of Personal Data. DSTI/ICCP/REG(2011)4/Final, Paris: Working Party on Information Security and Privacy.

———. n.d. "Country Statistics." Accessed December 2017. http://stats.oecd.org.

Orsini, Amandine, Jean-Frederic Morin, and Oran Young. 2013. "Regime Complexes: A Buzz, A Boom, or a Boost for Global Governance?" *Global Governance* 19: 27–39.

Osnos, Evan, David Remnick, and Joshua Yaffa. 2017. "Active Measures—What Lay Behind Russia's Interference in the 2016 Election—And What Lies Ahead?" *The New Yorker* 93 (3): 40–55.

Owens, William A., Kenneth W. Dam, and Herbert S. Lin. 2009. *Technology, Policy Law, and Ethics Regarding U.S. Acquisiting and Use of Cyberattack Capabilities*. Washington, DC: National Academic Press.

Oyedemi, Toks. 2015. "Internet Access as Citizen's Rights? Citizenship in the Digital Age." *Citizenship Studies* 19 (3/4): 450–464.

Papacharissi, Zizi. 2010. "The Virtual Sphere 2.0: The Internet, the Public Sphere and Beyond." In *Routledge Handbook of Internet Politics*, edited by Andrew Chadwick and Philip Howard. London: Routledge .

Penney, Jonathan. 2019. "The Right to Privacy: The End of Privacy Fatalism." In *Human Rights, Digital Society and the Law: A Research Companion*, edited by Marti Susi, Chapter 3. Abingdon, Oxford: Routledge.

Petkova, Bilyana. 2019. "Privacy as Europe's First Amendment." *European Law Journal* 25 (2): 140–154.

Pollicino, Oreste, and Marti Susi. 2019. "Internet and Human Rights Law: An Introduction." *European Law Journal* 25 (2): 120–121.

Powers, Shawn M. 2015. *The Real Cyber War: The Political Economy of Internet Freedom*. Urbana, IL: University of Illinois Press.

Putnam, Robert D. 1988. "Diplomacy and Domestic Politics: The Logic of Two-Level Games." *International Organization* 42 (3): 427–460.

Risse-Kappen, Thomas, Steve C. Ropp, and Kathryn Sikkink. 1999. *The Power of Human Rights: International Norms and Domestic Change*. New York, NY: Cambridge University Press.

———. 2013. *The Persisten Power of Human Rights: From Compliance to Commitment*. Cambridge: Cambridge Universit Press.

Rosecrance, Richard. 1996. "The Rise of the Virtual State." *Foreign Affairs* 75 (4): 45–61.

Schneier, Bruce. 2015. *Data and Goliath: The Hidden Battles to Collect Your Data and Control Your World*. New York, NY: W. W. Norton.

Singer, P. W., and Allan Friedman. 2014. *Cybersecurity and Cyberwar: What Everyone Needs to Know.* New York, NY: Oxford University Press.

Soh, Changrok, Daniel Connolly, and Seunghynn Nam. 2019. "The Main Challenges Related to Protecting Human Rights in the Internet." In *Human Rights, Digital Society and the Law: A Research Companion*, edited by Marti Susi, Chapter 6. Abingdon, Oxford: Routledge.

The Privacy Rights Clearinghouse. 2018. "Data Breaches." March. Accessed March 27, 2018. https://www.privacyrights.org/data-breaches.

Tolbert, Caroline J., and Ramona S. McNeal. 2003. "Unraveling the Effects of the Internet on Political Participation." *Political Research Quarterly* 56 (2): 175–185.

Voigt, Paul, and Axel von dem Bussche. 2017. *The EU General Data Protection Regulation (GDPR): A Practical Guide.* Cham: Springer.

Wallace, Helen, Mark A. Pollack, and Alasdair R. Young. 2015. *Policy-Making in the European Union.* Oxford: Oxford University Press.

Weiss, Thomas G. 2013. *Global Governance—Why? What? Whither?* Cambridge: Polity Press.

Wicker, Stephen B., and Stephanie M. Santosa. 2013. "Access to the Internet Is a Human Right." *Communications of the ACM* 56 (6): 43–46.

Wischmeyer, Thomas. 2019. "Making Social Media an Instrument of Democracy." *European Law Journal* 25 (2): 169–181.

Wolfsfeld, Gadi, Elad Segev, and Tamir Sheafer. 2013. "Social Media and the Arab Spring: Politics Comes First." *International Journal of Press/Politics* 18 (2): 115–137.

Zuboff, Shoshana. 2015. "Big Other: Surveillance Capitalism and the Prospects of an Information Civilization." *Journal of Information Technology* 30: 75–89.

CHAPTER 2

Digitized Data Protection as a Fundamental Human Right

It is important to analyze three areas to establish that a new norm of digital human rights has been created. This chapter tackles each of these in order. First, it is necessary to pinpoint the key elements that identify the establishment of a new human rights norm. To accomplish this job, I take a deep look at how prior international relations scholars have explained the development of other human rights norms. Second, norm emergence and acceptance specific to the European Union must be explained, given that EU states were the global source of origin for digital human rights. Institutional regime theory provides a recognized framework for this explanation, and I apply it to the birth of digital human rights. Lastly, I explore which interests within EU states would be most or least likely to promote a new norm, including which groups and individuals are more likely to push for the formalization of a digital human rights norm within national and EU laws.

Identification of New Human Rights Norms

New human rights practices are based upon human rights norms. Norms include expected "standards for appropriate behavior for actors [or a group of actors] who share specific identity or values."[1] To recognize

[1] Finnemore and Sikkink (1998, p. 891).

R. Dowd, *The Birth of Digital Human Rights*, Information Technology and Global Governance,
https://doi.org/10.1007/978-3-030-82969-8_2

the presence of a new human rights norm, it is useful to uncover the mechanisms and structures that facilitate creation of new human rights. Economic and social rights implementation requires three main elements: process mechanisms (M), agency and actions (A) by key actors and states, and pathways (P) whereby change is produced and responsible parties held accountable.[2] New economic and social rights can emerge through top-down efforts by states, or bottom-up, through social movements or civil society activity.[3] External pressures such as sanctions, reputational shaming, and treaty commitments also improve states' adoption of and compliance with new human rights.[4]

Norm emergence is a dynamic and evolutionary process. Within explanations for norm emergence, distinct patterns occur, key actors are identified, and their strategies for norm advocacy and formalization discovered. In a broad sense, when norm creation follows certain observable patterns, it increases the likelihood of successful dispersion. It often follows a progressive timeline—emergence, acceptance by an increasing cascade of states, and finally internationalization and general compliance.[5] Somewhere between steps one and two, a "tipping point" is reached when a critical mass of one-third of states adopts the norm, generating acceptance momentum. Norms with a wider scope of appeal—particularly those considered more democratic in origin—can have a greater chance of success.[6] If a new norm is not fully internalized, states will weigh potential sanctions for noncompliance against any gains obtained by violating the new norm. Prior punishments and overarching metanorms influence these decisions.[7]

Turning to sub-state actors' involvement in norm creation, a variety of actors promote new norms within domestic and international settings. The utilization of agency by individual actors matters, and through extensive framing efforts, norm entrepreneurs (NEs) draw attention to

[2] Hagland and Aggarwal (2011).

[3] Risse et al. (2013).

[4] Cardenas (2004), Hafner-Burton (2008), Hafner-Burton and Tsutsui (2007) and Hathaway (2002).

[5] Finnemore and Sikkink (1998).

[6] Finnemore and Sikkink (1998) and Sandholtz and Stiles (2009).

[7] Borrowing from Axelrod (1986), metanorms are overarching expectations about accepted norms and the possibility of punishment for non-compliance with the accepted norms.

a social or political problem and explain why it makes a difference to human rights outcomes.[8] Transnational advocacy networks (TANs) and NEs organize and promote a new norm, help states adopt the norm, and provide compliance monitoring.[9] Certain conditions breed higher success for norm advocacy efforts. These include having a good pre-existing environment of human rights provision and the development of new political opportunities for policy and behavioral change. If national institutions have multiple policy access points, TANs are more effective when bringing outside norms into a state, by employing information campaigns to promote the desired behavior.[10] Advocacy efforts vary according to role as well; epistemic experts work differently than "general" norm entrepreneurs.[11] Epistemic experts provide technical and substantive knowledge to governments setting them apart from norm entrepreneurs, whose emphasis centers on normative arguments.

Internationally, NEs utilize organizational platforms to amplify their norm promotion activities. They leverage the normative components of the identities of intergovernmental organizations (IGOs) to generate cognitive dissonance between value-based identities and existing practices. New norm adoption and compliance behaviors are difficult to ignore once this dissonance with stated values is acknowledged. Lastly, NEs match the new norm with existing IGO policy. This can facilitate grafting of new norms onto old norms, and establish congruence between the old and the new, making it easier for member states to justify adoption of the new norm.[12]

There are, however, important aspects of the new DHR (digital human rights) norm that are not directly addressed in the prior-mentioned literature, particularly as it involves the adoption of human rights norms *within EU law*. To explain DHR norm creation and adoption within the EU, we must address the policy-making process that establishes formal norm adoption; this is accomplished by applying regime theory to the topic of digital human rights in EU law creation.

[8] Finnemore and Sikkink (1998).

[9] Hawkins and Lloyd (2003), Price (1998) and Risse-Kappen (1995).

[10] Risse-Kappen (1995) and Stroup and Murdie 2012.

[11] Price (1998, pp. 620–626).

[12] Acharya (2004) and Hawkins and Lloyd (2003).

What Is a Regime?

In domestic policy-settings, the formalization of laws or policy preferences is referred to as institutionalization.[13] At the international level, the institutionalization of policy preferences around an issue which concerns multiple states is known as a *regime*. Stephen Krasner defined regimes as, "principles, norms, rules, and decision-making procedures around which actor expectations converge in a given issue-area."[14] European states have joined a variety of international regimes which are embodied in international organizations (IOs), including the United Nations (UN), the Organization for Economic Cooperation and Development (OECD), and the European Union (EU). Each IO has suggested policies related to the mission and goals of the organization. Each of the aforementioned regimes have suggested or mandated policies to handle the treatment of personal and cyber data that produced a trickle-down impact on national legislation for states that are members of the regime. Over time, a regime complex has emerged around the issue of digital human rights. A regime complex involves, "the presence of nested, partially overlapping, and parallel international regimes that are not hierarchically ordered."[15] Thus, important point one is: a digital human rights regime complex exists in the European Union as a result of overlapping, and at times, conflictual policy expectations at the national, regional, and international levels. The European Union process for the formation of new legislation has evolved over time, and the functional structure of making legislation has shaped digital human rights.

Regime Creation in the European Union

The EU legislative process is quite complex. The Maastricht Treaty created the European Union in 1992, and categorized issue areas into three groups.[16] "First pillar" issues focused on economic integration within the Single Area Market, as an extension of the European Economic Community (EEC) goals from the original Treaty of Rome, signed in

[13] North (1990).

[14] Krasner (1983, p. 185).

[15] Alter and Meunier (2009).

[16] The pillar structure was abolished with the passing of the Lisbon Treaty in 2007; Lisbon went into effect in 2009.

1957. National laws were to be superseded by EU laws in first pillar issues, through the power of supranationalism.[17] Otherwise, second and third pillar policies were decided using intergovernmentalism, in which the members made new policy decisions only when unanimously agreed. The "second pillar" outlined responsibilities and a balance of governance between the Union and the member states on common foreign and security matters. In the "third pillar", member states retained the highest level of national policy sovereignty; any issues not placed within the first and second pillars were third pillar topics.

Data policy started as a third pillar concern, meaning EU member states initially set their own data legislation with full sovereignty from the 1970s, when data digitalization began. However, with the signing of the Lisbon Treaty in 2007, EU policy-makers moved data policy to the first pillar, transforming it from an intergovernmental issue to a supranational policy issue in which all member states consider the EU law as binding within their countries. Three EU agencies are currently involved in the process of making new EU legislation; the executive body (the Commission) requests new legislation, and the legislative bodies (the Council of Ministers and Parliament) research and create new laws. It is important to isolate the digital human rights norm and new legislative protections from pre-existing human rights policies present in the EU in order to substantiate the claim that an entirely new norm is present. I now turn to the process of policy-making in the EU, involving both national and EU-level activity.

Legislation occurs at two levels in the European Union: the domestic level (internal to each member state) and regional level (with all EU members).[18] Policy-making at the national level is quite fluid, involving give and take between domestic interests, and requiring coordination between the public and private sectors. New human rights norms in democratic nations must be socially constructed in such a way that social and political actors accept the norm as democratically legitimate (i.e., it

[17] Supranationalism includes not only how the agreement is made for shared governance, but also the subjugation of national laws to the power of regional, or organizational laws. Member states must align the content of national laws with the regional law, or create new national laws to accomplish this goal.

[18] Putnam (1988).

is widely accepted by society).[19] Otherwise, the norm is less likely to become formal law.

Regarding supranational policy-making, the EU has long been accused of a democratic deficit.[20] The EU is perceived by some EU citizens as a distant organization, lacking legitimacy and connections to national cultural preferences, accusations which heightened in the 1990s and early 2000s.[21] In the past, EU democratic legitimacy was measured using "output legitimacy" such as national acceptance of EU legislative products. Since 2000, however, the EU has moved toward "input legitimacy."[22] Article 47 of the attempted EU Constitutional Treaty (2004), as well as Article 8b of the Lisbon Treaty (2007) increased stakeholder participation to promote input from EU administrators, academic researchers, and members of civil society in order to achieve a more representative outcome.

New norms are formally legitimized when adopted into legislation. Making digitized data protection a supranational legislative matter signals a formal legitimization of the DHR norm in the EU. This is especially true, given the change to collecting policy input from multiple stakeholders during the investigative phase of the EU legislation process. Therefore, new data protection legislation would indicate an institutionalized norm of digital human rights.

Who Creates Regimes, and Who Should Be the Primary Actors Interested in a Digital Human Rights Regime?

The development of a digital human rights regime is divided into distinct periods of change and involves multiple levels of political actors. I call the two time periods Phase I (1970–1999) and Phase II (roughly the late 1990s–2016); note there is some overlap with the two phases, because of the gradual change toward supranationalism. Data governance was managed at the national level during Phase I, but moved to the regional level of policy coordination during Phase II. Policy-making followed the trajectory given in Robert Putnam's two-level diplomacy

[19] Saurugger (2010).

[20] Moravcsik (2002).

[21] Magnette (2006), Moravcsik (2002), Rittberger (2005) and Saurugger (2010).

[22] Pollack (2015, p. 40).

model and Helen Milner's spatial negotiations arguments.[23] Putnam and Milner show that national policy-makers move back and forth between their national legislative environment and the international stage, seeking policy compromises that please their obligations in both arenas. At both the domestic and international levels, lawmakers utilize epistemic professionals to provide technical expertise regarding present needs and potential long-term implications of newly proposed policies.[24] Slightly differently from the role played by epistemic professionals, as new EU legislation is crafted, norm entrepreneurs can attempt to diffuse new norms throughout the international system by calling attention to issues of importance and attempting to network with elites who hold decision-making power.[25] Next, I look at how institutions and regimes are formed specifically regarding data governance.

The Three Structural Interest Groups

Recall that the causal argument proposes a distinct role for three key interests as digital human rights developed in the European Union—the economic world, the national security community, and human rights actors. I now turn to examine each of these structural elements, beginning with the economic and business environment.

Economic Interests

Economic interests are driven by voters, corporate actors, and the state in a complex interactive process. Economic voting research has uncovered mixed findings about the role of sector-based employment and voting responses. Voters can punish incumbent governments and hold those in political leadership responsible for economic downturns by withdrawing vote support.[26] Attribution of responsibility for periods of economic growth is less proven, however; voters seem more likely to hold governments accountable for reversal of prior economic gains, rather than a lack

[23] Milner (1997) and Putnam (1988).

[24] Epistemic professionals comprise a "network of professionals with recognized expertise and competence in a particular domain and an authoritative claim to policy-relevant knowledge within that domain or issue-area." See Haas (1992, p. 3).

[25] Finnemore and Sikkink (1998) and Keck and Sikkink (1998).

[26] Lewis-Beck and Paldam (2000).

of growth in general.[27] We do know that political and corporate interests can interact in ways that favor particular firms or sectors. Industries enjoy more political influence when broad public–private coalitions exist allowing firms to lobby on behalf of sectoral concerns.[28] If low levels of conflict exist between the desires of multiple political decision-makers, or if the interests of economic actors and politicians align, governments will pass public policies that are favorable for these firms.

Technology-related sectors are known contributors to the economic growth of European states as a result of their participation in the global marketplace during Phase I (1970s–late 1980s).[29] The economic contributions by technology firms to economic growth was quite consistent, and the EU tech sector expansion was driven by computer manufacturing, communications equipment, and later, software development.[30] Gains from ICT investment and diffusion varied among EU states after the late 1980s, and EU growth started to lag behind US performance. Despite the lag, EU states backed the growth potential in ICT throughout the 1990s and into the early 2000s, via investments in technology infrastructure.

Investments increased demands for telecommunications and internet services.[31] Between 1995 and 2000, the share of value added to the economy of OECD states by ICT firms averaged 9.5%, with some EU states seeing growth as high as 16.5%.[32] By 2011, growth had cooled somewhat to a European Union-wide mean of 6.0%, but again, averages for some states persisted above 11%.[33] By 2015, individual EU states growth plateaued, but still showed consistency in ICT value contributions, with Sweden earning >7% annually, while France, Germany, and the United Kingdom hovered around 5%.[34] The substantial contribution by ICT firms to economic growth helped member states experience growth

[27] Lewis-Beck and Paldam (2000).

[28] Michalowitz (2007).

[29] OECD (2003) andWorld Bank (2006).

[30] Colecchia and Schreyer (2001).

[31] Röller and Waverman (2001).

[32] OECD (2002).

[33] OECD (2018). Note: as of publication of this chapter, this reflects the most recently available OECD data.

[34] See OECD, Value added of the ICT sector and sub-sectors, 2015.

in technology-based industries simultaneous to the decline in contributions by other manufacturing sectors. In addition, the demand for persons with ICT skills remained steady from the mid-1990s, even in the aftermath of shocks such as the 2008 financial crisis. Eurostat reports cite that:

> More than two fifths (46 %) of large enterprises recruited or tried to recruit personnel for jobs requiring specialist ICT skills in 2018, while almost one third (30 %) of large enterprises reported that they had hard-to-fill vacancies for jobs requiring specialist ICT skills.[35]

In other words, both voters and firms had a vested interest in ICT-friendly policies, including policies that would impact data governance.

Security Interests

In addition to data legislation being driven by ICT dependence at the national level, the provision of national security has become a largely data-driven endeavor. We see evidence of data-driven security strategies employed in multiple areas: to locate and monitor threatening actors, as a defensive measure to detect terrorist activity, for use with offensive and defensive actions related to cybersecurity, and even crossing into the realm of economic espionage.

Since the 1970s, states have utilized digitized data as a surveillance tool within their larger defense arsenal to reduce security risks at the international, state, and sub-state levels. Digitized data is useful during proactive surveillance of state and non-state actors seen as potential threats to the states. Overt data surveillance is commonly performed by state authorities, though intentionally concealed for obvious reasons.[36] Covert surveillance via data collection and assessment allows for low levels of attrition and accountability, especially when contracted actors perform the surveillance on behalf of the state, at least until the perpetrating state is caught and "shamed."[37] Even if the proxies performing the surveillance espionage are publicly identified, the state behind the action will try to distance itself from the exposé. For example, US embarrassment when

[35] Eurostat (2020).

[36] Deibert (2013, 2020) and Kello (2017).

[37] Deibert (2013, 2020).

caught spying on German Chancellor Angela Merkel's mobile phone conversations resulted in public efforts by US officials to throw the focus on Edward Snowden, framed as an individual who acted in opposition to the security interests of his own state.[38]

Digitized data is a useful tool for shoring up national security not just in general, but also to protect against specific risks, such as terrorist attacks. Following the advent of the 9/11 attacks in the United States, countries worldwide increased use of public and private sector data for counter-terrorism efforts, heightened since 9/11.[39] The United Kingdom, Spain, and France, all of whom were EU member states during the years under examination, experienced a comparatively disproportionate numbers of deaths related to terrorism compared to other European states, and have all adopted data-heavy counter-terror measures.[40] These attacks necessitated government action to shore up the public trust in the current governments, as providers of social order and safety.[41] States responded to attacks and rising public fears with a variety of data-driven measures. Changes included more bilateral, collaborative border management, increased funding for technology for law enforcement, and additional legislation designed to facilitate and widen surveillance of potential perpetrators of future violence.[42] This last measure is significantly reliant upon access to "Big Data",[43] sometimes generated by governmental actors, at other times co-opted or coerced out of private sector data brokers such as Google or mobile phone service providers.[44]

[38] Johnson et al. (2014).

[39] Longo (2018).

[40] Alcantara (2017) and Global Terrorism Database. Terrorism related deaths, 1970–2016. UK = 2519, Spain = 1141, and France (1972–2016) = 492. See Chapter 3 for more details. Also see reports by Department of Homeland Security Emeritus Center of Excellence (2019) and Longo (2018).

[41] Chanley (2002).

[42] Deibert (2013) and Longo (2018).

[43] Big Data: "An approach to data analysis that aims to capture data comprehensively about a particular phenomenon, looking for patterns in the data" (Mayer-Schönberger and Ramge 2018, p. 77). Big Data is generated by data brokers or data profilers who correlate large quantities of seemingly unrelated data together in order to profile individuals based on larger patterns of behavior, online and offline.

[44] Deibert (2013) and Longo (2018).

First and foremost, data is used to assess the security risks associated with people or goods entering the state at airports or ports of entry by utilizing biometric and biographic data profiles to improve accuracy and speed of processing human movement across borders. Data aids in the movement of certain groups traveling into a country, through pre-screening processes such as the Global Entry program in the United States, Registered Traveler in the United Kingdom for some Commonwealth citizens, or visas required for non-EU citizens staying longer in an EU member state. Each of these accumulated data profiles on the approved travelers ensure that border flows are safe and expeditious, while simultaneously preserving state sovereignty and security. To monitor general public behavior, many countries rely on face recognition software tied to CCTV camera feeds watching the mass public, again a treasure trove of data, which can be used to identify persons of interest.[45] Though the extensive use of invasive screening processes may seem counterintuitive to the data privacy wishes of concerned citizens in democracies such as the United States and Europe, research shows that perceptions of threat by terrorism increase public willingness to forego civil liberties related to privacy.[46]

States don't limit their use of digitized personal data to aiding in control over physical space. Due to the diffusion of internet use and the propagation of data that occurs around its use, states see the cyber realm as another location over which to maintain their power, either for information surveillance, or for proactive measures of attack. States mine data for relevant pieces of information to surveil other states and a variety of non-state actors, such as politicians, diplomats, and high-profile economic actors. Key data conveys online identification, internet behavior, and yields meta-data (online traffic patterns).[47] Thanks to the low barriers for entry, both big and small states can enter this space and perform both defensive and offensive data collection against states or sub-state actors who are targets of national interest.[48] Unfortunately, the very nature of internet infrastructure means that vulnerabilities in cyber space

[45] Schneier (2015).

[46] Huddy et al. (2005) and Penney 2019.

[47] Meta-data: "categories of data, about data" (Mayer-Schönberger and Ramge 2018, p. 66).

[48] Clarke (2016) and Rosecrance (1996).

are often only exposed after an attack is perpetrated, giving offensive actors a seeming advantage over those seeking to deter cyber-attacks.[49] While differentiation between accidental data leaks and intentional system breaches are often poorly defined, digitized data loss is a potential casualty during both activities.[50] By example, thousands of individuals experienced data privacy loss during data breaches associated with the US Office of Personal Management and the attack on the German Reichstag, both of which took place in 2015.

Offensive cyber-attacks have yet to become the first option strategy of most states. Currently, digitized data surveillance is more a tool of defensive and/or economic espionage, less so than as an offensive weapon. Even when cyber-attacked, states have thus far been unwilling to react in kind with cyber retaliation, or with use of conventional weaponry; states resort to living in a condition of "unpeace" with one other.[51] This is broken by occasional outbreaks of open attacks if the target is seen to be vulnerable, or if it is economically useful to the aggressor state or its interests.[52] China in particular has been known to practice significant amounts of economic espionage to acquire intellectual property advantages for state-backed industries.[53] This topic will be explored more in subsequent chapters.

Digital Human Rights Interests

The final structural variable shaping EU data policies has been the action of legal and human rights advocates who encouraged rights-based data protections. First, prior scholarship revealed that human rights policies can be adopted as a result of both internal and external pressures, in a 'two-level' spatial environment.[54] Depending on the human rights issue, researchers found that both domestic and international level activity help explain policy success. Domestically, members of civil society push states

[49] Kello (2017).

[50] Liu (2019).

[51] Kello (2017).

[52] Kello (2017).

[53] Lee (2013) and Skinner (2014).

[54] Cardenas (2004).

to adopt particular human rights policies.[55] Civil society includes, but is not limited to "... human rights organizations, religious groups, political parties, and student organizations...".[56] While civil society can provide the vital impetus to push national policy-makers to adopt new human rights, it is the efforts of domestic *and* international actors within political structures that ultimately shape policy outcomes; it is neither all state nor all society that fully explains human rights activity and progress.[57] As data policy first emerged within the national legislatures of Europe, the causal pathway for digital human rights began at the domestic level, and later expanded into the regional level with EU-wide mandates, which we will visit more in Chapter 4.

Second, formal policy change has been conditional upon a new window of political opportunity opening in the legislative agenda space.[58] Reimann found that human rights advocacy is more successful when new political openness meets activism.[59] Tsutsui and Wotipka agree with Reimann; during the early stages of issue advocacy, domestic political opportunities are especially crucial to increase the numbers of citizens willing to support a cause.[60] We know several facts about how non-state actors promote new human rights policies within states and globally. Activists employ information campaigns, leverage relationships with high-profile actors or elites, and use rationalist arguments to pressure governments into developing new human rights policies. To further build pressure, domestic activists also combine efforts with outside networks, such as non-governmental organizations (NGOs) and transnational advocacy networks (TANs), especially if a state is resistant to change.[61]

Third, and most relevant to the arguments in this book, there is significant evidence that civil society is highly interested in the impact of technological change upon individuals' human rights.[62] Interviews with ICT (information, communications, and technology) activists in Europe

[55] Liu (2019).

[56] Cardenas (2004, p. 215).

[57] Risse-Kappen (1995).

[58] Tarrow (1998).

[59] Reimann (2006).

[60] Tsutsui and Wotipka (2004).

[61] Benford and Snow (2000).

[62] DeSimone (2010) and Magnusson and Iqbal (2018).

reveal that privacy and data protection are now high priorities for multiple human rights groups.[63] For instance, Irish activists worked to monopolize newspaper headlines in order to increase public awareness and pressure governments into data protections (this in response to the growing use of data as a commodity by telecommunications firms).[64] Other advocates utilized traditional social movement mechanisms, such as protests, to focus attention on needed changes.[65] In the late 1990s and early 2000s, still others brought court cases against states or some private sector firms, with the goal of pushing policy-makers into acknowledging that digitized data risks belong within the larger realm of fundamental human rights. ICT policy activism has created coalitions of multiple stakeholders, including individuals from industry alongside civil society actors.[66] This "networking" of rights-motivated activists (human rights insiders) and private sector industry representatives (outsiders) concerned with the impact of data use upon human rights reflects similarities with past networking efforts to convince states to adopt new human rights policies, such as with opposition to land mine use, or weapons bans.[67]

Fourth, involvement of epistemic experts elevated DHR activism to a level where it was taken seriously by government policy-makers. An epistemic community is "a network of professionals with recognized expertise and competence in a particular domain and an authoritative claim to policy-relevant knowledge within that domain or issue area."[68] Epistemic experts provide substantive expertise for governments who seek to alleviate the condition of imperfect information during the process of making new legislation. Use of technical advisors is markedly present during policy-making for laws that intersect new technology with legal rights concerns, as many politicians do not come from technology-based fields prior to serving in government. However, the advice given by epistemic experts is not void of ethical components. Epistemic experts communicate normative beliefs alongside technical knowledge. The normative aspects

[63] McIntyre (2008).

[64] McIntyre (2008).

[65] Kolb (2005).

[66] Löblich and Wendelin (2012).

[67] Finnemore and Sikkink (1998), Sikkink (2005) and Hintz and Milan (2009).

[68] Haas (1992).

of policy preferences shared among members of the professional community can thus diffuse throughout a governance system, as these individuals are used as consultants for multiple states and by international organizations.[69] The power of diffused norm-setting throughout the international system by networked advisors cannot be overstated.

In their landmark work on transnational advocacy, Keck and Sikkink identified networks of like-minded individuals from NGOs, social movements, foundations, media, trade unions, IGOs, or even sections of government.[70] These individuals design issue agendas, help set institutional procedures, and ultimately, influence state behavior through the crucial elements of "issue resonance, network density, and target vulnerability."[71] Applying these concepts to the emergence of DHR, professionals from within the legal and academic communities in the European Union created linkages from their own legal rights community, to government policy-makers, and ultimately, connected to the oversight bodies of data protection at the EU level. They used the consulting space they were given as a platform to frame and promote fundamental human rights for digitized data. As Haas notes,

> To the extent to which an epistemic community consolidates bureaucratic power within national administrations and international secretariats, it stands to institutionalize its influence and insinuate its views into broader international politics.[72].

Regime Convergence upon the Human Rights Model

The development of a digital human rights regime in the European Union relied upon (1) the necessity of a data governance regime in the EU, and (2) some force within the EU that would shape data governance toward the human rights model. EU states' coordinated efforts to create a Union-wide digital human rights regime can shed light on EU policy-making around other issues, and perhaps teach us more upon human

[69] Keck and Sikkink (1998), Meyer et al. (1997) and Sikkink (1993).

[70] Keck and Sikkink (1998).

[71] Keck and Sikkink (1998, p. 26).

[72] Haas (1992, p. 4). Note: I explore the role of epistemic actors extensively within Chapter 7

rights policy cooperation in other regions of the world. The two main EU laws protecting digital human rights - Directive 95/46/EC and the General Data Protection Regulation (GDPR) which passed in 2016—offer substantial proof of the digital human rights regime. These specific laws are explained in detail in Chapter 4. To establish the presence of an EU digital human rights regime, I apply each of the main international relations (IR) theories of realism, liberal institutionalism, and constructivism to the emergence of data protection laws in the early 1970s. After a comparative analysis, I discuss the trend after the mid-1980s, when EU data policy moved toward convergence upon the digital human right model.

Despite the fact that international regime creation has exploded since WWII, international relations theories attribute different reasons for the formation and maintenance of regimes. Each of the main IR paradigms explains an aspect of regime structure and functioning that underpins the creation of digital human rights. Realist regime theory describes the role of "hegemonic" or powerful states in creating regimes, a description of which applies to certain members of the EU.[73] Liberal institutionalism explains how and why a hegemon is not necessary for regime stability or continuity, and gives the reasons why EU states have not removed data protections set out years ago. Constructivism clarifies the contribution made by social factors and elite networks, including the adaptive influence of epistemic experts working with the EU Commission. I now examine each theory for its impact upon the digital human rights regime.

The Importance of Structure and Power

Realist theory argues that no state desires to create a regime which will enforce shared policy coordination, because it will impinge on the most sacred norm of states and governments: national sovereignty. This constraint can be overcome by utilizing systemic structure and states' positions within the structure which delineate certain roles. States' individual goals explain the willingness of states to create regimes, despite

[73] I use Robert Keohane's definition of a hegemonic state, where "one state is powerful enough to maintain the essential rules governing interstate relations, and willing to do so" (Keohane 1984 [2005], p. 35).

some fears of sovereignty loss.[74] Krasner notes that self-interested states will allow regime creation, negotiate terms via agreements, or will impose regimes upon less powerful states *when it matches the state's interests to do so*. Realists expect that regime initiation will be done by the predominantly powerful, or "hegemonic" states.[75] After all, these states have more resources to provide the public goods needed by the international community, and they have the political will and capacity to punish free-riders, again, should they wish to do so.[76]

As a trade-off for providing some public goods to member states of the regime, the hegemon expects to control the issue agenda in ways which progress that state's foreign policy goals.[77] Reaching agreement to form a regime is possible because less-powerful states will join the regime to free-ride on the provision of public goods of some kind, or to avoid sanctions by hegemonic states who control the issue agenda of the new regime. Therefore, according to realists, regime creation is most likely to occur when a dense issue space includes high levels of interdependence, raising the possibility of side payments to hesitant group members which offset the potential loss of sovereignty generated by policy-making for the regime.[78] In other words, where issue density is high, states and their representatives may seek side payments from other IGO member states over one supranational issue area, in order to agree to regime policies that potentially produce negative effects to domestic interest groups back home.

Several things challenge the rigidity of regimes. Internal contradictions can become apparent over time during application of the regime rules, or power shifts can occur within the international system that alter who fills the hegemonic space. Pure realism cannot explain why regimes will persist when the original purpose no longer exists, or if and when the hegemonic state which first created the regime begins to decline. Hegemonic Stability Theory (HST) speaks to this weakness in realism by proposing that after a hegemon declines in power, the regime it created may not necessarily

[74] *International Regimes*, 1983, Chapter 1: "Structural Causes and Regime Consequences: Regimes as Intervening Variables", by Stephen Krasner.

[75] Keohane and Nye (1989).

[76] Nye (2014) and Gilpin (1987, p. 100).

[77] Keohane and Nye (1989).

[78] Keohane, pp. 155–157, in Krasner (1983, 1995).

decay.[79] Scholars suggest: if other states continue to benefit from the framework of the regime, then regime instruments will be reshaped to adapt to shocks to the regime such as loss of the regime leader, but the regime itself may not die off altogether.[80] Realism provides the foundation for regime construction, but leaves gaps that can be supported by other international relations theories.

Institutions, Time, and Efficiency

Liberal institutionalism provides a supplemental framework to that of realism, and is based upon ideational concepts that can be applied to the formation of data protection in the EU. Recall that realism assumes that states' shared interests provide the motivation for states to forego sovereignty in particular areas and allow regime creation.[81] A liberal institutionalism counter-argument asserts that not only can regimes form, but they become self-perpetuating, given that regime rules will lock states into ongoing participation. These rules persist long after the original conditions for their creation have changed, ensuring regime longevity after the initial utility function has decayed. When we understand the nature of regimes to be long-term, membership in a regime signals credible commitments and future accountability to other states during multiple iterations of interaction around an issue. In addition to improving accountability, regimes reduce transaction costs, increase economies of scale, and enhance goods provisions to the group members as resources are pooled together. Finally, international regimes give voice to small and mid-sized states; they will work to preserve regimes as a leveling agent with more powerful states in a shared issue arena.[82] The data protection regimes created by the OECD and Council of Europe, and later by the European Union exemplify such long-standing regimes. EU member states that have joined these IGOs have made commitments to the accompanying missions and behavioral expectations for member states of each regime.

[79] Keohane (1984 [2005]).

[80] Ruggie (1982).

[81] Keohane (1984 [2005]).

[82] Chapter 5, "The Governance Problem in International Relations" by Peter Alexis Gourevitch, in *Strategic Choice and International Relations*, edited by David A. Lake and Robert Powell, 1999.

Returning to the power of hegemonic states, regime membership binds member states to the preferences of the states which achieved agenda control over the regime.[83] Early research scrutinized security regimes, but in the 1980s expanded to include economic regimes.[84] As security-based regimes are beyond the scope of this project, I focus on the economic regime findings. Economically speaking, individual governments wanted to take successful domestic economic policies and scale them up to the international level if seen as beneficial to the national economy.[85] What began with the individually beneficial goal of economic integration in the European Steel and Coal Community of 1951, led to exponential "mission creep" into multiple issue pillars involving economic, security, and justice affairs built into the Maastricht Treaty of 1992, which established the European Union.[86] Today, the *aquis communitaire* authorizes EU governance over multiple policy arenas, including trade, financial systems regulation, genetically modified agriculture restrictions, climate protections, intellectual property safeguards, and of interest to this book, internet and data governance.[87]

Both realist and institutionalist arguments rely upon the presence of social threats, but neither approach explains *how* social threats emerge or change.[88] Realism assumes security threats are the primary motivator, and liberal institutionalism assumes that other shared issues exist, secondary to the primary interest of protecting state security. Liberal institutionalism adds the element of domestic economic concerns for why states create, join, and cooperate with international regimes, including data regimes. Yet this paradigm lacks an explanation for how states determine their willingness for *which* interests will be carried into the international space. Wendt proposes that the main motive of states—protecting territorial and issue sovereignty—is actually a socially constructed and accepted norm,

[83] Keohane (1984 [2005]).

[84] Jervis (1982), Keohane (1984), Keohane and Nye (1989) and Krasner (1983).

[85] Moravcsik (1998).

[86] Bache et al. (2015).

[87] Drezner (2007) and Varveris and Panagopoulou (2019). *Acquis communautaire* is the core body of EU law, including Decisions, Directives, and Regulations, as well as court decisions, all of which are binding upon member states.

[88] Wendt (1992).

implying that the development of national interests is a more multi-dimensional and learned process, constantly evolving across time, and impacted by domestic interests.[89] The constructive theoretical approach provides the final missing piece to explain the emergence of a DHR regime in the EU.

Social Norms and Agency

Constructivists contend that the components of the international system are socially interactive and originate at the domestic level. Social actors build the domestic structure of states and set constraints for state behavior, which leads to desires for international constraints upon other states' behaviors.[90] These constraints can be seen inside institutional organizations, or regimes. Identifying the intersubjective nature of the international order and by implication the intersubjectivity of regimes illuminates the role played by states' identities, which have normative factors. Crucially, constructivism points out that the agency of individuals, including professional or epistemic actors, contribute to the evolution of domestic norms and identities which can be then be diffused throughout the international system.[91] By allowing for cross-interactions between the domestic and international spheres, the constructive approach acknowledges that identities and interests are constantly being reassessed for value and for instrumentality.[92]

Constructivism also offers explanations on how sociopolitical factors impact regime adaptation across time.[93] As just mentioned, domestic actors shape the political environment of national preferences. In addition to the preferences of the aggregate population, domestic elites and firms influence a state's foreign policy, which in turn shapes the strategies a state will pursue when negotiating internationally. As explained by Frieden, this process is implicit with changing preferences across time, meaning that

[89] Wendt (1992).

[90] Ruggie (1998).

[91] Haas (1992) and Keck and Sikkink (1998).

[92] Wendt (1992).

[93] Moravcsik (1997) and Wendt (1992).

not only are sub-state actors influential, time itself is a contributing variable to regime evolution.[94] Without the contribution of constructivism, the role played by non-state actors at multiple time points in determining policy changes in the EU would be completely overlooked. Constructivism thus provides important tools to explain the activity of sub-state actors to transform data regimes across time and space.

Taken together, each of the main IR theories supply reasons for states' willingness to adopt a data policy regime in the European Union. However, these theories don't fully explain the move toward a consensus around the digital human rights approach. This is where additional research is required.

Explanations of Identity-Based Policies and Policy Congruence

As mentioned in the introduction of this book, some data policy researchers and IOs such as the OECD expected data policy convergence at the global level, particularly due to early pressures placed upon multinational corporations to standardize data protections.[95] Yet these predictions did not uncover why *EU states* would choose a human rights-based policy as the convergence point, especially given the fact that early guidelines were driven by economic growth concerns, not human rights. Nor do these models explain the attempts by the EU to export high levels of DHR protections outside the EU. I propose that the wishes of the most powerful EU states became the end-point of policy convergence. France, Germany, and the United Kingdom had the largest populations, economies, and military capabilities, making these states the hegemonic powers of the European Union. Each of these states desired data policies founded on fundamental human rights, generating the energy for DHR to become the policy convergence point. The gradual and expanded scope of EU supranationalism simply provided the fallow ground for this to take root, and as a result, DHR became the framework that EU institutions used to push actors outside the Union toward compliance.

[94] Chapter 2, "Actors' Preferences in International Relations," by Jeffry A. Frieden, in *Strategic Choice and International Relations*, edited by David A. Lake and Robert Powell, 1999.

[95] Mueller (2010), Mueller (2017) and Newman (2008).

Regimes are large international organizations (IOs), created on the basis of one primary concern, but as institutionalism predicts, IOs have often experienced an expanded scope as members add new dimensions to the original institutional agenda, or as new members with new identities and goals are admitted into the group. The EU is an example of an IO that has adapted across time, and despite its many challenges, it is arguably one of the most successful international organizations established to date. Much of the success can be attributed to decisions taken around shared goals and values across the community. The EU began as an economic integration project, based on the belief that the increase of business exchange within Europe would reduce the likelihood of another world war. Yet EU competences have spread far and beyond merely economic goals, in a clear instance of "mission creep." Today, EU legislation includes economic, security, and justice affairs competences as seen in the primary organizational document, the Maastricht Treaty of 1992, which created the European Union as we know it today.[96] For the purpose of this book, I focus on the latter issues, justice affairs, as this area includes normative policies involving human rights and justice imperatives tied to EU identity, and therefore data governance for the Union members.

A "logic of appropriateness" on proper behavior is embedded within the identities and systems of many international organizations in which the member states are democracies, including the EU.[97] The EU has adopted multiple Directives and Regulations that incorporate mandates for appropriate behavior for public and private sector actors in the EU. Chapter 4 explores the various laws in detail. For now, it is important to highlight the process by which normative elements are inserted into these laws. There are multiple ways in which behavioral practices are approved.[98] Norm entrepreneurs frame new standards of appropriate behavior and attempt to influence the adoption of these behaviors via the content of new laws and policy.[99] I find evidence that norm entrepreneurs, together with epistemic advisors, proactively inserted the

[96] Bache et al. (2015)

[97] March and Olsen (2008, 2011).

[98] March and Olsen (1995).

[99] Finnemore and Sikkink (1998, p. 897).

frame of human rights around data policy in the EU at the national and regional levels of policy-making.

During the legislative process, policy-makers are often dependent upon the advice of key professionals.[100] This is especially true when a new issue emerges and lawmakers are aware of their lack of knowledge around the topic, such as is frequently seen with technological matters. Epistemic professionals fill this gap by providing much-needed information; in addition, they often interpret the information for lawmakers. Consultants also link state behavior tied to past or proposed policy as causes with effects. As Haas points out, experts bring socially constructed reality interpretations into this informational service.[101] Experts trained in legal framework for a country (or countries) can explain potential human rights outcomes if a certain policy is chosen. The need for technical expertise for ICT and other technology-based issue areas was patently present in this instance. Epistemic actors can and did shape human rights legislation and advocated for norm evolution around EU data protection legislation.

Epistemic experts are crucial actors in international policy-making.[102] Chronologically, when a new issue emerges, this generates a need for information on the emergent issue. The location of topical experts within the EU legislative process is important to the process of data governance, as they serve as central nodes of information within international organizations, including the EU. Epistemic experts are located between the need for new information and the policy-makers who need to make an informed decision about the content of new laws; they are conduits through which the law-making process flows. Thus, new legislation often depends on the organization having access to the information provision of these experts, but the information itself is not the only benefit they provide. Through their service as information providers, experts working within IOs *construct the narrative* about a particular topic.

In addition to their service as information providers, epistemic experts are fundamental to the policy legitimacy of international organizations such as the EU, as they serve to legitimize the legislative process.[103] Democratically organized institutions such as the EU depend upon

[100] Haas (1992).

[101] Haas (1992, p. 21).

[102] Lake and Wong (2007).

[103] Barnett and Finnemore (1999).

consensual decisions and the necessity of policies chosen with rational decision-making, which requires looking at the costs and benefits to the whole community of any potential legislation.[104] Epistemic actors provide rational-legal legitimacy through their acknowledged expertise on a specific issue—having technical experts involved reduces the appearance of political grandstanding or manipulation by any specific state or subset of states. It is rational for policy-makers to follow the parameters proposed by the expertise of those possessing the most knowledge, especially when the experts are chosen from multiple member states and should collectively offer a more objective perspective than that of any one state's respective national interests.[105]

While epistemic expertise allows policy-makers to make informed decisions, and lends democratic accountability to the policy-making process, these individuals also have a uniquely high amount of access to lawmakers, above that of general interest groups or other stakeholders within civil society. Little research has been done to investigate the normative framework these experts transmit as they serve as information-providers to EU decision-makers.[106] Policies aren't set once and remain static; through time, needs change, and prior norms or goals shift. Policies must also shift to accommodate sociocultural changes.[107] What role do epistemic experts play in not only shaping initial legislation, but also promoting change across time? The key to answering this question lies within the structure of the EU legislative machine.

Data policy was initially a third pillar issue: EU member states could set their own data legislation with full sovereignty. After the Lisbon Treaty went into effect in 2009, EU policy-makers moved data policy into the first-pillar space, transforming it from an intergovernmental issue to a supranational policy issue.[108] By mainstreaming data concerns, this led to a top-down, rather than bottom-up data governance model. Krook and True note that "internal discussions" become quite powerful in a top-down policy environment of human rights provision.[109] From the

[104] Jančiūtė (2017).

[105] Penney, see p. 105.

[106] Haas (1992, p. 35).

[107] Krook and True (2010, p. 108).

[108] Jančiūtė (2017) and Petkova (2019, p. 148).

[109] Krook and True (2010, p. 117).

point of Lisbon activation, EU bureaucrats had a much-widened scope of authority to define and shape data policy, given that it had moved to the first pillar. Directive 95/46/EC not only solidified the norm of digital human rights, but it created a permanent, standing advisory committee, known as the Article 29 Working Party (WP 29), whose sole purpose was to investigate ongoing concerns about data governance and provide technical expertise to the Commission and Council. This mandate gave them the power to create a logic of appropriateness specific to the topic of digital human rights, as they had a monopoly on shaping "normative capital" and offer exclusive expertise over data governance.[110]

To continue to "guide behavior and stabilize expectations" in a given issue area, IOs establish policy-monitoring agencies. The primary ongoing function of these agencies is to ensure compliance; member states' behaviors must be regularly monitored.[111] Oversight agencies are staffed with a "rational bureaucracy" who provide a form of social legitimization of the policy and any associated implementation practices.[112] The role of "rational bureaucrats" in norm promotion is clearly defined in the epistemic community and norm entrepreneurship literature previously mentioned. If agency-like structures are created to oversee EU data legislation compliance, and the agencies are staffed with epistemic experts having significant input into DHR provision and compliance, this would provide additional evidence of the creation of a digital human rights norm in the European Union.

Gains vs. Losses: Policy Adaptation Across Time

External Policy Pressures upon EU States

As will be shown in Chapter 3, the early years of data legislation focused on the need for data mobility to support growth in the nascent ICT sectors of European countries and their trade partners, what Jančiūtė refers to as a "market making legal base."[113] The OECD originated the first international effort at harmonization of data processing policies, as a result of the desire among members to prevent disruption to data

[110] Legro (1997, pp. 35–37).

[111] Tilly (1990).

[112] Finnemore (1996).

[113] Jančiūtė (2017, p. 2).

use during the onset of computer technology diffusion.[114] The OECD's progress on recommendations followed conferences held in 1974 and 1977, during which attendees looked at the topics of data privacy, citizens' access to information about data, and cross-border data mobility. The OECD's policy experts, Peter Gassman (German engineering and economics consultant), Louis Joinet (French drafter of French *Informatique et Liberté* law), and Professor Peter Seipel (Swedish Professor of Law), made several recommendations regarding data controls. They raised concerns about "reconciling fundamental but competing values such as privacy and the free flow of information."[115] The subsequently released document, *OECD Guidelines Governing the Protection of Privacy and Transborder Flows of Personal Data,* included eight core principles:

- Limit personal data collections to lawful means, preferably with data subject consent
- Collect personal data only for specified purposes, and limit data use to these original purposes
- No disclosure of personal data without either the data subject consent *or* the authority of the law
- Provide security measures against unauthorized data access or disclosure
- Provide a transparent policy concerning personal data
- Data subject rights should be allowed to confirm any data held, and data should be corrected/ erased, when requested by the data subject

Member governments were encouraged to incorporate the OECD Guidelines into national practices, but no formal enforcement mechanisms existed. Concurrent to the work being done by the OECD on setting guidelines for data use, was activity taken by the Council of Europe, also dealing with data protection measures.

The origin of the Council of Europe (CoE) data protection regime began in the late 1960s. The CoE Legal Committee received two motions from the Consultative Assembly of 1967, requesting that the Committee

[114] Gassman (1976) and OECD (2011, p. 15).

[115] Gassman, pp. 127–141; H. P. Gassman (2010) and OECD (2011, p. 19).

examine the impact of technological developments upon privacy.[116] In 1973 the CoE adopted Resolution 73 (22), recommending privacy protections for individuals' data held by electronic databanks within private sector firms. At the 236th meeting of the Ministers' Deputies, the CoE passed Resolution (74) 29, *On the Protection of Privacy of Individuals Vis-à-vis Electronic Data Banks in the Public Sector*; this resolution noted the increased use of computerized data banks within the public sectors of member governments, and expressed similar fears to those raised by the OECD consultants previously discussed. Resolution 74 (29) suggested data protections to include:

- Inform the public of government use of electronic data banks for storage or processing of personal information
- Keep information current and use it only for designated purposes
- Create storage time limits
- Set precautions and codes of conduct to limit misuse of information
- Restrict databank access to authorized users, with necessity of use
- Maintain data subject anonymity when using data for statistical purposes

The CoE final treaty, thereafter, known as Convention 108, was finalized on 28 January 1981, with protections for personal data during automatic processing. It was the first truly international regime for personal data protection based upon a treaty signed by the members of an international organization. Original signatory states from the EU included France, Germany, and Sweden. The CoE regime had much more impact on the EU states than did the OECD Guidelines for two main reasons: it asked specifically for "data protection" rather than data privacy, and it invited regional institutions such as the EU to push their member states for implementation.

When combined together, national laws, EU data regulations, and the recommendations by the OECD and Council of Europe regarding data protection generated a regime complex for digital human rights. During Phase I (1970–mid-1990s), EU states had national data laws that at times rivaled or competed with neighbor states, or were in conflict with the recommendations of the OECD and/or the CoE, which will be further

[116] Fuster (2016, p. 83).

Fig. 2.1 Digital human rights regime complex

explained in Chapter 6.[117] EU states dealt with some intersection of data governance goals, but at other times, competing demands for diverse data management policy content. See Fig. 2.1 for a graphic representation of the overlapping interests that impacted EU digital human rights during this period.

Internal Policy Pressures upon EU States

As mentioned, Directive 95 established a permanent working committee, the Article 29 Working Committee (hereafter WP 29), whose sole purpose was to oversee data legislation matters for the EU. The Commission, Council of Ministers, or Parliament periodically asked WP 29 for updates on data use and governance. More commonly, data policy changes originated from WP 29, whose mandate allowed the committee to suggest amendments to "safeguard the rights and freedoms of natural persons with regarding to the processing of personal data, and on any

[117] Drezner (2007).

other proposed Community measures affecting such rights and freedoms."[118] The committee was comprised solely of the directors from each national data protection agency. As Chapter 7 reveals, these individuals frequently had a career history as legal professionals or social science academics; both fields embrace norms of human rights provision and protection.

WP 29 vastly expanded the scope of data protection rights and cemented the digital human rights regime in the EU. The committee submitted annual reports, opinion statements, and recommendations to the Commission and Council. These reports served to keep both bodies apprised of societal changes in data use and treatment, as well as to recount compliance efforts by member states. Most importantly, across time the reports made clear suggestions for an expanded range of data protections for all EU states. For example, the committee pushed for the right to have data forgotten, asked for data subject consent before data collection and use, set data retention practices for mobile phone and ISP firms, and outlined when states could and could not transport data during threats to national security.[119] As a result of multiple amendments to Directive 95, and the addition of several outside pieces of legislation involving aspects of data governance, it was eventually necessary to replace the Directive with a more comprehensive piece of legislation capable of housing the majority of EU data mandates in one policy. The General Data Protection Regulation (GDPR) replaced Directive 95 in 2016. The GDPR merged prior EU recommendations and filled gaps due to technological and political changes, thereby expanding data protection mandates in the EU. It also fundamentally altered the global landscape of data protection by requiring third party countries to provide digital human rights to EU citizens, when using their data. I explore these changes in detail in Chapters 6 and 8.

Theoretical Support and Hypothetical Expectations

To summarize, new human rights norms emerge when constructed by social and/or political actors. Norm development and formalization

[118] *Competences*, p. 4, Directive 95/46/EC.

[119] ISP: Internet service provider.

inside the EU involves legislation at the national and regional/EU level. Two-level negotiations require policy compromises to ensure domestic interests are appeased and international commitments are kept. Rigorous debate between multiple stakeholders occurs during the norm birthing process. Regime theory expects domestic institutions and international regimes to protect and preserve policy that matters to the most powerful states and to particular interest groups. There are three key groups in the EU for whom data policy is crucial both domestically and internationally. The ICT sector identifies data as a powerful economic commodity and would like to keep control over how data is collected, processed, stored, and moved. Government security ministries, law enforcement, and criminal prosecutors see data as a tool for protecting state sovereignty and national security. Lastly, European legal professionals and human rights advocates have increasingly identified data use and abuse as a component of fundamental human rights, and used their consultative power to promote digital human rights. Note that I do not expect these interests to be mutually exclusive, but I do anticipate a need to prioritize when these interests are at conflict.

Given these facts, I expect national data legislation to evolve as follows:

> *EU states with large-scale economic dependence on ICT firms will pass economic commodification polices* ***(create a national institution),*** *protecting the use of personal and/or cyber data (i.e., digitized data) for profit.*
>
> *EU states with a history of numerous domestic terrorist attacks will promote securitized policies for digitized data* ***(create a national institution),*** *resulting in state and law-enforcement gaining access to the databanks of both public and private sectors.*
>
> *EU states which utilize legal experts or academics based in human rights disciplines as legislative consultants during the law-making process will extend human rights protections over data legislation* ***(create a national institution).***

To formalize the new DHR norm at the EU-level, specific political opportunities must exist for new supranational legislation. Making EU law requires the EU Commission to open the policy agenda for a new issue area, after which the EU Council of Ministers and Parliament respond favorably as co-legislative bodies. As this occurs, individual member states desire to influence the direction of policy congruence, and legal and academic policy advisors practice norm advocacy that aligns with the norms of their professions. The creation of DHR laws clearly signals new norm emergence and nominal acceptance of the new norm across a majority of EU member states. Bureaucratic agencies should then be established to manage oversight and compliance; this further signals new norm institutionalization. Once initiated, these oversight agencies will become entrenched. Subsequent chapters reveal the evolutionary process of the EU data regime complex, as well as the areas of policy compromise reached in the wake of changing internal and external conditions.

As evidence of the development of a DHR regime at the EU level, I expect the following:

> *The EU Commission will ask for data policies to be added to the legislative agenda of the EU Community, opening the door for a formalization of the norm of digital human rights.*
>
> *As a result of their hegemonic power, the policy preferences of more powerful EU states will become the convergence point for EU data policy.*
>
> *Legal and human rights experts serving in an advisory capacity to the EU institutions (Commission, Council of Ministers, Parliament) will advocate for fundamental human rights protections for digitized data, creating an EU digital human rights regime.*

Methodological Tests

This book utilizes a variety of methods to test the theoretical argument and expectations just introduced. As noted in the section on human rights norm emergence, the initial stages typically involve rhetorical discussions over the necessity of the new norm and attached behaviors. These debates between legislative actors occur during the origination of new laws, and take place at both national and regional levels, therefore, it is necessary to examine the debates during the debate phase of policy initiation. I assess a variety of communications at both national and EU levels, using established research practices such as case studies and text analyses. To ensure testing robustness, I also incorporate descriptive statistics and standardized modeling of key variables within the causal argument. Case studies and historical process-tracing in Phase I provide a structured, focused, and systematic approach to uncovering the causal factors of the EU policy output.[120] Regarding Phase I, when process-tracing of individual cases is combined with case comparisons, this creates a powerful, synergistic tool

[120] Bennett and Checkel (2015), George and Bennett (2005) and Herb (2017).

for comparative historical analysis.[121] There are numerous past examples comparative political science literature incorporating this combination of methods, such as Skocpol's *States and Social Revolutions* and Wood's *Forging Democracy from Below*.[122] Finally, descriptive statistics support the structural arguments made at the national level for the three independent variables (economic commodification of data, data securitization due to national security threats, and the presence of legal rights experts serving as consultants for data policy advice). The content of data laws to emerge at the national serve as the dependent variable. The full methodology is discussed more within in Parts II and III.

National Cases

Germany, the United Kingdom, and Sweden are the national cases. This choice reflects both a "most similar" and "least similar" selection approach. The case states are developed economies with democratic regimes, as well as being EU, OECD, Council of Europe, and UN Member States (i.e., an overlap of regime memberships). Similarity in organizational membership allows for the regime complexity argument to be controlled in the respect that the IO memberships are all the same. Economic indicators reflect additional similarities; each of these countries have high levels of international trade in GDP (Germany 43.6%, UK 31.2%, Sweden 47.14%),[123] and high average incomes in GDP per capita (Germany $56,689; UK $48,651; Sweden $55,243; all in USD).[124]

Dissimilarities include population sizes (Germany 83.1 million, the UK 66.8 million, Sweden 10.2 million),[125] dates of accession to the EU (West Germany 1958, UK 1973, Sweden 1995),and participation in the Eurozone (Germany participates, the UK and Sweden do not). An additional dissimilarity is location: Germany is in central Europe, the UK in western Europe (non-continental), and Sweden is in northern Europe (also non-continental). Dissimilar factors allow me to rigorously test the argument that policy convergence should occur across multiple states (recall that the

[121] Herb (2017).

[122] Skocpol (1994) and Wood (2007).

[123] https://stats.oecd.org, 2020 data.

[124] OECD Database, National Accounts at a Glance, 2021 data.

[125] World Bank World Development Indicators, Population 2019 figures.

1980s literature expected technology policy convergence among democracies). Finally, the independent variables of epistemic expert involvement (highly prominent in Germany and Sweden), economic dependence on ICT firms (highest in the UK, lower in Germany and Sweden), and frequent security/terrorist attacks (highest in UK) show variance in the independent variables as recommended by King, Keohane, and Verba when conducting qualitative social science research.[126]

Time Frames

Data times measure from 1970 to 2018, contingent upon data availability. Beginning in 1970, state agencies and private sector firms began computerizing data management and storage. National policies appeared from early in the 1970s to cover data practices. By the 1990s, government offices and academic research facilities adopted internet use, which then spread to business sectors. Computer networks capable of data exchange across large distances grew, and governments incorporated cyber data policies into their larger data legislation from the 1990s forward. Individual states decided how and when to implement elements of human rights protections within domestic data policies.

I employ several "markers" for the birth of a new human rights norm. Initially, individuals working within governments and intergovernmental organizations (IGOs) make statements to introduce a new norm and favorably frame its necessity. Next, the pro-norm discourse is spread throughout the executive and legislative bodies. Following this, the norm is adopted by several member states in an IGO, providing evidence of "shared understandings among states."[127] Finally, policies can be altered across time to reflect accommodations to changing conditions.

The Role of Text Analyses

Additionally, I looked for written documentation of positive declarations and pro-data protection discourse during legislative sessions, agenda-setting meetings, or other points during the policy-initiation process of

[126] King et al. (2012).

[127] These methods mirror those of UN sanctioning practices; see Hawkins and Lloyd (2003, p. 441).

both the national legislatures of member states, and the executive and legislative bodies of the EU. At the EU level, I searched for textual content promoting digital human rights in the key policy-making bodies: The Commission, the Council of Ministers, or Parliament. If the new DHR norm follows prior emergence patterns, I expected to find discourse narratives tying protection of individuals' digitized data to the existing human rights framework of the EU, with links to EU identity based upon liberal values, including the right to privacy. This does not explain *why* certain states or individuals decided to introduce the new norm, nor does it measure the scope of norm compliance after emergence. However, it does uncover *if* and *how* digital human rights were born in the EU and in which location(s) the effort began.

I further outline a second useful set of expected norm promotion activities based upon prior models which utilize clear conceptual definitions, and subsequently provide measures for testing the presence of norm adoption.[128] The new norm must be consistently applied across society to the activities of public and private sector actors. Although new norms may conflict with the self-interests of some parties involved, a state or IO will acknowledge the "rightness" of the norm, despite these potential costs. Finally, the norm must have a basis in "…moral or ethical character."[129] Text analysis will thus combine a clearly defined set of parameters for the norm of digital human rights and search for key markers to measure the presence of the norm inside the relevant documents. Important texts should utilize:

1. Statements by governmental actors and advisors tying new EU data legislation to fundamental human rights
2. Positive discourse about DHR by officials within the executive and legislative bodies
3. Digitized data protection laws created by the EU, as a result of the above-mentioned efforts

To trace the emergence of digital human rights, I located an appropriate corpus of documents found within the EUR-Lex database using a

[128] Goertz and Diehl (1992, p. 634).

[129] Goertz and Diehl (1992, p. 639).

set of a priori search terms about data processing, which will be explained at length in the next chapters.

EU Development of DHR Laws

Recall that I have three expectations at the *regional* level: a new opening will occur for DHR on the EU legislative agenda, human rights advocates will take a significant role in shaping the formalization of the new norm, and powerful states should push to have policy congruence matching their national preferences.

First, I looked for legislative agenda discussions about data governance, beginning in 1970. My focus primarily occurred around the behavior of the various EU Commission presidents, as the Commission is the starting part for new legislation. Then, I looked at the responses by the Council of Ministers and the EU Parliament, who share co-legislative responsibilities for crafting the content of new laws. To map out these activities, I relied upon historical process-tracing within the official records of the Commission, Council, and Parliament, again within the EUR-Lex database, using key search terms explained in the chapters ahead.

Next, I examined the level of influence of the most powerful EU states—France, Germany, and the UK—upon the EU data policy-making process. According to the argument, individual states will push other member states toward specific policies, based upon the salience of the three structural elements in each country. I measure levels of economic dependence upon the ICT sector by looking at the value of the ICT sector upon the national economy, as well as by measuring the additive export effects of ICT to the economy. The Global Terrorism database helps identify the impact of domestic security problems upon preferences for using data in security surveillance, via gross measure of numbers of domestic terror incidents from the 1970s to 2014. Once laws emerge at the EU-level, the formal presence of a digital human rights regime will be evidenced by:

1. DHR laws which apply to public and private sectors
2. Consistency on how DHR laws are applied to all member states
3. Economic sanctions for violators

Extensive content analysis thus reveals the degree to which the national data policies of France, Germany, and the United Kingdom match the content of subsequent EU data legislation.

Finally, to gauge the role of legal and human rights experts in pressuring the EU to pass data protection, I searched for the presence of individuals from these professions in positions of authority related to technical information provision during the pre-legislative phase, and given the power of oversight once DHR laws exist. Again, I relied upon process tracing and text analysis of EU legislative documents involving advisory reports requested by the Commission, Council, and Parliament.

In the next section, I look at the origin of EU data governance, to the countries of Sweden, Germany, and the United Kingdom in the early 1970s.

Bibliography

Acharya, Amitav. 2004. "How Ideas Spread: Whose Norms Matter? Norm Localization and Institutional Change in Asian Regionalism." *International Organization* 58: 239–275.

Alcantara, Chris. 2017. "46 Years of Terrorist Attacks in Europe, Visualized." July 17. Accessed May 16, 2018. https://www.washingtonpost.com/graphics/world/a-history-of-terrorism-in-europe/.

Alter, Karen J., and Sophie Meunier. 2009. "The Politics of International Regime Complexity." *Perspectives on Politics* 7 (1): 13–24.

Axelrod, Robert. 1986. "An Evolutionary Approach to Norms." *The American Political Science Review* 80 (4): 1095–1111.

Bache, Ian, Simon Bulmer, Stephen George, and Owen Parker. 2015. *Politics in the European Union*. Oxford: Oxford University Press.

Barnett, Michael N., and Martha Finnemore. 1999. "The Politics, Power, and Pathologies of International Organizations." *International Organization* 53 (4): 699–732.

Benford, Robert D., and David A. Snow. 2000. "Framing Processes and Social Movements; An Overview and Assessment." *Annual Review of Sociology* 26: 611–639.

Bennett, Andrew, and Jeffrey T. Checkel. 2015. *Process Tracing: From Metaphor to Analytic Tool*. Cambridge: Cambridge University Press.

Cardenas, Sonia. 2004. "Norm Collision: Explaining the Effects of International Human Rights Pressure on State Behavior." *International Studies Quarterly* 6 (2): 213–231.

Chanley, Virginia A. 2002. "Trust in the Government in the Aftermath of 9/11: Determinants and Consequences." *Political Psychology* 23: 469–483.

Clarke, Richard A. 2016. "The Risk of Cyber War and Cyber Terrorism." *Journal of International Affairs* 70: 179–181.

Colecchia, Alessandra, and Paul Schreyer. 2001. "ICT Investment and Economic Growth in the 1990s: Is the United States a Unique Case? A Comparative Study of Nine OECD Countries." OECD Science, Technology and Industry Working Papers 2001/07, Paris: OECD.

Deibert, Ronald J. 2013. *Black Code: Surveillance, Privacy, and the Dark Side of the Internet*. Toronto: McClelland & Stewart.

———. 2020. *Reset: Reclaiming the Internet for Civil Society*. Toronto, ON: House of Anansi Press.

Department of Homeland Security Emeritus Center of Excellence. 2019. "National Consortium for the Study of Terrorism and Responses to Terrorism." Global Terrorism Database (GTD). University of Maryland.

DeSimone, Christian. 2010. "Pitting Karlsruhe Against Luxembourg? German Data Protection and the Contested Implementation of the EU Data Retention Directive." *German Law Journal* 11 (2): 291–317.

Drezner, Daniel W. 2007. *All Politics Is Global: Explaining International Regulatory Regimes*. Princeton, NJ: Princeton University Press.

Europa. 2019. "Enterprises Using Cloud Computing Services, 2014 and 2018 (% of Enterprises)." July 17. Accessed July 2019. https://ec.europa.eu/eurostat/statistics-explained/index.php/Digital_economy_and_society_statistics_-_enterprises.

European Parliament. 2019. "EU Parliament." Accessed April 20, 2019. http://www.europarl.europa.eu/external/html/euenlargement/default_en.htm.

European Parliament and the Council of the European Union. 1995. "Directive 95/46/EC of the European Parliament and of the Council of 24 October 1995 on the Protection of Individuals with Regard to the Processing of Personal Data and on the Free Movement of Such Data." Directive. Brussels: Official Journal of the European Communities.

European Union. 1973. "Information Memo, P-63-73." *SEC (73) 4300 Final*.

Eurostat. 2020. *Digital Economy and Society Statistics—Enterprises*. Statistics Explained, Digital Economy and Society, European Union, Brussels: Eurostat, 23.

Finnemore, Martha. 1996. "Norms, Culture, and World Politics: Insights from Sociology's Institutionalism." *International Organization* 50: 325–347.

Finnemore, Martha, and Kathryn Sikkink. 1998. "International Norm Dynamics and Political Change." *International Organization* 52 (4): 887–917.

Flaherty, David H. 1989. *Protecting Privacy in Surveillance Societies: The Federal Republic of Germany, Sweden, France, Canada, and the United States*. Chapel Hill, NC: University of North Carolina Press.

Frieden, Jeffry A. 1999. "Actors and Preferences in Internationtal Relations." In *Strategic Choice and International Relations*, by David A. Lake and Robert Powell, 39–76. Princeton, NJ: Princeton University Press.

Fuster, Gloria González. 2016. *The Emergence of Personal Data Protection as a Fundamental Right of the EU*. Cham: Springer.

Gassman, Hans Peter. 1976. "OECD Guidelines Governing the Protection of Privacy and Transborder Flows of Personal Data." *Computer Networks* 5 (2): 127–141.

———. 2010. "30 Years After: The Impact of the OECD Privacy Guidelines." Organisation for Economic Cooperation and Development, March 10.

George, Alexander L., and Andrew Bennett. 2005. *Case Studies and Theory Development in the Social Sciences.* Cambridge, MA: MIT Press.

Gilpin, Robert. 1987. *The Political Economy of International Relations.* Princeton, NJ: Princeton University Press.

Goertz, Gary, and Paul F. Diehl. 1992. "Toward a Theory of Interational Norms: Some Conceptual and Measurement Issues." *Journal of Conflict Resolutoin* 36 (4): 634–664.

Goodin, Robert E., James G. March, and Johan P. Olsen. 2011. "The Logic of Appropriateness." In *The Oxford Handbook of Political Science*, edited by Robert E. Goodin. Oxford: Oxford University Press.

Gourevitch, Peter Alexis. 1999. "The Governance Problem in International Relations." In *Strategic Choice and International Relations*, by David A. Lake and Robert Powell, 137–164. Princeton, NJ: Princeton University Press.

Haas, Peter M. 1992. "Epistemic Communities and International Policy Coordination." *International Organization* 46 (1): 1–35.

Hafner-Burton, Emilie M. 2008. "Sticks and Stones: Naming and Shaming the Human Rights Enforcement Problem." *International Organization* 62: 689–716.

Hafner-Burton, Emilie M., and Kiyotera Tsutsui. 2007. "Justice Lost! The Failure of International Human Rights Law to Matter Where Needed Most." *Journal of Peace Research* 44 (4): 407–425.

Hagland, Ladawn, and Rimhjim Aggarwal. 2011. "Test of Our Progress: The Translation of Economic and Social Rights Norms into Practice." *Journal of Human Rights* 10: 494–520.

Hathaway, Oona A. 2002. "Do Human Rights Treaties Make a Difference?" *The Yale Law Journal* 111 (8): 1935–2042.

Hawkins, Darren, and Joshua Lloyd. 2003. "Questioning Comprehensive Sanctions: The Birth of a Norm." *Journal of Human Rights* 2 (3): 441–454.

Herb, Michael. 2017. "Discussion of Cross-Case Analyses." Atlanta, GA: Georgia State University, Political Science Department, April 3.

Hintz, Arne, and Stefania Milan. 2009. "At the Margins of Internet Governance: Grassroots Tech Groups and Communications Policy." *International Journal of Media and Cultural Politics* 5 (1–2): 23–38.

Huddy, Leonie, Stanley Feldman, Charles Taber, and Gallya Lahav. 2005. "Threat, Anxiety, and Support of Antiterrorism Policies." *American Journal of Political Science* 49 (3): 593–608.

Jančiūtė, Laima. 2017. "EU Data Protection and 'Treaty-Base Games': When Fundamental Rights Are Wearing Market-Making Clothes." In *Data Protection and Privacy: The Age of Intelligent Machines*, 1–31. Oxford: Hart Publishing.

Jervis, Robert. 1982. "Security Regimes." *International Organization* 36 (2): 357–378.

Johnson, Loch K., Richard J. Aldrich, Christopher Moran, David Barrett, Glenn Hastedt, Robert Jervis, Wolfgang Krieger, et al. 2014. "An INS Special Forum; Implications of the Snowden Leaks." *Intelligence and National Security* 29 (6): 793–810.

Keck, Margaret E., and Kathryn Sikkink. 1998. *Activists Beyond Borders: Advocacy Networks in Transnational Politics.* Ithaca, NY: Cornell University Press.

Kello, Lucas. 2017. *The Virtual Weapon and International Order.* New Haven, CT: Yale University Press.

Keohane, Robert Owen. 1983 [1995]. "The Demand for International Regimes." In *International Regimes*. Ithaca, NY: Cornell University Press.

———. 1984 [2005]. *After Hegemony: Cooperation and Discord in the World Political Economy.* Princeton, NJ: Princeton University Press.

Keohane, Robert Owen, and Joseph S. Nye Jr. 1989. *Power and Interdependence: World Politics in Transition.* New York, NY: Harper Collins.

King, Gary, Robert O. Keohane, and Sidney Verba. 1994 [2012]. *Designing Social Inquiry: Scientific Interference in Qualitative Research.* Princeton, NJ: Princeton University Press.

Kolb, Felix. 2005. "Chapter 5: The Impact of Transnational Protest on Social Movement Organizatios, Mass Media and the Making of ATTAC Germany." In *Transnational Protest and Global Activism.* Lanham, MD: Roman & Littlefield.

Krasner, Stephen. 1983. *International Regimes.* Ithaca, NY: Cornell University Press.

Krasner, Stephen D. 1995. "Compromising Westphalia." *International Security* 20: 115–151.

Krook, Mona Lena, and Jacqui True. 2010. "Rethinking the Life Cycles of International Norms: The United Nations and the Global Promotion of Gender Equality." *European Journal of International Relations* 18 (1): 103–127.

Löblich, Maria, and Manuel Wendelin. 2012. "ICT Policy Activism on a National Level: Ideas, Resources and Strategies of German Civil Society in Governance Processes." *New Media & Society* 14 (6): 899–915.

Lake, David A., and Wendy Wong. 2007. "The Politics of Networks." *SSRN*, May 12. Accessed February 10, 2020. https://papers.ssrn.com/sol3/papers.cfm?abstract_id=1004199.

Lee, John. 2013. "Cyber Kleptomaniacs." *World Affairs* 176: 73–79.

Legro, Jeffrey W. 1997. "Which Norms Matter? Revisiting the 'Failture' of Internationalism." *Internationtal Organization* 51 (1): 31–63.

Lewis-Beck, Michael S., and Martin Paldam. 2000. "Economic Voting: An Introduction." *Electoral Studies* 19: 113–121.

Liu, Hin-Yan. 2019. "The Digital Disruption of Human Rights Foundations." In *Human Rights, Digital Society and the Law: A Research Companion*. Oxford: Routledge.

Longo, Matthew. 2018. *The Politics of Borders: Sovereignty, Security, and the Citizen After 9/11*. Cambridge: Cambridge University Press.

Lynn III, William J. 2010. "Defending a New Domain: The Pentagon's Cyberstrategy." *Foreign Affairs* 89 (5): 97–108.

Magnette, Paul. 2006. "Democracy in the European Union: Why and How to Combine Representation and Participation?" In *Civil Society and Legitimate European Governance*, edited by Stijn Smismans. Cheltenham: Edward Elgar Publishing.

Magnusson, Lars, and Sarfraz Iqbal. 2018. "Implications of EU-GDPR in Low-Grade Social, Activist and NGO Settings." *International Journal of Business and Technology* 6 (3): 1–7.

March, James G., and Johan P. Olsen. 1995. *Democratic Governance*. New York: Free Press.

———. 2008. "The Logic of Appropriateness." In *The Oxford Handbook of Public Policy*, edited by Robert E. Goodin, Michael Moran and Martin Rein. Oxford Handbooks Online.

March, James G., and Johan P. Olsen. 2011. "The Logic of Appropriateness." In *The Oxford Handbook of Political Science*, edited by Robert E. Goodin. Oxford: Oxford University Press.

Mayer-Schönberger, Viktor, and Thomas Ramge. 2018. *Reinventing Capitalism in the Age of Big Data*. London: John Murray.

McIntyre, T.J. 2008. "Data Retention in Ireland: Privacy, Policy and Proportionality." *Computer Law & Security Report* 24: 326–334.

Meyer, John W., John Boli, George M. Thomas, and Francisco O. Ramirez. 1997. "World Society and the Nation-State." *American Journal of Sociology* 103 (1): 144–181.

Michalowitz, Irina. 2007. "What Determines Influence? Assessing Conditions for Decision-Making Influence of Interest Groups in the EU." *Journal of European Public Policy* 14 (1): 132–151.

Migdal, Joel S. 1988. *Strong Societies and Weak States: State-Society Relations and State Capabilities in the Third World*. Princeton, NJ: Princeton University Press.

Milner, Helen. 1997. *Interests, Institutions, and Information*. Princeton, NJ: Princeton University Press.

Moravcsik, Andrew. 1997. "Taking Preferences Seriously: A Liberal Theory of International Politics." *International Organization* 51 (4): 513–553.

———. 1998. *The Choice for Europe: Social Purpose and State Power from Messina to Maastricht*. London: University College London Press.

———. 2002. "In Defense of the 'Democratic Deficit': Reassessing Legitimacy in the European Union." *Journal of Common Market Studies* 40 (4): 603–624.

Mueller, Milton L. 2010. *Networks and States: The Global Politics of Internet Governance*. Cambridge, MA: Massachusetts Institute of Technology Press.

———. 2017. *Will the Internet Fragment?: Sovereignty, Globalization, and Cyberspace*. Cambridge: Polity Press.

Newman, Abraham L. 2008. *Protectors of Privacy: Regulating Personal Data in the Global Economy*. Ithaca, NY: Cornell University Press.

North, Douglass C. 1990. *Institutions, Institutional Change and Economic Performance*. Cambridge: Press Syndicate of the University of Cambridge.

Nye, Joseph S. 2014. "The Regime Complex for Managing Cyber Activities." Paper Series No. 1, Global Commission on Internet Governance, Waterloo, ON; London, UK: Centre for International Governance Innovation and the Royle Institute for International Affairs.

Organisation for Economic Cooperation and Development. 2001. *ICT Value Added: Total, % of Value Added, 2011* Innovations and Technology. Paris: OECD.

———. 2002. *Measuring the Information Economy*. Paris: OECD.

———. 2003. *ICT and Economic Growth Evidence from OECD Countries, Industries and Firms*. Business Performance and Policies. Paris: OECD.

———. 2011. *Thirty Years After the OECD Privacy Guidelines*. Paris: OECD.

———. 2017. *Digital Economy Outlook 2017*. Paris: OECD.

———. 2018. *ICT Total, % of Value Added, 2011 (Indicator)*. ICT Database. Paris: OECD.

———. 2019. "National Accounts at a Glance." Accessed April 2019. https://stats.oecd.org/Index.aspx?DataSetCode=NAAG.

———. n.d. "Trade in Goods and Services." Exports/Imports, % of GDP.

Penney, Jonathan. 2019. "The Right to Privacy: The End of Privacy Fatalism." In *Human Rights, Digital Society and the Law: A Research Companion*, edited by Marti Susi, Chapter 3. Abingdon, Oxford: Routledge.

Petkova, Bilyana. 2019. "Privacy as Europe's First Amendment." *European Law Journal* 25 (2): 140–154.
Pollack, Mark A. 2015. "Theorizing EU Policy-Making." In *Policy-Making in the European Union*, edited by Mark A. Pollack, Alasdair Young and Helen Wallace, 12–45. Oxford: Oxford University Press.
Price, Richard. 1998. "Reversing the Gun Sights: Transnational Civil Society Targets Land Mines." *International Organization* 52 (3): 613–644.
Putnam, Robert D. 1988. "Diplomacy and Domestic Politics: The Logic Of Two-Level Games." *International Organization* 42 (3): 427–460.
Röller, Lars-Hendrik, and Leonard Waverman. 2001. "Telecommunications Infrastructure and Economic Development: A Simultaneous Approach." *The American Economic Review* 91: 909–923.
Reimann, Kim D. 2006. "A View from the Top: International Politics Norms and the Worldwide Growth of NGOs." *International Studies Assocation* 50: 45–67.
Risse, Thomas, Stephen C. Ropp, and Kathryn Sikkink. 2013. *The Persisten Power of Human Rights: From Compliance to Commitment.* Cambridge: Cambridge Universit Press.
Risse-Kappen, Thomas, ed. 1995. *Bringing Transnational Relations Back In: Non-state Actors, Domestic Structures and International Institutions.* Cambridge: Cambridge University Press.
Rittberger, Berthold. 2005. *Building Europe's Parliament: Democratic Representation Beyond the Nation State.* Oxford: Oxford University Press.
Rosecrance, Richard. 1996. "The Rise of the Virtual State." *Foreign Affairs* 75 (4): 45–61.
Ruggie, John Gerard. 1982. "International Regimes, Transactions, and Change: Embedded Liberalism in the Postwar Economic Order." *International Organization* 36: 379–415.
———. 1998. "What Makes the World Hang Together." *International Organization* 52 (4): 855–885.
Sandholtz, Wayne, and Kendall Stiles. 2009. *International Noms and Cycles of Change.* Oxford: Oxford University Press.
Saurugger, Sabine. 2010. "The Social Construction of the Participatory Turn: The Emergence of a Norm in the European Union." *European Journal of Political Research* 49: 471–495.
Schneier, Bruce. 2015. *Data and Goliath: The Hidden Battles to Collect Your Data and Control Your World.* New York, NY: W. W. Norton.
Sikkink, Kathryn. 1993. "Human Rights, Principled Issue-Networks, and Sovereignty in Latin America." *International Organization* 47 (3): 411–441.
———. 2005. "Patterns of Dynamic Multilevel Governance and the Insider-Outsider Coalition." In *Transnational Protest and Global Activism*, edited

by Donatella della Porta and Sidney Tarrow. Oxford: Rowman & Littlefield Publishers Inc.

Skinner, Christina Parajon. 2014. "An International Law Response to Economic Cyber Espionage." *Connecticut Law Review* 46 (4): 1165–1207.

Skocpol, Theda. 1994. *States and Social Revolutions in the Modern World*. London: Cambridge University Press.

Soh, Changrok, Daniel Connolly, and Seunghynn Nam. 2019. "The Main Challenges Related to Protecting Human Rights in the Internet." In *Human Rights, Digital Society and the Law: A Research Companion*, edited by Marti Susi, Chapter 6. Abingdon, Oxford: Routledge.

Stroup, Sarah S., and Amanda Murdie. 2012. "There's No Place Like Home: Explaining International NGO Advocacy." *The Review of International Organizations* 7 (4): 425–448.

Tarrow, Sidney. 1998. *Power in Movement: Social Movements and Contentious Politics*. Cambridge: Cambridge University Press.

Tilly, Charles. 1990. *Coercion, Capital and European States*. Cambridge, MA: B. Blackwell.

Tsutsui, Kiyoteru, and Christine Min Wotipka. 2004. "Global Civil Society and the International Human Rights Movement: Citizen Participation in Human Rights International Nongovernmental Organizations." *Social Forces* 83 (2): 587–620.

University of Maryland. 2018. "Global Terrorism Database." Accessed March 2019. https://www.start.umd.edu/data-tools/global-terrorism-database-gtd.

van Ark, Bart, Johanna Melka, Nanno Mulder, Marcel TImmer, and Gerard Ypma. September 2002. "ICT Investment and Growth Accounts for the European Union, 1980–2000." Final Report on ICT and Growth Accounting, for the DG Economics and Finance of the European Commission, University of Groningen & the Conference Board, Brussels; Centre d'études prospectives et d'informations internationales (CEPII). Paris, Brussels: EU Commission.

Varveris, Alexandros, and Fereniki Panagopoulou. 2019. "The Challenge of Personal Data Protection in the Digital Era and Global Responses." In *Human Rights, Digital Society and the Law: A Research Companion*, edited by Marti Susi, Chapter 18. Abingdon, Oxford: Routledge.

Wendt, Alexander. 1992. "Anarchy Is What States Make of It: The Social Construction of Power Politics." *International Organization* 46 (2): 391–425.

Wood, Elisabeth Jean. 2007. *Forging Democracy from Below: Insurgent Transitions in South Africa and El Salvador*. Cambridge, NJ: Cambridge University Press.

World Bank. 2006. *Global Trends and Policies*. 2006 Information and Communications for Development. Washington, DC: World Bank.

———. 2016. "World Development Indicators Database." Population 2016 Figures. https://data.worldbank.org/indicator/SP.POP.TOTL

PART II

The Early Years—National Origins of Digital Human Rights

Digital human rights in Europe began at the state level, in the first mover countries of Sweden and West Germany. As mentioned in Chapter 2, while the United Kingdom did not legislate as early as the other two countries, the case is relevant because of its hegemonic status in the EU and on the global stage.[1] Though the types of laws each state adopted reflect similar concerns with data management practices and potential privacy losses, the contributing factors behind creating their respective laws differ in important ways. Archival searches in the legislative records for all three countries reveal the origination point for their national laws, as well as provide a window of understanding into the motive for their data legislation. Content analysis of historical documents yields a common lexigraphy among the case countries. Before explaining the findings, let me first outline the process of uncovering these diverse state experiences.

National Laws on Data Governance (1970–1999)

During the early years, public sector bureaucracies and private sector firms digitized manual or paper-based data during the adoption of computer technology. With the transition from manual data to computer databanks,

[1] Hegemony denotes states possessing comparatively more military and/or economic capacity, which gives them the ability to influence other states' practices and therefore, alter the international system itself.

personal data handling lost human oversight and switched to fully automatic processes. States chose how these activities would be legislated, in terms of protecting data privacy and security during databank creation, data processing, and storage. States also faced decisions on whether the new laws should apply to both state and non-state actors, in accordance with the preferences of the three main groups of actors expected to have the greatest interest in data policy content: the Information, Communications, and Technology (ICT) sector, national security providers, and the human rights community. The wording of laws discloses whether a state prioritizes:

·use of digitized data as an economic commodity, and/or
·use of digitized data for security purposes of the state, and/or
·provision of digital human rights protections for individuals' digitized data.

I do not assume the three main preferences generate mutually exclusive types of laws. However, when the preferences of interest groups come into conflict, lawmakers prioritize which of the three uses of data are granted the most leverage. To measure this outcome, I analyze national laws introduced or passed in the case states from 1970 to 1999 regarding general personal data (largely pre-internet data).

To date, there is no single standardized method for assessing textual content within social science, due to the diverse nature of the materials we study.[2] However, researchers agree that content analysis should identify thematic patterns within written texts and other communications.[3] Before assessing the actual documents, an *a priori* coding framework is written to capture the importance of specific expected content and any positive/negative sentiments indicative of feelings of support or lack of support for the key interests (in this case, the economic or security value of data, or the need to protect it).[4] It's important to locate and assess key documents from the beginning of the legislative process through to

[2] Chong and Druckman 2011, "Standardized guidelines on how to identify (or even how to define more precisely) a frame in communication do not exist.", p. 240.

[3] Rubin and Rubin 2005.

[4] Chong and Druckman 2011, p. 240; Rubin and Rubin pp. 207–211. Recommended steps include locating the issue/person/event of interest, isolating the relevant topics based on the research question, inductively creating original frames using past literature, and then choosing appropriate material to analyze.

Table 1 National Law Coding Scheme

	Positive mention per sentence	Negative mention per sentence	Net Score
Economic use of data	0, 1	0, 1	0
Security/law enforcement access	0, 1	0,1	0
Protect data/privacy rights	0, 1	0, 1	1
TOTAL			0 = economic use of data 0 = security/law access 1 = protect data

Example: Sweden's 1998 Personal Data Act, Section 1 *Reads, "Be it enacted as follows. General Provisions, Purpose of this Act*, Section 1: *The purpose of this Act is to protect people against the violation of their personal integrity by processing of personal data."*

the creation and implementation of the new laws. The presence and use of particular content frames within data laws reveal the importance of certain issues within a society when the law was made. Counting the frequency of content frames exposes topic salience. Mentioning an issue in either a positive or negative light signifies either support or opposition for a particular area.

For this project, the content of each legislative document is coded for prioritizing the data economy, granting data access freedoms to national security actors, and/or assigning protections for digital human rights. The coding scheme is seen in Table 1. As I discuss each case, I will mention the coded results of key documents, and in so doing, demonstrate support for the argument I've made thus far.

Net score coding accounts for the possibility of multiple goals happening simultaneously. For example, if the law includes positive or negative word associations when discussing any of the three frames (data commodification, security use of data, protecting data privacy), the net score in each of the three categories will denote the hierarchy among policy preferences for data treatment. For laws that treat data as an economic commodity, there will be more content that discusses keeping data open for economic or business use, giving permission for data movement across borders, and/or granting data controllers the ability to destroy or keep data indefinitely. Laws that "securitize" data grant priority access to government actors for security purposes such as enabling law enforcement or criminal investigators permission to collect or retrieve data from either public or private sources. Such demands include court orders to allow for data surveillance, creating a list of set requirements for data processors ("controllers") to submit data when requested from state officials, and/or mandates to retain data for certain periods of time for use by government officials during criminal investigation or prosecution. In some cases, the laws might require cross-border data mobility during international terrorist investigations or prosecution, so that state officials can assist partner states with security processes. Finally, laws that legalize digital human rights stipulate protection for personal data, such as limiting how processors collect, store, maintain, or re-use data (including selling or moving data to third parties). Additional protections might require data subject consent for any of the prior mentioned activities, or granting data subjects the right to revoke such privileges later. If the net score is equal for all three preference areas, it will be noted. If there are inequalities among the net scores of the three influential factors, I note which scores ranked highest. Now let's look the domestic interests concerned about data governance, one by one.

Measuring the Data Economy, Security Threats, and Human Rights Advocacy

Economic Impact of Data

EU states with large-scale economic dependence on ICT firms pass economic commodification polices protecting digitized data for profiteering. While in theory the economic commodification of data consists of an attempt by public or private actors to achieve monetary gains from *any* digitized data, it is primarily a profiteering tool of the private sector. Data commodification occurs with personal data collected and held on individual computers or computer networks, or cyber data created by individuals' participation in online websites and during use of smart phones and third-party apps and/or social media. Data in these forms can be attached to personal identity, or anonymized, but it is being used heavily for the purposes of generating profit by multiple types of industries, including firms that operate as "data brokers." Data brokers are private sector collectors, users, processors, and storers (i.e., "controllers") of personal or cyber data, i.e., profiteers making money off of any type of digitized data generated by and about individuals.

The emergence of the digital economy gave birth to digital markets and data brokers, for whom data is the new money. The OECD notes,

> "The Digital Economy incorporates all economic activity reliant on, or significantly enhanced by the use of digital inputs, including digital technologies, digital infrastructure, digital services and data. It refers to all producers and consumers, including government, that are utilising these digital inputs in their economic activities."[5]

In Phase I (1970–1999), firms profited by using data in multiple ways, such as computerizing data, and/or creating greater data storage and movement technology for use during business practices. The OECD and World Bank began indirectly measuring various aspects of economic gain from the data-rich ICT sector in the 1990s, including growth of the manufacturing, telecommunications, retail, insurance, and financial services sectors, each of whom used digitized data in some capacity.[6] To measure the economic impact of data commodification, this book utilizes the most consistently available data measures found within the *2017 Enter the Data Economy Report*, as well as variables used by the International Monetary Fund (IMF) when measuring the digital economy.[7] These include ICT services exports (% of service exports), investment in ICT supplies (% of total non-residential gross fixed capital formation),[8] high tech exports (% of manufactured exports), and insurance and financial services (% of services).[9] Data sources are identified where the data is discussed in each section. To compare the influence of the ICT sector in each state, I use the descriptive statistics of the aforementioned economic variables.

Although crucial to the data governance choices of the case states of Sweden, Germany, and the UK, data commodification practices of the

[5] OECD 2020.

[6] See OECD Digital Economic papers series, or World Bank annual reports on Information and Communications for Development.

[7] European Commission 2017, IMF 2018.

[8] https://data.oecd.org/ict/ict-investment.htm.

[9] Note the data ranges for the key measures: ICT services exports (1961–2016), investment in ICT supply (1985–2016), high technology exports (1988–2016), and insurance and financial services (1985–present). ICTservices exports, investment in ICT supplies and high-tech exports data found in the World Development Indicators database. Science and Technology indicators. Insurance and financial services sector data is sourced from the OECD.

ICT sector weren't the only influence upon domestic legislation. Now let's look at the role of data as a surveillance tool of national security interests.

Security Incidents

Domestic attacks against state or non-state targets are a breach of state sovereignty, including attacks on territorial spaces and physical infrastructure, whether military or civilian targets. Domestic security threats often drive governments toward information gathering behavior, thus making digitized data surveillance a useful tool in keeping countries safe. EU states with a history of numerous domestic terrorist attacks promote securitized policies for digitized data, resulting in state and law-enforcement gaining access to the databanks of both public and private sectors. The Global Terrorism data (GTD) records the frequency of such attacks (bombings, personal attacks, etc.) bounded within a state's territorial space.[10] To discuss national level legislation, as I look at each states' process for setting data legislation, I utilize GTD statistics on domestic terror attacks. Though cyber-attacks have become increasingly common since the early 2000s, they were uncommon in Phase I. Now lets' look at the human rights aspect of data governance.

Digital Human Rights

Digital human rights (DHR) is the term I introduced in Chapter 1 to describe rights-based legal protections for digitized data; these rights first applied to digitized personal data, and later to cyber data. The application of human rights protections over all types of digitized data is largely attributable to the influence of specific non-state actors. Digital human rights legislation is more likely in EU states in which legal experts or academics based in human rights disciplines are used as legislative consultants during the process of making data legislation and/or monitoring compliance with such laws. This argument follows the logic in the human rights and social movements research, with proven links between the pressure applied by advocates who seek new or strengthened human rights

[10] https://www.start.umd.edu/gtd/about/. The GTD is organized by the University of Maryland researchers and holds open-source, reliable data on terrorist events around the world from 1970–present, with approximately 200,000 cases.

protections and use their influence to achieve positive government policy responses.[11] Promoters of new human rights norms and policy practices are known as "norm entrepreneurs."

Research shows that norm entrepreneurs (NEs) use a variety of tools to achieve their goals. NEs pressure states with "strategic use of information to garner attention...[12] Media coverage is a key component of information campaigns, for promoting public awareness, building urgency and social movement size, and to increase funding.[13] Unfortunately, tallying digital human rights advocacy is difficult for the early years of data legislation, as organized advocacy, such as with NGOs dedicated to this mission, did not emerge until the mid to late 2000s.[14] Furthermore, measuring public advocacy such as through information campaigns and protests is impossible, because major news outlets did not digitize contemporary newspaper content until the mid to late 1990s, and backdated content wasn't added to the Lexis-Nexis academic repository. This left no easy way to access the news coverage about DHR advocacy by civil society during Phase I. A proxy measurement for digital human rights advocacy is needed.

As outlined in Chapter 2, epistemic experts can and do alter policy outcomes by drawing on community norms within their profession, and incorporating these norms within their policy recommendations given as government advisors. Government records documenting the data legislative process contain information on committees, consultations, public hearings, and other investigations utilizing expert advisors, making these materials ideal for tracing certain professions' influence upon data legislation outcomes. I also provide the professional training and backgrounds of the director of each country's data protection authority agency (DPA), as the leadership of the agency has the opportunity to mold the mission of the agency toward her/his own liking. According to my theory, DPA officials coming from legal, jurist, and judicial backgrounds will promote

[11] Keck and Sikkink 1998, Tarrow 1998, Tsutsui and Wotipka 2004.

[12] Stroup and Murdie 2012.

[13] Benford and Snow 2000, Kolb 2004.

[14] See Ron, Ramos, and Rodgers 2005. For example, the European Digital Rights association (EDRi) was formed in 2002 to advocate for data protection and other types of protections for digital content across Europe. Also see the UN list of interested stakeholders who file regular reports with the UN High Commissioner for Human Rights regarding the right to data privacy.

data protection rights, more so than persons from a business, ICT, non-legal, or non-academic profession. I visit this concept again in a later chapter, when I look at the role of epistemic professionals within the EU consultative environment. For now, know that the normative training that legal and human rights professionals receive shapes their policy content suggestions. Admittedly, the shortcoming of looking to the profession of legislative consultants is that one cannot directly establish the motives for individuals beyond the recorded statements, but when available, personal quotes and official texts reveal the priorities these individuals *intentionally wished to convey* as they provide expertise to lawmakers.

To summarize, digital human rights laws in the European Union first emerged in the case countries of Sweden and West Germany, but later spread to powerful states such as the UK. During examination of these case countries, I first look at the laws themselves. Content analysis brings to light the priority and hierarchy given to three main structural interest groups: data commodification allowances for the ICT industries, data access to facilitate national security provisions, and finally, digital human rights protections. Moving from 1970 forward when computer networking first emerged, I then examine how each of the three interests contributed to the types of data laws made in each country. This assessment relies upon descriptive statistics on economic gains from the digital economy, numbers of domestic terror incidents, and the presence of epistemic advisors drawn from legal and/or academic backgrounds. Now, to examine each country in turn.

Bibliography

Benford, Robert D., and David A. Snow. 2000. "Framing Processes and Social Movements; An Overview and Assessment." *Annual Review of Sociology* 26: 611–639.

European Commission. 2017. *Enter the Data Economy: EU Policies for a Thriving Data Ecosystem.* Brussels, BE: European Union.

International Monetary Fund. 2018. "Measuring the Digital Economy." Washington, DC: International Monetary Fund.

Keck, Margaret E., and Kathryn Sikkink. 1998. *Activists Beyond Borders: Advocacy Networks in Transnational Politics*. Ithaca, NY: Cornell University Press.

Kolb, Felix. 2004. "The Impact of Transnational Protest on Social Movement Organizations: Mass Media and the Making of ATTAC Germany." *Transnational Processes and Social Activism*, edited by Donatella della Porta and Sidney G. Tarrow. Lanham, MD: Rowman & Littlefield.

Ron, James, Howard Ramos, and Kathleen Rodgers. 2005. "Transnational Information Politics: NGO Human Rights Reporting, 1986–2000." *International Studies Quarterly* 49: 557–587.

Stroup, Sarah S., and Amanda Murdie. 2012. "There' No Place Like Home: Explaining International NGO Advocacy." *The Review of International Organizations* 7 (4): 425–448.

Tarrow, Sidney. 1994. *Power in Movement: Social Movements and Contentious Politics*. Cambridge: Cambridge University Press.

Tsutsui, Kiyoteru, and Christine Min Wotipka. 2004. "Global Civil Society and the International Human Rights Movement: Citizen Participation in Human Rights International Nongovernmental Organizations." *Social Forces* 83 (2): 587–620.

CHAPTER 3

Sweden: A History of Informational Access

Sweden passed the first national data protection law among European Union states, thus formalizing the norm of digital human rights. There were two main reasons for this bold step. First, when a new digitized census was proposed for 1970, people feared personal information would become forever publicly accessible, violating privacy and risking loss of personal integrity. Second, oversight on compliance with the data protection law was granted to a Data Inspection Board (DIB), led by individuals who made protecting digital human rights a proactive, rather than reactive, responsibility. Sweden's model for data governance would go on to inspire multiple other European states, and provide a reproducible model for how to legislate and enforce digital human rights.

Sweden was the earliest European Union member state to create a national data protection law. The Data Act of 1973 (*Datalagen*) prevented "undue encroachment" on individual privacy present within personal data, albeit with a caveat explained in a moment. The law addressed personal data collection, treatment, and storage, defined the properties of a data subject, and described the level of permission required from the data subject in order to collect and use personal information.[1]

[1] "Data subject" is a term frequently used among data laws in multiple states and refers to the individual(s) about whom the data is collected.

R. Dowd, *The Birth of Digital Human Rights*, Information Technology and Global Governance,
https://doi.org/10.1007/978-3-030-82969-8_3

Perhaps most importantly, the law served as a template for subsequent legislation adopted in many western European states.[2]

The 1973 law set the pattern of government-driven digital human rights found in multiple laws. First, the narrative within the subsequent Swedish data policies as well as rhetoric used by data authorities takes the stance that personal data *must* be state-protected, not private-sector driven. The top-down model of governance is absolutely crucial to the legislative direction taken by the Swedish government. This model went on to influence the data policy stance taken by numerous other EU states, and finally, the EU itself. Second, note that the Swedish language does not have a word that directly translates into "privacy" in English, but references to the protection of the data subject's *integritet*, or "integrity" are frequently referenced. As I will show, the narrative shifts across time away from mere privacy protections, toward a broader list of identity-based human rights components which need protecting within digitized data, a model which is duplicated within the European Community as time unfolds. Since 1973, Swedish data controllers have been obliged to prevent personal data breaches from happening, or suffer a variety of penalties, including fines, prosecution, or even imprisonment, with a variety of penalties, including fines, prosecution, or even imprisonment. Such punitive measures continued thereafter in Sweden and were adopted elsewhere for data protection breaches.[3] In other words, Sweden took a very hardline stance toward personal data protection as a fundamental human right which is easily seen within the content of all Swedish data legislation from 1970 forward.

The *Datalagen* was the first of thirteen laws passed during Phase I that affected personal data in any way. Seven laws deal exclusively with data governance.[4] Three laws had a mix of priorities, including some mention of data commodification and/or security access for digitized data. The

[2] Flaherty (1989) and Fuster (2016).

[3] "Data controllers" is defined as individuals, businesses, or public actors who are responsible for data collection and management of information regarding data subjects in any form.

[4] These laws include the 1973 Data Act (*Datalagen*), the 1973 Credit Information Act (*Kreditupplysningslagen*), the 1974 Debt Collection Act (*Inkassolagen*), the 1978 Act on Names and Pictures in Advertising (*Om Namn Och Bild I Reklam*), the 1980 Secrecy Act (*Sekretesslag*), amendments to the Credit Information and Debt Collection Acts in 1981 and the Data Act in 1982, the 1987 Ordinance with Instructions for the Data Inspectorate (*Förordning med instruktion för datainspektionen*), and finally, the 1998

Table 3.1 Select Swedish data laws, Phase 1 (1970–1999)

Year	*Name of Law*	*Description*	*Net Score*
1973	Data Act (*Datalagen*)	Prevention of loss of personal privacy through data use	+19 Protect data +2 Economic use
1973	Credit Information Act (*Kreditupplysningslagen*)	Regulate licensing for credit and debt collection firms that collect data; Created the Data Inspection Board (DIB)	+31 Protect data
1980	Secrecy Act (*Sekretesslag*)	Allows for data movement between governmental authorities	+8 Security use +7 Protect data +5 Economic use
1998	Personal Data Act (*Personuppgiftslag*)	Regulate identity data among "data controller" firms in Sweden. Align Swedish national laws with EU Directive 95/46/EC	+19 Protect data +3 Economic use +1 Security use

1973 Data Law allowed for data commodification, and the Secrecy Law permitted data commodification and security access, as long as data protections were in place. The 1998 Data Law overwhelmingly expanded the scope of data protections, in accordance with the demands of the supranational EU Directive 95/46/EC, which is discussed more to come. Using the a priori scheme mentioned earlier, I find that **the majority of Swedish data laws prioritized digital human rights**, primarily above the other two interests. Table 3.1 reveals the coded analysis of Swedish data legislation using a select list of laws.

Conditions prior to the establishment of new laws help us understand why laws were created and identify which interest groups the laws may serve. Let's now turn back time, to examine key social, political, and cultural experiences in Sweden which directly shaped data protection.

Tracing Swedish Data Legislation

In the early 1960s, mechanized record and data management expanded in Sweden. Yet expanded technology adoption did not generate public concern over personal data use until the late 1960s. This change is due to

Personal Data Act (*Personuppgiftslag*). Swedish Law Repositories located at http://www.riksdagen.se/sv/ and https://www.regeringen.se/.

two factors: the nature of Swedish governance and policy decisions taken in the country at the time.[5] The Swedish government has often taken a proactive stance toward policy-making, rather than wait until sociopolitical conditions became negative and needed correction.[6] Existing laws allowed open access to most government archives by members of the press and the public.[7] When the government proposed a population wide census for 1970, concerns arose over the ways that census data would be managed and who would have access to the personal data collected, once it was in the archives.[8] Anxieties centered around the possibility that anyone could look up very personal information about friends, neighbors, and colleagues, within the digitized census databank. The government responded to the public outcry by calling in academics and jurists who could offer legal advice to the Riksdag (parliament) on how to frame the law to protect individuals while gathering the necessary data.

The census was but one example of events that exacerbated public worries over digitized data collection. Many feared the adoption of a new national identification number system (PINs) for all members of Swedish society, particularly in light of the upcoming census digitization. PIN data included birthdate and sex, and these ID numbers were to be attached to service provision, similar to social security numbers in the US. Theoretically speaking, due to the law of open records access to government files, anyone in society could retrieve others' personal information, including their PIN. Finally, additional reservations existed around the possibility of linking census data and personal PINs to the data in other government databanks. Who would be allowed to access the full extent of digitized data across the linked government databanks, and for what purpose?

The Riksdag delayed the census and established a new committee in 1969 to investigate the matter further.[9] The Royal Commission released

[5] Bennett (1992).

[6] Elmore et al. (1986, p. 221).

[7] Freedom of Press Act (*Tryckfrihetsförordning*, 1949:105) and multiple versions of the Secrecy Act, dating back to 1937.

[8] Bennett (1992, pp. 62–63) and Newman (2008, pp. 42–50).

[9] In the interim, the Supreme Administrative Court, the highest civil court in the country, issued a 1971 ruling that magnetic tapes used for storing citizens' information were de facto documents, making them subject to public access similar to other documents under the Freedom of the Press Act. This ruling raised even more questions as to what

their findings in a 1972 report, "Computers and Privacy," and concluded that the proposed ways of collecting and storing data did indeed present,

> ... new threats to personal privacy. Compared with information kept in documents it is principally a matter of degree, but the difference is such that the situation has changed in a decisive way.[10]

Following this report, the Riksdag passed the Data Law in April of 1973, which set initial restraints on data treatment by public and private actors. The creation of the investigatory commission by the Riksdag and the passing of the 1973 law set the foundation for digital human rights as a normative practice in Swedish data policy. All data laws during Phase I equated the protection of all personal, digitized data with the necessary preservation of individuals' "integrity." Importantly, the law solidified the protection of personal data by forming a Data Inspectorate Board (DIB), permanently responsible for monitoring compliance with the law. It is clear that for the case of Sweden, data governance laws fell within the realm of fundamental human rights. I now look deeper into how the three interest areas contributed to this outcome.

Data Commodification and the Economy

Before looking at the role of data commodification in influencing data governance, it's important to understand a bit about the country's economic history and health. Sweden adopted a social welfare economy in response to changing political pressures and the worldwide economic depression of the 1920s and 1930s.[11] The main government solution to ensure economic health involved an understanding reached between the Swedish Employers Association (SAF), the Swedish Trade Union Confederation (LO), and the government in 1928. Known as the Saltsjöbaden agreement, this three-way coordination format established an interactive economic policy model for the country. Politically, the Social Democrat Party controlled the government for over 40 years, from 1932 to 1976,

limits should be set for document access, and the allowable parameters for automatic data processing (ADP) under the Freedom of Information Act. See Flaherty (1989).

[10] Sweden, Commission on Publicity and Secrecy of Official Documents, 1972 (*Computers and Privacy*, p. 6).

[11] Magnusson (2000).

giving them agenda-setting power over economic policy. Over the years, governments periodically intervened to jumpstart stalled growth, rather than let market forces determine outputs. Generally speaking, these two factors—the tripartite Saltsjöbaden agreement and having the same party in power over such a long time period—meant that policy-makers received significant input on the potential economic impact of new policies from members of the corporate and labor communities.[12]

Certain sectors contributed more to economic growth than others. After World War II, the economy hinged on manufacturing of consumable goods and some agricultural components to provide the bulk of GDP growth. Sweden experienced a severe recession in the 1970s, and the national currency (krona) was overvalued. As a result, traditional manufacturing exports fell and unemployment grew. The recession deepened into a near depression. After an election in 1976, the government began to experiment with the core "Swedish economic model." Hoping to jump-start export demands, the krona was devalued three times between 1976 and 1981, with drops over 10% each time. Despite the corrections to currency values, making Swedish imports more attractive to the global market, there was still a reduced demand for traditional manufactured goods. Production fell in the historically strong sectors of shipbuilding, iron, steel, and mining, dropping between 30 and 50% from 1974 to 1982. To make matters worse, industrial management faced increased wage competition from overseas. The resulting dependency of economic growth upon ICT sectors increased as well.

In the1980s and 1990s, ICT growth picked up, while other types of manufacturing declined. When the Social Democrats returned to power in 1982, PM Olof Palme introduced an economic and trade policy "third way" for Swedes, liberating financial markets and releasing capital flows. The government struggled to get the balance right between support for redundant workers and support for the nascent tech sector. Resource transfers could not compensate for deficient export volume related to inconsistent external demands for ICT goods and services. In sum, during the 1990s, Sweden experienced growth lags, combined with deflation, both producing negative economic effects.

[12] Tripartite coordination is a form of corporatism whereby the government meets with industrial management and labor representatives when setting some aspects of economic policy.

Table 3.2 ICT services sector contribution, Sweden, 1970–1999[13]

Years	*ICT services exports, % of services exports*	*Investment in ICT supplies, % of total non-residential gross fixed capital formation*	*High-tech exports, % of manufactured exports*	*Insurance and financial services, % of commercial services exports*
1970–1974	8.70	*	*	7.03
1975–1979	14.11	*	*	5.09
1980–1984	23.76	*	*	4.97
1985–1989	14.91	15.65	12.53	7.75
1990–1994	15.15	20.75	15.00	8.22
1995–1999	26.38	26.21	19.03	2.79

*No data available for these years
Data sources World Bank, OECD

[13] Statistics are 5-year means. Magnusson 2000; OECD 2021; World Bank 2021.

Recall from Chapter 2, that EU states with significant economic dependence upon ICT firms would be more likely to pass data policies protecting data commodification. Though Swedish economic planners had a pattern reducing negative effects to labor when conditions changed in the global marketplace, the 1970s recession made such policies unsustainable. Exports fell temporarily among the previously growing tech-based industries, but the economic contributions by the ICT domain gradually replaced the prior importance of traditional manufacturing. Table 3.2 reveals an upward trend of growth in the ICT sector during Phase I, in three out of four measures. The greatest increases were seen in ICT services exports (these nearly doubled from 1970 to 1979 and again in the 1990s) and in investment in ICT supplies. Other than insurance and financial services, all changes were positive.

Since economic contributions correlate with employment levels, labor demand indirectly contributes to policy preferences by members of the public who will blame or attribute their income levels with government support for the sector of their employment. In fact, the fastest growing firms in Sweden from 1955 to 1980 were those in technological fields.[14] Out of 250,000 persons employed in manufacturing, 85,000 people

[14] Utterback et al. (1988).

worked in technical engineering firms. Interviews of executives at 77 firms revealed that 25% of these firms formed after 1955 had revenues above $1 million USD by 1980. In addition, engineering-based firms employing at least 20 people between 1955 and 1980 were independently owned in Sweden, making tech-based entrepreneurship a significant portion of the start-up businesses of the time.[15] Compared to the other two cases which I examine next, Sweden falls in the middle of the three countries in terms of employment in technology industries.

The increasing importance of ICT growth should drive a demand for data commodification policies. However, as you will see, though Swedish ICT firms experienced generally positive growth and provided a significant number of jobs, these contributions did **not** track with data commodification being built into a majority of the laws. I return to this puzzling fact shortly.

Security Concerns and Digitized Data

The next area which could shape data governance is the risk of national security threats. Security threats include any attack against state or non-state targets that could be perceived as a breach of state sovereignty, including assaults on general locations or key infrastructure. The more frequent and numerous are security attacks, data access for security, police, and law enforcement personnel will become more important as an offensive and defensive tool.[16] From 1970 to 1999, the country experienced a total of 13 fatalities and 39 injuries related to the above definition of domestic security incidents.[17] Among the case states, Sweden suffered the least number of such events, with the most activity in 1975, 1990, 1992, and 1999.

The years of heightened attacks represent unusual events and are disconnected from any organized and long-term security threats to the state. The 1975 attack on the Germany embassy in Stockholm was perpetrated by the German Baader-Meinhof, or "Red Army Faction" militia group, an extreme Marxist and anti-Semitic group active in Germany

[15] Utterback et al. (1988); approximately 85,000 out of 250,000 firms.

[16] There were no cyber-attacks in Sweden during this period, due to the nascent condition of the computer industry as a whole. Cyber-offensive attacks among the case states did not begin until after 2005.

[17] Global Terrorism Database.

from approximately 1970–1998. The RAF used violent means such as bombings, kidnappings, and gun battles with police as a part of their wider goals to generate a revolution against what they believed was the disproportionate power of industrialized states.[18] During the 1975 attack, five RAF members held embassy staff hostage, while making demands for the release of 26 RAF group members imprisoned in Germany. Swedish security forces and German authorities refused to negotiate with the militants, who set off an explosion that blew up the embassy, and caused burns and injuries to members of the group and to hostages in the building. Two people died.[19] Though this event represents the most significant security attack in Sweden during Phase I, the overall goal had been to target the German government and its policy, rather than any political entity specific to Sweden.

The other security attacks during Phase I affected isolated individuals or groups. The most political attack was the 1986 assassination of PM Palme, attributed to a then-unknown gunman. The shooter suddenly appeared on the streets of Stockholm and shot Palme as he was leaving the theater with his wife one evening. A petty criminal was convicted in 1989, but this ruling was later overturned in 2004.[20] Multiple theories abound as to the root cause of Palme's death, including accusations against arms dealers from India, Kurdish rebels from Turkey, or perhaps Stig Engstrom, a former witness interviewed by police after the killing. To this day, no concrete proof has been offered as to the motivation behind Palme's assassination, nor has the real killer been caught.

Following the prime minister's death, additional small-scale, targeted incidents occurred in the 1990s. A far-right Swedish extremist by the name of John Ausonius ("the laser killer") shot members of various Stockholm immigrant communities in 1991–1992.[21] Ausonius was convicted in 1995 of 11 attacks, and one death. On April 5, 1992, the Iranian embassies in nine countries including Sweden were simultaneously invaded by rebel group members in opposition to the government of Iran. Approximately 50 protesters set fire to two buildings and six cars

[18] Moghadam (2012).

[19] BBC News (2005).

[20] Anderson and Cowel (2018).

[21] Martin (2018).

associated with the Iranian diplomatic core in Stockholm. The ambassador's wife and children were treated for shock, but thankfully, no one was killed. 1999 ended with a peak of activity in the summer, with two incidents purportedly involving neo-Nazi groups. Investigative journalist Peter Karlsson and his son were injured during a bombing of their car on June 28 in Nacka. Karlsson had been researching the activity of the neo-Nazi group, the Ariska Bordraskapet ("Aryan Brotherhood").[22] Less than a week later, two policemen suffered several injuries when investigating a stolen car that exploded when they approached it.[23] This crime was attributed alternately to either another neo-Nazi group, the Nationalsocialistick Front (NSF), or to Hells Angels.

Sweden experienced a total of 39 persons injured, and 13 deaths from domestic terror-related attacks between 1970 and 1999. While these events were certainly disturbing and disruptive, they did not represent a larger pattern of security risks endemic to the entirely Swedish society. How does the data align with the argument on security threats motivating the need for personal data as a surveillance tool to protect national security? Given the low volume and isolated nature of domestic attacks in Phase 1, there was little pressing need for extensive data surveillance to control a widespread security threat. Providing security access to digitized data remained less of a priority for Swedish policymakers.

We've now seen the importance of data as an economic commodity, and the limited value of personal data to national security interests. The human rights element of digitized data remains the only area unexplored in Sweden.

Digital Human Rights

In Chapter 2, I proposed that the epistemic community of legal professionals and academics were the main actors involved in advancing digital human rights in the European Union. In the case of Sweden, a history of government accountability laid the foundation upon which human rights advocates capitalized when advising parliament on potential data legislation.

[22] Nordic Business Report (1999).

[23] Younge (1999).

As mentioned before, Swedish society has a precedent of what Anderson calls the "principal of public access to official documents."[24] This practice dates back to the eighteenth century, when the "Caps," or *mössorna* party, passed the Act of 1766 to reverse censorship practices made by the prior party in power, the "Hats" (*hattarna*). Importantly, freedom of access to information was coupled with norms requiring government accountability. Since the creation of this landmark act, the press and public have enjoyed legal access to government files.[25] Only minor revisions to access and secrecy laws have been made since.[26]

Beginning in the 1960s, all manual government and private sector records gradually shifted to computer storage. From 1963, the Swedish government collated databanks for population registration, land and automobile records, and social services, all under the management of the Central Bureau of Statistics, or *Statistiska Centralbyran* (SCB).[27] In another example, the taxpayer's registry accumulated data on 6.5 million people, retrieving local-level paper sources of public tax records, and transferring them to computers.[28] The private sector adopted data digitization within wider goals to organize trade and improve the financial bottom line for many industries, though this was of much less concern to the public and lawmakers, due to the nature of government records access as compared to private record-keeping.[29]

The expansion of computer-based government record-keeping was generally supported among members of parliament. The few who raised concerns early on, such as Minister of Justice Kurt Hugossen, worried that businesses were tapping into local housing authorities' records to canvas for marketing and advertisement.[30] Public opposition to personal data computerization began with the proposed 1970 Housing and Population Census, which triggered a larger debate on data treatment.[31] From

[24] S. V. Anderson (1973, p. 420).

[25] S. V. Anderson (1973).

[26] S. V. Anderson (1973, p. 422); revisions took place in in 1810, 1812, and 1949.

[27] Bennett (1992).

[28] Flaherty (1989).

[29] Johansson (1993, pp. 63–80).

[30] Ilshammar (2007).

[31] Census data was collected in Sweden every five years. Prior censuses had occurred in 1960 and 1965.

the perspective of the population, fears centered on the potential for census records being linked to other types of governmental records, virtually reversing the anonymity related to non-census record collections.[32] Additional doubts arose with the difficulty in correcting false information once smaller pools of data were combined in large databanks. Eventually, the Riksdag delayed the 1970 Census to investigate the potential of losing anonymity and personal privacy during digitization of government records. From this time point on, voters sought accountability in connection with digitized record-keeping.[33]

Parliament responded by frequently forming committees to advise the Riksdag on proposed data laws. These committees typically included civil servants, legal officials or jurists, members of the press, and academics.[34] In January of 1969, Kaj Björjk and Kurt Hugosson introduced bills to protect citizens' rights to privacy. Both MPs wanted parliament to take up privacy violations within existing legislation, such as the Secrecy Act. The government established the Committee on Publicity and Secrecy Legislation (*Betänkande Offentlighets- och sekretesslagstiftningskommittén*, or OSK) in April, 1969.[35] The makeup, findings, and suggestions made by the OSK had enormous impact upon future Swedish data legislation.

First, the OSK members brought to the committee a diverse background of expertise in politics, statistics, public administration, Ministry of Justice bureaucracy, and legal jurisprudence academia. Four of the five political parties in the Riksdag at the time had members sitting on the OSK. Rune Hermansson, a Social Democrat and the OSK Chairman, previously served as a judge of appeals and a minister with the Department of Justice between 1960 and 1966. The other committee members consisted of Erick Adamsson (parliamentary council chairman), Allan Eriksson (philosophy academic), Jan Freese (court of appeals lawyer, Assistant Secretary of the committee), Hans-Olaf Hansson (actuary), Kurt Hugosson (parliamentarian), Sven-Erik Larsson (former farmer, then career parliamentarian), Karl-Olof Lidin (assessor), Åke Polstam (parliamentarian), Edmund Rapaport (statistician), Kent Skoog (consultant),

[32] Bennett (1992) and Ilshammar (2007).

[33] Magnusson (2000, p. 255) and Ilshammar (2007, p. 23).

[34] S.V. Anderson (1973), Flaherty (1989), Fuster (2016) and Ilshammar (2007).

[35] Ilshammar (2007, p. 23).

Hans-Olov Stark (ministry of justice civil servant), Erik Svedberg (parliamentarian), and Per Svenonius (public management expert). Altogether, their combined experience was extremely heavy in the areas of legal jurisprudence, meaning their professional norms were heavily steeped in human rights.

The OSK committee had a two-fold mandate.[36] First, they were charged with balancing the protection of individuals' privacy while simultaneously allowing for the Swedish norm of public access to records. The task was challenging to say the least. Under Hermansson's leadership, the OSK presented an initial report to the Minister of Justice Lennart Geiger on June, 1972, and suggested serious revisions to the current Freedom of the Press Act. However, the most innovative components of the report called for an entirely new data act, and importantly, asked for a new governmental agency which would supervise the protection of computerized data. These two recommendation laid the foundation for digital human rights in Sweden.

The OSK-proposed bill was presented to the Riksdag in February of 1973, and became the Data Act of 1973 (*Datalagen*).[37] It functioned as a standard-setting piece of legislation for multiple reasons. First, the law placed responsibility for insuring fair data treatment upon a variety of actors within private sector firms and public sector agencies. Because the law applied to both public and private databanks, the norm of digital human rights applied to all areas of digitized data management in Sweden. All databanks holding personal data would be required to obtain a registration license with the government oversight agency, known as the DIB. (Only the Riksdag itself was exempt from this requirement.) By registering all databanks collecting personal data, the law allowed manual record-keepers to continue their current practices unchanged, but set new expectations for those using digitized data. Lastly, it was the first application of law to mandate digitized data practices, meaning that the government would be aware of all databanks holding digitized data, and could inspect data practices on site, ensuring high levels of compliance.[38] Multiple scholars note the human rights model set by Sweden for data

[36] Ilshammar (2007, p. 34). Dr. Ilshammar conducted multiple interviews with OSK members as a part of his academic research and work as a statistician.

[37] Flaherty (1989, p. 93).

[38] Bennett (1992, p. 161).

Table 3.3 DIB Directors-General, 1970–1999

Years served in DIB	*Name of Director General*
1973–1977	Claes-Göran Källner
1977–1987	Jan Freese
1986–1989	Mats Börjesson
1989–1992	Stina Wahlström
1992–1998	Anitha Bondestam
1998–2004	Ulf Widebäck

legislation, whose example was later followed by numerous European states.[39]

The Datainspektionen (Data Inspection Board, hereafter, the DIB) delivered a novel approach to the oversight of digitized data, seen in the composite of board leadership and the scope of powers given to the board.[40] The DIB was comprised of ten members chosen by the Riksdag, and fulfill four-year terms. The initial board consisted of four legislators, a trade union representative, one person drawn from industrial management, a member of public administration, and a few researchers. A Director-General (DG), chosen from candidates with judicial experience, would lead the agency. DGs and eight Deputy-Directors were permitted to serve indefinite terms. The DIB also held authority to license data banks, supervise compliance, and administer various tasks related to these responsibilities. It held autonomous oversight over the implementation of gaining data subjects' consent for the collection of their personal information, and supervised the digitized data management post collection. From 1973 to 1983, the DIB largely focused on licensing databanks. After the law was revised in 1982, the scope of responsibilities expanded to add on-site inspections. Aside from the makeup of the DIB and the scope of the agency authority, the Director-Generals of the DIB influenced data practices in profound ways due to their unique leadership styles. As the initial DG, Källner brought his legal expertise to the DIB, having served as a court lawyer beginning in 1955, as a minister of the Interior after 1963, and as the Head of the Department of Civil Affairs just prior to accepting the DG position (Table 3.3).

[39] Bennett (1992), Flaherty (1989) and Fuster (2016).

[40] Bennett (1992, pp. 161–170).

Without a doubt, however, the greatest long-term impact to DHR in Sweden came through the efforts of Jan Freese, the second Director-General (DG) of the DIB in Sweden.

Freese advocated for digital human rights within Sweden, and later outside the country when called as a consultant on data governance for multiple international organizations in Europe. Freese saw himself as a policy-maker, not just a policy implementer. Prior to his time at the DIB, he worked as a court of appeals lawyer and judge from 1964 to 1973. Once at the DIB, he leveraged his role as DG to openly promote the importance of data protection as a fundamental human right, including reaching out to the media and the public. Noting the lack of a word in Swedish equivalent to the English word "privacy," Freese argued that the spirit of the 1973 law essentially promoted an, "individual's right to be left alone."[41] In 1978, Freese actually opposed a tighter reconceptualization of the word "integritet" in a proposed revision of the 1973 law, preferring instead to give the DIB more leverage to interpret levels of encroachment against data protection. He also actively opposed linking databanks from multiple agencies, stating,

> The road to 1984 is paved with good intentions. Besides that, you can't compare apples and pears – two data banks could have different rules for collection, and then can affect the quality of information.[42]

Freese supported DHR throughout Europe and globally during the 1970s and 1980s, writing multiple documents and working papers regarding data protection as a fundamental human right, and speaking at numerous data policy conferences.[43] Among the leadership of national data protection agencies in Europe, Freese served the second longest term of service, second only to Spiritos Simitis in Germany.[44] Although he left the DIB in 1986 to accept another position, he left an enormous legacy of empowerment for DHR in Sweden.

None of the directors following Freese aggressively sought media exposure for the agency's efforts to the degree of Freese's efforts, however

[41] Flaherty (1989, p. 105).

[42] Wicklein (1982, p. 205).

[43] Flaherty (1979, 1989) and Ilshammar (2007).

[44] Flaherty (1989) and Fuster (2016).

they did work with the Riksdag to shape proposed legislation that would impact their work with data protection. After Freese, the management of the DIB switched to Mats Börjesson. Börjesson served from 1986 to 1989, focusing mainly on "guiding" the DIB through implementation of the 1982 Data Law revisions, rather than acting as a policy innovator as had Freese.[45] While many if not all DGs had legal expertise similar to Freese (for instance, Wahlström and Widebäck were attorneys and legal consultants for the Riksdag), subsequent DGs kept the "status quo" of the DIB functionality, following the pattern of professionalization and civil service created by Källner and sustained by Freese.

Similar to what happened in other EU states, national data law revisions were necessary due to changing technology and political conditions. In 1978, the Riksdag revisited the Data Law, wishing to add mandates on the burden of protection over more "sensitive data" such as health problems, criminal history, etc., that may have inadvertently been exposed to public access as a result of the ambiguous wording of the 1973 law. A new advisory commission, the *Datalagskommittén*, or Data Act Committee (DALK) issued assessment reports regularly between 1976 and 1984.[46] DALK suggested new protections for sensitive data, but the core areas of the 1973 law remained intact. In 1997, the data law was overhauled again to comply with the 1995 Directive passed by the EU Commission (Directive 95/46/EC). To summarize, there is very significant evidence to show legal experts chosen to give policy advice, conduct regulatory committee research, and lead the DIB moved forward the agenda of digital human rights for Sweden. Though Swedish data protection laws contain mentions of security use for data, and certainly for data commodification, the overarching approach taken in Swedish legislation is that of providing and protecting digital human rights.

Bibliography

Anderson, Stanley V. 1973. "Public Access to Government Files in Sweden." *American Journal of Comparative Law* 21 (3): 419–473.

Anderson, Christina, and Alan Cowel. 2018. "Was the Killer of Sweden's Leader in 1986 Under Investigators' Noses All This Time?" May 24. Accessed

[45] Flaherty (1989, p. 128).

[46] DALK Report on the Revision of the Data Act, *Statens offentliga utredningar* (1978: 54, pp. 340, 341).

September 16, 2018. https://www.nytimes.com/2018/05/24/world/europe/sweden-olof-palme-killing.html.

BBC News. 2005. "On This Day—24 April." Accessed September 2016, 2018. http://news.bbc.co.uk/onthisday/hi/dates/stories/april/24/newsid_2523000/2523095.stm.

———. 2017. "Swedish 'Laser Man' Ausonius on Trial for 1992 German Murder." December 13. Accessed September 18, 2018. https://www.bbc.com/news/world-europe-42340711.

Bennett, Colin J. 1982. *The Concept of Open Government and Its Interpretation and Development in British Politics.* Cardiff: University College of Cardiff.

———. 1992. *Regulating Privacy: Data Protection and Public Policy in Europe and the United States.* Ithaca, NY: Cornell University Press.

Butchart, R. L. 1987. "A New UK Definition of the High-Technology Industries." *Economic Trends* 400: 82–88.

DALK. 1978. "DALK Report on the Revision of the Data Act/Statens ofentliga utredningar."

Dworkin, Gerald. 1973. "The Younger Committee Report on Privacy." *The Modern Law Review* 36 (4): 399–406.

Elmore, Richard, Gunnel Gustafsson, and Erwin Hargrove. 1986. "Comparing Implementation Processes in Sweden and the United States." *Scandinavian Political Studies* 9: 209–233.

Flaherty, David H. 1979. *Privacy and Government Databanks.* London: Mansell.

———. 1989. *Protecting Privacy in Surveillance Societies: The Federal Republic of Germany, Sweden, France, Canada, and the United States.* Chapel Hill, NC: University of North Carolina Press.

Fuster, Gloria González. 2016. *The Emergence of Personal Data Protection as a Fundamental Right of the EU.* Cham: Springer.

Government of Sweden. 1949. "Tryckfrihetsförordning (Freedom of Press Act)."

———. 1972. *Computers and Privacy.* Royal Commission. Stockholm: Commission on Publicity and Secrecy of Official Documents.

———. 1985. *Public Attitudes to Data-Processing in the Information Society.* Data inspektionen. Stockholm, SW: Swedish Central Bureau of Statistics.

Ilshammar, Lars. 2007. "When Computers Became Dangerous: The Swedish Computer Discourse of the 1960s." *Human IT* 9 (1): 6–37.

Johansson, Magnus. 1993. "Informationssamhällets rötter ur ett svenskt perspektiv." In *Brus över landet: om informationsöverflödet, kunskapen och människan*, edited by Lars Ingelstam and Lennart Sturesson. Stockholm: Carlssons.

Magnusson, Lars. 2000. *An Economic History of Sweden.* London: Routledge.

Martin, David. 2018. "'Laser Man' John Ausonius Receives Life Sentence in Frankfurt." February 21. Accessed May 5, 2020. https://www.dw.com/en/laser-man-john-ausonius-receives-life-sentence-in-frankfurt/a-42672805.

McKinsey & Company. 2006. *Sweden's Economic Performance: Recent Development, Current Priorities (Executive Summary)*. McKinsey Global Institute. New York, NY: McKinsey & Company .

Moghadam, Assaf. 2012. "Failure and Disengagement in the Red Army Faction." *Studies in Conflict & Terrorism* 35: 156–181.

New Scientist. 1976. "Protection for Whose Data?" July.

Newman, Abraham L. 2008. *Protectors of Privacy: Regulating Personal Data in the Global Economy*. Ithaca, NY: Cornell University Press.

Nordic Business Report. 1999. "Swedish Journalist Documenting Neo-Nazis Injured in Car Bomb." M2 Communications, July 5.

OECD. 1976. *Establishing Institutional Structures to Monitor and Enforce Data Protection*. Policy Issues in Data Protection and Privacy. OECD Informatics Studies. Paris: Organization for Economic Cooperation and Development, 83–94.

———. 2000. *A New Economy? The Changing Role of Innovation and Information Technology in Growth*. Information Society. Paris: Organisation for Co-operation and Economic Development.

———. 2020. *Roadmap Toward a Common Framework for Measuring the Digital Economy*. Paris: OECD.

———. 2021. ICT Investments, *OECD*.

University of Maryland. 2018. *Global Terrorism Database*. Accessed March 2019. https://www.start.umd.edu/data-tools/global-terrorism-database.gtd.

Utterback, James M., Marc Meyer, Edward Roberts, and Loren Reitberger. 1988. "Technology and Industrial Innovation in Sweden: A Study of Tech Firms Formed Between 1965 and 1980." *Research Policy* 17: 15–26.

WDI. 2021. World Development Indicators, *World Bank*.

Wicklein, John. 1982. *Electronic Nightmare: The Home Communications Set and Your Freedom*. Boston, MA: Beacon Press.

Younge, Gary. 1999. "Car Bombs Explode Sweden's Self-Image." *Guardian Weekly*.

CHAPTER 4

Germany: Digital Human Rights and a History of Invasive Surveillance

Germany created a very specified conceptualization of digital human rights within their data protection laws, which, similar to the Swedish law, occurred in the early 1970s. What contributed to this early legislation? In a word: history. Both the Nazi and East German regimes had controlled public behavior during the twentieth century using secret surveillance networks to collect vast amounts of personal information. When data computerization began in the 1970s, human rights ideals and constraints upon government power were so deeply imbedded in the sociopsychological values of society, that data treatment was quickly identified as a human rights matter. The national work done by German politicians and the international efforts by German legal experts not only permanently fixed digital human rights within German law, their impact crossed borders to influence other EU states and international organizations, making these rights a salient, and indeed most necessary, component of international law.

Second only to the impact made by Sweden's 1973 data protection law, Germany helped set the European standard for digital human rights. As will be discussed further in subsequent chapters, German human rights experts not only advocated for digital human rights in their own country, they also advised other European states and international organizations during the 1970s and 1980s, during a time when data computerization raised fears over privacy losses. To understand the evolution and impact

R. Dowd, *The Birth of Digital Human Rights*, Information Technology and Global Governance,
https://doi.org/10.1007/978-3-030-82969-8_4

of German laws and political actors within Germany, it is necessary to look at the focus of the German laws. I trace the creation of laws at the regional, or *die Länder* level, explain the national laws of West Germany prior to unification, and outline the data laws chosen by a united German state after 1990.

German data legislation aims to balance two concerns: providing law and order on one hand, and setting limits for state use of personal information on the other hand. In the early years, data protection was seen as an extension of the "rights to a personality" or *persönlichkeitsrechte.*[1] Until the Constitution of 1949 was deemed inadequate to perform the task of protecting one's personality by way of data about them, neither governmental and non-state actors showed any interest in making laws specific to data protection. Thus, digital human rights emerged gradually, across time. First, let's look at the data protection laws in Germany from 1970 to 1999.

Germany created a total of 12 laws dedicated to data protection during Phase I.[2] As with the case of Sweden, I analyzed each law, creating a net content score which reveals the prioritization of either data commodification, data as a security tool, or protecting data with digital human rights.[3] As seen in a selection of these laws coded in Table 4.1, digital human rights were clearly prioritized well and above the other two interests in Germany, with an even higher prioritization for DHR than seen in the case of Sweden.

Three elements stand out as shaping German data legislation. The most powerful component is tied to the history of aggressive state surveillance during the Nazi regime of the 1930s and 1940s, and the Stasi monitoring

[1] Basic Law of 1949, Article 1(1); Bennett (1992, pp. 1–2), and Flaherty (1989, p. 22). Note: there is no provision for privacy rights within the Basic Law.

[2] For the remainder of this chapter, "Germany" will be used to refer to the federal level of governance that occurred in West Germany prior to 1991, and to the re-unified state after 1991.

[3] The full list of laws with data governance content in Phase I: 1970 Population Micro Census Law, the 1971 Telecommunications Universal Services Act, the 1977 BDSG (Data Protection Law), a 1983 Census Act, the updated version of the BDSG of 1990, a 1995 Broadcasting Act for North-Rhine Westphalia, and the 1996 Telecommunications Act; numerous acts passed in 1997—the Telecommunications Universal Service Ordinance, the Digital Signature Act, the Act on the Protection of Personal Data Used in Teleservices, a law for Telecom Customer Protection, and a Postal Act. See the German Law Repository (University of Oxford), and Bundesgesetzblatt Online.

Table 4.1 Select German data laws, Phase I (1970–1999)

Year	*Name of law*	*Description*	*Net score*
1977	Data Protection Law *Bundesdatenschutzgesetz* (BDSG)	First national data protection law, protecting against misuse during automatic processing	+89 Protect Data +2 Economic use +7 Security use
1983	Census Act	Discusses the protections required by the Basic Law, regarding personal data collected during the national Census. Also regulates use of data collected for statistical and public administration purposes	+46 Protect Data +5 Economic use +2 Security use
1990	Data Protection Law Bundesdatenschutzgesetz (BDSG)	Revision of the 1977 law on federal level personal data protections. Includes responsibilities of federal Data Protection Officer, the mandates on data secrecy and transmission provisions, and rights afforded to data subjects	+142 Protect Data +30 Economic use +23 Security use
1996	Telecommunications Act	Regulations regarding service installation, fee scheduling, environmental protection, and other aspects of telecom service provision. Also creates Regulatory and Advisory bodies	+27 Protect Data +18 Economic use +8 Security use
1997	Act on the Protection of Personal Data Used in Teleservices	Charges tele-service providers with protection of personal data during telecom service provision	+31 Protect Data +4 Economic use +1 Security use

in East Germany, both of whom left a remarkable imprint upon society. Second, the federal law-making process itself presented several challenges, allowing regional policymakers to actively promote digital human rights. Lastly, the policy-making environment contained multiple stakeholders with interests in data policy outcomes, whose efforts altered the types of laws made in Germany. Let's now examine these in turn to better understand the German case.

Past Aggressive State Surveillance

All federal laws that emerged after World War II rest upon the foundations of the *Grundgesetz*, which is the basic constitution for the country. The law provides for fundamental human rights, bound in such statements as, "Human dignity shall be inviolable. To respect it shall be the duty of all state authority."[4] It outlines distinct obligations for the federal government, and constrains federal and regional state authorities, or *die Länder*, from certain behaviors. Over fifty changes have been made to the Basic Law since 1950, yet the framework provided by the Basic Law shapes all legislation in Germany, including that of data governance.

Computer adoption began in the 1960s, effecting government practices. Automatic data processing (ADP) advanced bureaucratic efficiency, and use of ADP by public and private actors escalated throughout the decade.[5] During that time, *die Länder* authorities set up data centers for administrative planning purposes, but that was the limits of initial data controls.[6] In the late 1960s, German public authorities began to discuss introducing some sort of regulations regarding data computerization, primarily by the government, during the quick and widespread diffusion of digitized personal data use. Public authorities collected population statistics and general demographic data for civic planning and scientific research purposes, and stored the information on government databanks. Databanks would then be tapped by multiple public authorities, for the purposes of using data collected by other agencies. Understandably, the historical legacy of Gestapo mechanisms left by the Nazis led to a

[4] Grundgesetz, Artikel 1 (Basic Law, Article 1).

[5] Riccardi (1983).

[6] Bennett (1992) and Liedtke (1980).

universal desire within society for open accountability by central government authorities regarding personal data accumulation.[7] Given the public fears over an intrusive state surveillance, legislating data fell underneath the umbrella of larger human rights matters in the eyes of lawmakers and the public.

Initially, data governance was added to laws focused on other topics, and treated as a minor matter. The 1953 Basic Law on Statistics is the first German law affecting personal data management, albeit indirectly. The statistics law allowed for data collection at the federal and regional state levels. The 1953 statistics law remained the only law that included some element of data governance for many years. Despite the increase of personal data collections and government data bank linking, digitized data use was virtually unlimited. By example of the initially lenient stance, another administrative law, the 1970 Census Law, permitted "widespread data dissemination under controlled conditions,"[8] including when correcting local population registries, for scientific research, and for local planning needs, as long as confidentiality was protected (data subjects' names were removed).[9] This permissive attitude was also reflected in the leverage allowed to public authorities to collect and disseminate individuals' data collected by universities, as found within the 1971 Law for Statistics on Higher Education. On the books, these laws looked as if personal data had *some* protections, but in reality, government agencies such as the Statistics Bureau that collected personal data had little power and no authority to enforce data confidentiality. From the late 1960s until 1977, regional states took on the largest amount of responsibility for evaluating the risks associated with personal data processing and storage, until a federal law specific to personal data was passed. Once a federal data protection law passed, everything changed. First, I'll discuss the law itself, followed by the causal factors in its creation.

The 1977 *Bundesdatenschutzgesetz* (BDSG), or the "Law on Protection Against the Misuse of Personal Data in Data Processing," was the first and subsequently, the main federal level German law explicitly protecting personal data. The law prohibited misuse of personal data connected to a specific physical person, during all phases of data use, including "storage,

[7] Bennett (1992, p. 5) and Flaherty (1979, p. 141).

[8] Flaherty (1979, p. 153).

[9] Flaherty (1979).

communication, modification and erasure."[10] As pointed out by Professor Hans Peter Bull, one of the first national Data Protection Commissioners, data protection was a means to an end in Germany.[11] The main legal goal remained protecting the population from general harm, and data protection was simply a tool for achieving that goal. The BDSG applied only to commercial data, and required data anonymization and use of data only for pre-specified tasks. The law also mandated that inaccuracies be corrected, and once the original task was complete, data be erased. Violators could be punished with prison time. As seen in Table 4.1, Germany added additional data legislation after 1977, but the BDSG remains the bedrock for data governance for the country and followed a clear mandate for providing digital human rights. The process by which Germany finally arrived at adopting federal data protection legislation was quite political.

Politics and Personal Data

To the creation of German data regulations, as the numbers of public and private actors using databanks grew, the public expressed more concerns about data management practices, and politicians were drawn into the debate. Some citizens worried that data breaches and unauthorized databank linkages would become reality as the government made use of personal identification numbers while administering public programs. Eventually, the Green party adopted the issue of data protection within its regular party platform of environmental protections and civil liberties advocacy, and the party challenged the government to address the issue.[12] The German parliament (Bundestag) requested investigation into data protection in 1969, and established an interparliamentary working group to investigate the matter. The group submitted a draft proposal in January of 1970 for a "preliminary plan for the protection of privacy against the misuse of automatically processed personal data."[13] Brandt's SPD government didn't respond and the draft bill created by the working group was tabled until December 1971, despite having the support of the majority of political parties in the Bundestag.[14]

[10] Dammann (1977).

[11] Flaherty (1989, p. 34).

[12] Bennett (1992, pp. 74–82).

[13] Bull (1984, p. 104).

[14] Simitis, *Chancen und Gefahren der elektronischen Datenverarbeitung* (1971); Federal Republic of Germany, Bundestag, *Drucksache*, 6/2885, December 1971.

Though politicians now recognized the need for more specific data protection laws, they faced a governance challenge due to overlapping power mandates.[15] In reality, the Bundestag and the regional state governments shared legislative capabilities. It was the regional states that had acted first to protect digitized data, when the German state of Hesse passed the first data protection law of any kind in the world. The law applied to automatically processed data, and established an independent Data Protection Commission to oversee application of the law. Rheinland-Pfalz followed suit in 1974 with a similar law.[16] One by one, the regional states set up a data commission office to protect automatically processed data, and these offices operated independently of national authorities until the national law was passed in 1977. Once the BDSG became law, officials at both regional and federal levels of government had to negotiate levels of responsibility where jurisdictional overlap existed.

Creating consensus on a federal data law was impossible until disagreements among the various stakeholders involved could be solved. The first area of contention concerned the scope of application. For instance, the ICT sector wanted data protection laws to apply equally to those keeping manual files as well as to those holding computerized or ADP data. Otherwise, the ICT sector could be commercially disadvantaged by any new law which only applied to automatically processed data, disproportionately increasing costs and administrative burdens for their industry.[17] Second, some delayed the vote, worried over the level of specificity in the proposed law, which was much more detailed than the Hessian law, requiring more of government bureaucracies. As a result, industry representatives *and* public administrators objected during public hearings on federal data protection in late 1972. To overcome these objections, revisions were needed to remove the causes of concern for both groups.

A year later, on November 29, 1973, another draft was presented to the Bundestag by the Brandt government. The latest version was not only stronger than *die Länder* laws, it also had weaker enforcement mechanisms. Once again, a proposed data protection law was met with continued opposition. Bargaining continued through two more public hearings, a change in government leadership through Scheel (FDP Party)

[15] Flaherty (1979, 1989); Simitis, Spiros, "2 DVR 138 1973; Simitis, Spiros (1978).

[16] Bennett (1992, pp. 77–90).

[17] Flaherty (1989, p. 22).

to Schmidt's Chancellorship (SPD party), and a series of meetings on the topic by the Federal Interior Committee from 1974 to 1976. It was crucial that all efforts be made to resolve the disagreements over the levels of stringency behind the law and the type of enforcement body necessary to support it.[18]

In the final stages of negotiations, the government invited legal experts to make recommendations on the type of oversight authority they believed to be essential. Spiros Simitis, the Data Protection Commissioner for Hesse, strongly encouraged officials to create an independent federal agency, rather than utilize the self-regulatory model preferred by industry leaders.[19] The CDU and CSU parties wanted control to fall under the umbrella of the Federal Audit Office, rather than be an independent agency, keeping controls in the hands of parliament. The regional state data protection agencies were also in an uproar, contending that an independent national DPC would threaten the power of *die Länder* to oversee regional public agencies' use of data. A new committee, the Joint Conference Committee, designed a compromise in July of 1976, but the regional states were still displeased, and requested the committee to reconsider, which it refused. It seemed inevitable that no data legislation would please all parties, and the government moved forward with a vote in parliament. Though the CDU and CSU disapproved, a majority in the Bundestag endorsed the bill on November 10, 1976. Two days later it passed, with formal opposition on record by Bavaria, Baden-Württemburg, Rheinland-Pfalz, and Schleswig–Holstein. The BDSG took effect on January 1, 1978. Although no one group was totally pleased with the final version of the law, data protection was legalized in Germany at the federal level.[20] In total, it took 39 months from the meeting of the first government commission on data policy in 1973, to the making of an actual law in 1977.[21]

In order to better understand the emergence of the powerful and pervasive norm of digital human rights, let's look at the contributing factors to the content of data legislation in Germany. We know that

[18] Bennett (1992, pp. 68–81).

[19] OECD (1976).

[20] Dammann (1977, pp.70–107).

[21] Bennett (1992, p. 59).

Sweden's laws were most heavily influenced by sociocultural expectations about government accountability, combined with the importance of human rights. Would Germany be more influenced by the commodification of data, the needs for security access to data, or human rights advocacy? Given the importance of social and economic recovery after World War II, we will first look at the economic factors.

Data Commodification and the Economy

Assessing the economic importance of data in Germany requires a look at several components. First, we need to understand the general history of the economy and the approach taken by government planners toward development. We also need to look at how World War II and the merging of two countries altered economic health and therefore, strategic planning. Finally, we'll look at the emergence of the ICT sector and the contribution made by this industry to economic growth in Germany.

The West German approach to balancing economic gains with social outcomes after World War II followed the *Soziale Marktwirtschaft* model, combining decentralized autonomy for businesses with social protections for individuals.[22] This method has historical roots in learned experiences during industrialization and the interwar years of the twentieth century. Industrialization produced multiple social problems not adequately solved by the Marxist socialist system. On one hand, German economists in the 1930s–40s observed the failure of contemporary economic planners in the Soviet Republic to accurately predict and match production goals to current and future social conditions.[23] On the other hand, while market-based systems such as those used in the US and United Kingdom produced greater economic opportunities than did pure socialist systems, these systems failed to provide social protections for individuals in the event of market gaps.[24] In other words, thanks to the socio-cultural desires to blunt any potentially damaging effects of market and economic instability, no single sector would have the power to overtly influence lawmaking and economic strategy, even if it was economically powerful.

[22] Siebert (2005).

[23] German economic planners were trained in the Freiburg school of the 1930s, following the ordoliberal school of thought. See Mardellat (2011).

[24] Berman (2006).

Table 4.2 German exports, % of GDP

1950	13.7%
1960	21.2%
1970	26.4%
1980	31.1%
1990	22.8%
2002	35%

Data source Siebert (2005)

World War II decimated the West German economy and production capabilities. After the war, policymakers focused on crucially important repairs in order to re-establish growth in the German economy. The Deutschmark was stabilized.[25] Rationing ended in 1948, and prices allowed to fluctuate with market demands. GDP growth responded positively to the economic initiatives, with levels above 8% from 1951 to 56, and again from 1959 to 1961. Admittedly, economic growth was not consistently positive in the post-war era; the country suffered economic recessions facilitated by oil crises in 1973 and 1979. By the 1980s, GDP had fallen to 2%, and labor productivity was half of what it had been in the 1960s. To mediate the falling growth, the government opened internal markets to free trade, and joined the General Agreement on Tariffs and Trade (GATT) in 1951, signaling a willingness to forego gross protectionism. From 1950 to 1970, the state pursued an aggressive export-led growth plan which relied upon low wages and production of high-tech engineered goods, including the ICT space.[26] Exports increased, only slowing during the merge of the two states in 1990. By encouraging growth in export-driven sectors, policymakers inadvertently supported ICT industries, with some unintended effects (Table 4.2).

Export-driven growth produced several challenges. Labor coordination in Germany relied upon corporatist meetings between trade unions, firms, and government officials to set wage policies and adjust for market downturns. Essentially, the government could not change economic plans or trade policy without also being prepared to soothe the worst of negative

[25] Siebert (2005, pp. 12–14).

[26] Ahearn and Belkin (2010).

effects to the labor market.[27] If some sectors made employees redundant due to shifts in external demands, social welfare programs provided up to 67% of full-pay for an unlimited period for workers, effectively de-incentivizing work-seeking. As a result of fluctuating demand, and market shifts, unemployment rose after 1970, reaching 10% of the working age population.[28] Critics blamed an overreliance upon exports, rather than changes in domestic consumption.[29] Despite these challenges, no political parties were willingly to promote the fiscal reforms which would require cutting taxes and reducing social welfare spending to improve the imbalanced national budget.

In the 1990s, adjusting economic, fiscal, and trade policy took place within an atmosphere of merging two countries' economies. Prior to unification, the West German economy had price stability, a balanced budget, and a 5% surplus in current accounts. After December 1990, policy-makers set about privatizing East German industries, and setting the currency exchange ratio between the Ostmark/DDM and the Deutschmark. West German social benefits were immediately granted to East German residents, including early retirement and unemployment pay. To pay for the extension of social welfare benefits to an additional 16 million people, the government issued bonds, greatly increasing government debt. Rather than reduce social benefits to any citizens, German policy-makers continued to pursue export-led growth, and hoped that exports would offset the spending. The united-state focused support on export-heavy industries, while providing a social safety net for those negatively affected by the merge of two states. The shifts in the global manufacturing space toward an ICT dominant world paved the way for potential levels of influence by data-driven businesses upon data governance.

ICT and Global Competition

All of Europe sought to catch up to the successes of the US and Japan, both of whom had invested heavily in R & D for the ICT sector.[30]

[27] Hall and Soskice (2013).

[28] 0.7% of the population was unemployed in 1970. Ahearn and Belkin (2010).

[29] Ahearn and Belkin (2010).

[30] Australian Financial Review (1988).

Germany had relied heavily upon mature industries such as steel and traditional manufacturing. OECD analysts found one reason for the clear lag in German R&D in newer industries was the "insider system" of close relationships between firms and banks.[31]

> *First, to finance new industries, the financial system needs to facilitate the process of creative destruction. Such a system differs from one primarily geared towards the accumulation of physical assets in large, stable firms in well-established industries, which were the basis for much economic growth in the post-war period.*[32]

In addition, Germany relied much more upon the use of others' inventions, again a form of contracting out R & D, and often purchased existing foreign tech firms.[33] To facilitate adoption of advanced ICT, the country depended on university rand as a whole fell back on developing "engineering excellence" since institutional incentives for creative measures did not exist. Between 1980 and 1996, the contribution of ICT to output growth fluctuated from 1.4% (1980–1985) to 3.6% (1985–1990) then fell again to 1.8% (1990–1996).[34] The only area where Germany took a leading role within ICT during Phase I lay in the area of secure server hosting top domain names.[35]

Table 4.3 shows that the ICT sector expanded during Phase I. Significant growth occurred in ICT services exports, which essentially doubled from 1971 to 1999. This growth was matched in other areas of ICT. Insurance and financial services exports rose the most, from 1.16% to

[31] OECD (2000).

[32] OECD (2000, p. 33).

[33] OECD (2000, p. 38). Also see www.digitalhumanrightsbook.com for full data sets.

[34] OECD (2000, p. 50).

[35] OECD (2000, p. 66).

Table 4.3 ICT services sector contribution, Germany, 1970–1999

Years	*ICT services exports, % of services exports*	*Investment in ICT supplies, % of total non-residential gross fixed capital formation*	*High-tech exports, % of manufactured exports*	*Insurance & financial services, % of commercial services exports*
1970–1974	12.74	*	*	*
1975–1979	14.63	*	*	0.75
1980–1984	15.70	*	*	1.34
1985–1989	16.28	10.78	4.83	2.89
1990–1994	21.88	13.42	12.97	6.00
1995–1999	27.52	14.71	14.76	14.60

Data sources World Bank, OECD; *No data available for these years

16.64% by 1999.[36] No data is available during the two recessions (1973–1974, 1979–1980) to determine what, if any, impact was felt by ICT investments and high-tech exports. What is also noticeable when looking at annual changes, is the reductions in growth for the ICT sector during unification. Only ICT services exports managed consistently upward growth from 1990 to 1994 without any down years. The other three areas retracted temporarily; insurance and financial services fell by over 50% in 1991, but quickly bounced back. Though the country increased investments, the majority of the export growth experienced by ICT was due to services-based industries, and not products exports.

How can one explain the lack of influence on ICT firms to shape data governance in Germany despite the fact that these industries were certainly growing and contributing heavily to the economy? ICT during Phase I did not contribute as much as did manufacturing exports. Furthermore, the way in which economic and labor policy planning occurred meant that policymakers had to incorporate workers' concerns alongside management preferences when supporting data-dependent ICT firms. When workers in traditional sectors were negatively affected by decreased demand for traditional exports, planners focused on income replacement and supports for ailing sectors, rather than solely shift allegiance to the new industries. Also remember, policymaking took place in a domestic environment fraught with multiple interest groups. Simply put,

[36] Annual data set available on www.digitalhumanrightsbook.com.

while ICT growth was economically important, sectoral support paled in comparison to government priorities in the area of security and human rights. In fact, it was the invasive nature of past security policies which clearly violated human rights, which had the greatest impact upon data governance in Germany. To explain government surveillance practices, I look at threats to state security in Germany,

Security Concerns and Digitized Data

For security actors to be interested in using personal digitized data within their normal activities, and therefore care about data policy, the state needs to have a history of domestic security attacks. Such incidents motivate law enforcement to use data-driven surveillance to increase prevention and improve public protection. West Germany (RFD) faced numerous attacks during Phase I, primarily caused by the activities of radical left gangs and Neo-Nazi groups.

West Germany was the base location for a domestic terror group known as the Baader-Meinhof group, previously referenced in the Swedish case discussion. Also called the RAF (*Rote Armee Fraktion),* the group operated from the 1960s to the 1980s, and perpetrated the bulk of domestic terror attacks that occurred in Germany during Phase I.[37] This extremist group originated within the left-leaning student movement organizations (SMOs) that arose in the mid-1960s in Germany. Initially, student organizers and the RAF shared similar ideology and a disdain for several government policies. Their areas of agreement would eventually diverge from one another, as the RAF sought more violent activism to push against the German government.

A large student protest movement emerged during the 1960s in West Germany, driven by deep discontent with university and state authorities over faculty backgrounds and educational quality.[38] There were several contributing factors to student frustrations. After World War II, many German universities had retrenched many of their existing faculty who had been complicit in or at least compliant with National Socialist (Nazi) policies. This presented a staffing crisis and a shortage of teaching

[37] No data on domestic security incidents was available for East Germany during the period from 1970 to 1990. The data in Table 4.4 reflects West German data from 1970 to 1990, and data for the unified state after 1990.

[38] Becker (1977).

instructors, as universities failed to quickly replace faculty. In response to the shortage, universities then reversed the decision and rehired previously fired faculty, despite their political and ideological history. To make matters worse, German higher education had become largely antiquated compared to other systems, adding further to student discontent.[39] Subject matter fell behind the quality of the US and Germany's neighbors in Europe.

German students felt that university administrators were largely unresponsive to students' concerns over the non-democratic personal views of rehired faculty, the outdated facilities, and the lower quality content being provided to students. Student movement activists framed university authorities as authoritarian figures, similar to the Weimar Republic and Nazi regime leaders, who had forced compliance upon the public and de-legitimized any forms of opposition. Former student activist Daniel Cohn Bendit, who later founded the Green Party, recalled in a 2007 interview that the protest movement's anti-fascist ideology was motivated by a desire "to make up for the fight against fascism that their parents had not led... but we failed to distinguish between the meaning of 'resistance' in a fascist state and that in a democracy."[40] In short, the SMOs saw state activities to suppress or manage the protests against government policies and university administration as anti-democratic behavior.

Protest leaders contextualized the problems as a pattern of ideological and political dominance by many powerful countries—West Germany, the US, or any other state seen as disenfranchising members of society. Student protests came to head during the summer 1967, around a scheduled visit to Berlin by Reza Pahlevi, the Shah of Iran.[41] Comments made by the Shah during newspaper interviews prior to his visit were perceived by German students to reflect a leader largely out of touch with the plight of impoverished Iranians. The leader of the Socialist Student Association, Rudi Dutschke, planned a protest for June 2. The location would be just outside the Berlin opera, where the Shah, his wife, and German dignitaries were set to attend a performance of *The Magic Flute*.[42] After creating a huge uproar outside the theater entrance during the arrival of

[39] Becker (1977).

[40] Der Spiegel (2007) and Musolff (2011, p. 66).

[41] Aust (2008) and BBC (2016).

[42] Preece (2010).

the politicians and diplomats, a majority of students dissipated. Police with truncheons chased the remaining 1000 protesters; many were injured and hospitalized after being attacked.[43] One student, Benno Ohnesorg was shot and killed by an armed officer. Ohnesorg's death served as a symbolic catalyst for some present at the Berlin protest. It was from this point that some within the student groups began to mount a more violent response to "fascist" police and state authorities.

No longer happy to launch general protests, RAF founders Andreas Baader and Gudran Ensslin self-identified as "resistance fighters," working on behalf of the underprivileged against the Federal Republic of Germany.[44] Baader and Ensslin wanted the state to reveal the "true nature of its fascist tendencies and act with violence against students." Thus, what was needed was more aggressive actions to provoke the state to react in retaliation. In addition to West German targets, countries such as the US that were allied with West Germany were considered appropriate targets.[45] RAF leaders correlated the American military actions in the Vietnam war as an example of imperialist aggression to suppress the socialist North Vietnamese. Further targets included Israelis, because according to one RAF propaganda pamphlet, "The Jews displaced by fascism have become fascists themselves, who in collaboration with US capital want to exterminate the Palestinian people."[46]

The group solidified its membership base and accelerated plans for violence. Moving forward, the group only planned and executed attacks designed to result in significant damage to property and/or life.[47] First, they committed arson attacks on two department stores in Frankfurt in April of 1968. Several of the group members dispersed throughout West and East Germany in 1970 to evade police, eventually arriving in Jordan for "formal training." There they journeyed to a camp outside Amman, to live and work alongside guerillas hoping to free Palestine from Israeli control.[48] This arrangement would serve as the basis for their later partnership with the People's Front for the Liberation of Palestine (PFLP), an

[43] della Porta (1999, pp. 71, 72).

[44] Musolff (2011, p. 62).

[45] Musolff (2011).

[46] Musolff (2011, p. 63).

[47] Aust (2008).

[48] Aust (2008, pp. 65–70).

Table 4.4 Security incidents, Germany (West and East), 1970–1999

Peak year	*Fatalities*	*Injuries*	*Casualties*
1972	23	45	68
1976	4	36	40
1977	6	2	8
1980	17	218	235
1982	5	44	49
1985	9	114	123
1986	9	242	251
1991	10	35	45
1992	17	217	234
1994	2	85	87
1999	3	47	50
Total, All Years, Phase I	**139**	**1304**	**1443**

Data source Global Terrorism Database

ideologically similar and violent terrorist group. The RAF often aligned with groups seeking Marxist revolutions worldwide and desirous of an overthrow of the nation of Israel, both identified as "righteous causes."[49] As Table 4.4 shows, RAF violence contributed significantly to peak levels of domestic terror attacks in Germany

For the purpose of explaining the role of security threats in shaping data policy, I'll focus on the perpetrators and targets during the years of most intense activity, highlighting the events with the most impact.

1972 began an era of multiple domestic terror events perpetrated either by the RAF or their partner organizations. Once RAF members returned to Germany, they put their terrorist training to use by bombing the V-Corps headquarters of the US Army Officers Club on May 11, 1972, during which one person died and thirteen were injured. After the Springer-owned, extreme right newspaper *Deutsche Nationalzeitung*, called for student protest leader Dutsche to be stopped due to his radical views, the RAF bombed the Springer Press building in Hamburg on May 19, 1972. This attack resulted in over $100,000 in damages and left 24 people injured.[50] The highest profile domestic terror event of

[49] Becker (1977, p. 15). The PFLP aided violent Japanese, South American, and German terrorist groups.

[50] Aust (2008, pp. 31–32); also Global Terrorism Database.

1972 involved an attack by five members of a Palestinian terrorist group called the Black September Organization (BSO). They invaded the closed Israeli athletic compound at the Munich Olympics on September 5, took hostages and tortured athletes. A failed rescue by FDG authorities during a hostage exchange for Arab prisoners resulted in the deaths of 16 persons during a violent shoot-out, including the deaths of nine Israeli hostages, five terrorists, and one German police officer.[51] After a series of tipoffs by the public, RAF leaders were gradually arrested. Ironically, three founding members, Baader, Baader's lover Ulrike Meinhof,[52] Ensslin, and recent recruits Holger Meins and Ian Carl Raspe continued to plan assassinations and killings while in prison awaiting trial. By the spring of 1976, each of these individuals had either committed suicide or died by hunger strike while awaiting hearings.

After their deaths, other RAF followers kept the movement going by way of targeting public venues, particularly involving travel.[53] A sister group, the *Revolutionaïre Zellen*, or "Revolutionary Cells," killed sixteen people during the June 1976 bombing of the Frankfurt headquarters of the US Army, and later carried out a December attack at the Frankfurt US Air Force Officers Club, during which eighteen were hurt. On June 27, 1976, the Revolutionary Cells and the PFLP combined efforts to hijack an Air France plane en route from Tel Aviv to Paris. After making a touchdown in Athens, hijackers forced the pilot to fly to Entebbe, Uganda, after which Jewish passengers were separated from those who were non-Jewish, and the Jewish group held for hostage and ransom. Israeli paratroopers stormed the plane, freeing the hostages and killing the terrorists.[54] In 1977, PLO and German terrorists captured Lufthansa flight #181 on its way to Frankfurt, demanding the release of eleven RAF and Palestinian terrorists being held in prisons in Germany and Turkey.[55] While refueling

[51] CBS (2016).

[52] Meinhof had been associate with the group first as a journalist covering their activities in the left-leaning *kronket* publication, then later ideologically supporting their radical causes, including helping Baader escape from prison for a theft charge back in 1970.

[53] Musolff (2011).

[54] Musolff (2011, p. 63).

[55] Preece (2010, p. 152) and BBC (2016).

in Mogadishu, the plane was retaken by GSG-9 forces and all four terrorists were killed.[56] Airports and public venues were popular targets for the group, as members of the RAF also bombed the Frankfurt Alitalia airport hub in 1985 (3 died, 42 injured), the Rhein Air base (2 died, 20 injured), and then the La Belle Discotheque in West Berlin in 1986, during which 230 suffered injuries.[57]

The RAF movement began to lose momentum after 1990; as the majority of attacks occurred to a variety of targets suffering acts of violence by neo-Nazi extremists. In 1991, they attacked a Polish truck entering Germany and assaulted a Bonn home for immigrants. The largest incident occurred when 400 Neo-Nazis struck a police unit guarding a hostel frequented by foreign visitors in August of 1992. Later, in 1994 neo-Nazis assaulted another police unit in Bremen and attacked a group of Turkish immigrants. The most significant single attack at the latter part of Phase I took place in February of 1999. Two hundred Kurdish rebels stormed the Israeli Consulate in Wilmersdorf, Germany, during which three people died, and 43 were hurt.[58] In total, 139 people died, and 1304 were injured during domestic terrorist actions in Phase I, from 1970 to 1999. For twenty years, the government dealt with numerous attacks by a variety of anti-state terror groups, certainly creating a need for data surveillance.

Some within the larger population saw responses to domestic terror as a test of the restored democracy, a sort of trial on how the government would balance democratic rights against state surveillance accountability.[59] State authorities chose a multi-layered approach and developed two legislative goals to take into account public concerns.[60] The first goal sought to avoid "enemies of constitutional democracy" using the "grounds of the rule of law" to legally violate the principles of the state.[61]

56 Tanner/*NYTimes* (1977). Following the failed rescue of hostages at the Munich Olympics, Interior Minister Hans-Dietrich Genscher launched a new program, the Grnzschutzgruppe-9, or GSG-9, which would be a SWAT-like task force designated to intervene during future crisis terror events.

57 The attack on the discotheque was a joint effort between RAF and the Anti-American Arab Liberation Front. See Global Terrorism database.

58 Global Terrorism Database; University of Maryland 2018.

59 Hanshew (2010).

60 Katzenstein (2003).

61 Katzenstein (2003, p. 740).

Any new laws dealing with terrorism came under judicial review by the *Bundesnachrichtendienst*, or Constitutional Court, to ensure compliance with all constitutional rights outlined and protected in the Basic Law of 1949.[62] The second goal required clear control of state surveillance and information accumulation, under mandates of accountability. The latter was, of course, tied to the extensive surveillance practices under the Nazi regime. Together these approaches allowed the state to respond in a balanced way to current threats, while keeping in mind negative associations of past invasive state surveillance. Though general legislative content would be filtered through the need to ensure constitutional rights, even to those accused of terrorist behavior, the state obligation to restore public security remained. This last obligation was met with political differences between the parties rotating in control over the government.

German parties differed in their approaches to reducing domestic terrorism by means of data surveillance. The Social Democrats (SPD)-Free Democrats (FDP) coalition held majority power from 1969 to 1982. The SPD wanted to balance calm responses to the increased terror activities with legal constraints to avoid heady use of government power, it therefore modernized police and public management, and incorporated the use of new technology during reforms of the 1970s.[63] The Christian Democratic Union (CDU) led the government from 1982 to 1998. CDU/CSU leaders framed the ongoing domestic terrorism as indicative of weak and ineffective SPD security policies in 1970s and 1980s.[64] Counterterrorism efforts therefore shifted to proactive policing, as prevention would be better than catching criminals after terrorist acts had been committed. This led to a series of changes highly linked to personal data gathering and therefore, to data governance.

The government increased the size of staff at the Federal Criminal Office (BKU) and new agency head Dr. Horst Herold promoted computerized technology as a rational way to administer justice while simultaneously avoiding the human biases of past governments.[65] Additionally, Hans-Dietrich Genscher, then Minister of the Interior, expanded the budget and staff of the Bundeskriminalamt (BKA), or Criminal Police

[62] Schwartz (2002).

[63] Hanshew (2010).

[64] Hanshew (2010).

[65] Hanshew (2010).

Office, and centralized criminal investigative power. This last decision reduced the ability of *die Länder* officials to localize the handling of counterterrorism.[66] Most notable, in regards to digitized data use—the BKA was given power to use personal data as an information-gathering tool.[67] Herold also developed a computerized dragnet technique of profiling potential terrorists by cross-referencing multiple government databases and compiling a central record in the PIOS computer system used by the Suppression of Terrorism department (TE) and the Special Branch (ST). However, while German law allowed much leverage to security actors on the ability to collect personal data, there were clear limits on how long it could be stored (not above six months). The Constitutional Court was willing to punish the Federal Intelligence Service (BND) for overreach when sharing data across multiple agencies, in violation of digital human rights.[68]

In general, Germany shifted to a proactive counterterrorist agenda during Phase I, and expanded international cooperation efforts to stop previously successful terrorist groups. These plans included widening the scope of surveillance techniques. In the 1990s, German law enforcement utilized wire-tapped land lines, cellphones, and email content to monitor telecommunications by suspected criminals and terrorists.[69] The *Bundesnachrictendienst* or Constitutional Court allowed surveillance of "letters, conversations, or communications" involving personal and digitized data to search for evidence of behavior threatening to state survival or democracy. Law enforcement and security personnel received authorization for "strategic surveillance" involving telephone, satellite, or other communications, if needed to prevent an armed attack against the state. Security officials increased data surveillance to prevent all forms of illegal actions against the state, including terrorism. Security personnel opened cooperation in regional and international counter-terrorism programs: German officials pushed for and achieved a European secretariat of Interpol in 1986, and promoted the creation of Europol during the Maastricht treaty negotiations in the early 1990s.[70]

[66] Hancock (1994).

[67] Herold (1968).

[68] Schwartz (2002).

[69] Schwartz (2002).

[70] Katzenstein (2003).

To summarize the impact of security threats to German data surveillance, and therefore data governance: The Federal Republic of Germany experienced a significant number of domestic terrorist threats during Phase I, much more than in Sweden, but as we are about to see, at levels five times less than the incident totals in the UK. The number and frequency of domestic terror incidents led to gradual increases in the use of security use of digitized data. Authorities expanded access to data acquisition as a tool for improving domestic security from 1970 to 1999. However, despite the increase in violence, neither the political nor social will was present to grant unimpeded access to personal data. The shadows of restrictions upon personal expression and loss of dignity experienced under the Nazi regime remained in the collective memory, and politicians never lost site of the sociocultural importance of civil and political rights. The SPD government of the 1970s worked diligently to enshrine fundamental human rights and to protect via legal institutions the rights to democratically protest the government in power. Even after the more conservative CDU party came to power in 1982, it was unwillingly to sanction the highly intrusive use of digitized data surveillance. Several scholars attribute this self-imposed restriction to an underlying "civility" and "dignity" within the definition of individual self-determination in Germany's culture.[71] The constitutional framework for individual protections on dignity was largely unchanged once it was granted by the Basic Law of 1949. To address why the protection of these rights are so strong in Germany, I now turn to examine the last piece of the puzzle: the contribution to data governance made by legal professionals and human rights activists.

Digital Human Rights

Digital human rights legislation in Germany began at the regional state level. In 1970 the state of Hesse passed the first data protection law in the world.[72] The law mandated data security measures and required review of all new data processing technology for use in public administration prior to implementation. The Hessian law also established government oversight of data protection through an independent Data Protection

[71] Bennett (1992), Fuster (2016), and Schwartz (2002).

[72] G.V. Gl. Hessen 625, W. Germany (Data Protection Act of the Land of Hesse).

Commission (DPC), accountable to report back to the regional state parliament. Following Hesse, Rheinland-Pfalz passed their own data protection legislation in 1974. The Rheinland-Pfalz law granted supervisory power to a committee comprised of *Ländtag* (regional parliament) members and two judges, thus differing from the Hessian law. Notably, in Rheinland-Pfalz, data protection mandates only applied to *das Länd* administrative agencies.[73] Other *Länder* followed suit with their own data protection laws.[74] As a whole, German data protection laws prioritized digital human rights, largely due to two dynamics: a strong social norm for fundamental human rights within the Basic Law of 1949 and the advocacy of the legal community during the data legislation process.

The Basic Law of 1949 is the Constitution for Germany, and therefore the foundational framework for all of German law. The Basic Law formally codified protection for human rights within German society and by the government. Different actors during the process of creating data legislation in Germany utilized the wording of the 1949 law as justification for protecting personal or digitized data. Outside of Germany, privacy protection was the primary human rights concept referenced by others advocating for digital human rights, however, the German language has no specific word for privacy, so when discussing digitized data protection as a fundamental human right, German human rights advocates cited *persönlichkeitsrechte*, or the "right to a personality" found within Article 1(1) of the Basic Law.[75] The right to develop and express one's personality is also conditionally protected within Article 2(1), as long as someone does not violate general constitutional order.

The legal community drove the narrative of demand for digital human rights in Germany, rather than parliamentary ministers, administrators of data processing technology, or the ICT sector itself, as seen in Sweden and the United Kingdom. Professor Spiros Simitis, a trained and practicing jurist, authored the Hesse 1970 Data Protection Act.[76] Simitis immigrated to West Germany to study jurisprudence. After university, he became the Professor of Labour and Civil Law in Gießen and Frankfurt,

[73] Bennett (1992, pp 78, 151) and Hondius (1980).

[74] Bonn passed data protection legislation in 1976.

[75] Bennett (1992, pp. 74–82).

[76] Der Spiegel (1977).

as well as at UCLA-Berkeley. Simitis promoted personal data protection in Hesse and elsewhere in Europe, as a part of a larger network of legal professionals who actively advocated for adoption of a regulatory framework based on human rights constraints for the computerization of personal data. At the National Conference of Lawyers in 1972 (*Deutsche Juristentag*), the group created an international data protection group to research the topic.[77] Simitis' role in expanding data protection beyond the RFG into EU level legislation is examined further in subsequent chapters.

In addition to the concerns of the legal community, opinion polls revealed public fears over computer network linking across sectors, particularly regarding the widespread sharing of personal ID numbers during automatic data processing (ADP), and the risks associated with use of ADP during the population census collection. Within ten years, opinion shifted away from trust in government management of personal data, toward an increased fear of ADP by public authorities. In 1976, 62% of people polled said the state should be able to know as much as possible about residents, but by 1983, 65% of the public felt the state should have as little access as possible to their personal information as was possible.[78] Recall that this period of distrust was highest during the height of the RAF domestic terror spree, when security authorities increased their information surveillance techniques during efforts to stop the groups' repeated terror attacks.

Within the realm of politics, the Bundestag initiated a resolution in 1969 for a "preliminary plan for the protection of privacy against the misuse of automatically processed personal data" which failed to garner significant support.[79] Controversy emerged over an early draft to enact data protection, as some opposed the more stringent nature of the proposed federal law. The ICT industry also complained of potential discriminatory practices, asking for data use restrictions to apply to manual data and not just to digitized files. As a result of the push-back, the bill died in 1971.[80] From 1972 to 1976, the Interior committee held multiple public hearings to work out compromises, and called on expert testimony by human rights advocates to discuss the legality of new data

[77] Bull (1984).

[78] Flaherty (1989, p. 25).

[79] Bull (1984, p. 104).

[80] Flaherty (1989, p. 22).

restrictions. Spiros Simitis attempted to direct the parties toward support of a federal law with an independent control authority, rather than a loose self-administering surveillance model.[81] The CDU and CSU parties fought over whether the control body would be within the Federal Audit Office, rather than be independent as Simitis had promoted. Despite disagreement over the independence aspect of the DPC, the *Bundesdatenschutzgesetz* (BDSG) legalized data protection on 27 January 1977.[82] It's important to outline the extent of data controls imbedded within the BDSG to determine if digital human rights were indeed protected.

The law defined personal data as "details on the personal or material circumstances of an identified or identifiable physical person."[83] The purpose of the BDSG was to "ensure against the misuse of personal data during storage, communication, modification, and erasure (data processing) and thereby to *prevent harm* to any personal interests of the person concerned that warrant protection."[84] To "prevent harm" required data processors to fulfil three main tasks. First, personal data could be stored only as long as necessary for completion of a legitimate task—it had a time limit. Second, manual and automated data files must be protected—it set broad application on protecting all types of personal data. Finally, data subjects possessed the right to be informed of personal data existence, have their incorrect data amended, request that their data be restricted from additional use, and demand their personal data be deleted—data subjects had legal rights. As the first federal Data Protection Commissioner stated, the bill was to act, "As a kind of human rights protection in a technological society."[85] The BDSG was amended or updated in 1994, 1997, and 2001.[86] The 1997 and 2001 changes reflected the necessity of maintaining compliance with EU data law directives, including Directive 95/46/EC which will be discussed in Chapter 6.[87]

[81] Bennett (1992) and OECD (1976, pp. 83–94).

[82] The bill passed, but was opposed by several Länder, including Bavaria, Baden-Württemburg, Rheinland-Pfalz, and Schleswig–Holstein.

[83] Riccardi (1983, p. 249).

[84] Flaherty (1989, p. 30).

[85] Flaherty (1989, p. 31).

[86] Bennett (1992, p. 212).

[87] Flaherty (1979).

Table 4.5 Commissioners of the national data protection commission, FRG

Years served in DPC	*Name of commissioners*
1978–1983	Hans Peter Bull
1983–1988	Reinhold Baumann
1988–1993	Alfred Einwag
1993–2003	Joachim Jacob

To safeguard compliance, the BDSG created a new national-level, independent Data Protection Commission (DPC), led by a federal Commissioner. The new agency operated in tandem with the Federal Ministry of the Interior and was responsible for recommending updates to the law and giving advice to ministers or public authorities about special regulations for data protection. Initially, the DPC provided information solely to the Bundestag and Interior Ministry; later, the DPC was given power to serve as ombudsman over data protection violation complaints made by individuals. Going forward, each public agency needed a data protection officer who could ensure that the agency maintained compliance with the BDSG. All data processors were to be registered with the DPC authority. Lastly, the DPC produced an annual report on the state of data protection in the FRG; this report was submitted to the Bundestag for review on an annual basis (Table 4.5).

As with the Swedish data agency directors, the German DPA during Phase I all came from previous careers in legal and/or academic positions; the Data Protection Commissioners (DPCs) also typically chose personnel with legal training.[88] The legal training and experiences of the DPCs informed their management of the Commission and each director promoted digital human rights, albeit using different styles. The first Commissioner, Hans Peter Bull, set a framework for DHR advocacy, albeit from a state-based perspective. Bull earned a doctorate of law in 1963 and subsequently worked as an attorney and academic until 1967. Bull was a member of the Social Democrats when appointed as the first federal DPC, but saw himself as a federal civil servant, and used his platform to focus national attention on the social effects of computer technology diffusion. To Bull, state bureaucrats including that of the Commission provided a functional service for the state, not directly

[88] Flaherty (1989, pp. 48–57).

serving the public. When it became apparent that Bull may not be reinstated after his 5-year term ended, there was some discussion of Hessian Commissioner Spiros Simitis becoming the next federal Commissioner. In the end, Bull was succeeded by Dr. Reinhold Baumann, who had been a lawyer for 30 years within the federal Ministry of the Interior. His leadership style was more "managerial" than Bull's and placed more emphasis on public concerns rather than state's interests.[89] After Baumann retired, the DPC became much more aggressive against state infringement of DHR.

Dr. Alfred Einwag was appointed in 1988, and set the stage for direct confrontations between the DPC and security officials. Einwag acquired his doctorate in law from the University of Munich in 1952, after which he worked for district government offices and the Ministry of the Interior until 1964. His other public service posts included advisement on legal matters for the Federal Border Police after 1964. Ironically, it was his familiarity with police activities which fueled his resistance against invasive data practices by law enforcement. During his tenure, Einway criticized the copious use and accumulation of vast quantities of personal digitized data.[90] He was also quite vocal about the invasive nature of using data during employment screening processes, complaining that they were, "... a clear breach of the law." To Einwag, security actors and corporations were often given a free pass by the Federal Office for the Protection of the Constitution, or BfV (*Bundesamt für Verfassungsschutz*), who at times, ignored the civil rights components of the law when considering behavior by either group.[91] Einwag wasn't afraid to push back against digital human rights infringement; his more aggressive leadership paved the way for his successor to tackle new technological applications for personal data creation and use.

Joachim Jacob was appointed to lead the DPC in 1993. Similar to his predecessors, he also held a doctorate in law. His prior positions included working in the Ministry of the Interior, and as a consultant to State Secretary Günter Hartkopf of the FDP. Where Bull and Baumann focused upon enforcing basic practices, and Einwag faced off against law enforcement and firms, Jacob's approach centered on security cameras used by

89 Flaherty (1989 p. 48).

90 Der Spiegel (1989).

91 Der Spiegel (1992).

government and the private sector. He routinely clashed with firms over video surveillance techniques, which he believed violated personal privacy as well as data use parameters. In a 2001 interview, he warned that CCTV use needed to be examined on a "case by case basis" and be weighed against the privacy interests of individuals.[92] Even after leaving the DPC, he advised companies seeking to "ensure that the data protection regulations are fully complied with."[93] Thanks to Jacob and Einwag, Phase I ended with a more aggressive Data Protection Commission.

Each DPC had liberty to choose her/his personnel, and the majority of agency staff were lawyers or jurists. Unfortunately, due to the conditional nature of career advancement within civil service, it was difficult for any DPC to keep staff for very long, as trained staff frequently left for other positions within the Ministry of the Interior. This practice made long-term continuity and speedy action on data protection infringement complaints an ongoing problem for the agency. In spite of these challenges, regardless of who led the DPC, digital human rights were consistently enforced and each director showed a willingness to oppose security officials or other actors, if they felt German data protections outlined in legislation were at risk.

Though the BDSG firmly established digital human rights, and provided a strong oversight body with the authority to investigate violators, the fulfillment of the law was challenged by two political events during Phase I. In the first instance, public opposition to computerized data use arose around the proposed 1983 national Census. An opinion survey conducted by the Klaus Lange Society for Mathematics and Data Processing discovered that 81% of the public surveyed feared a loss of personal privacy during census collection.[94] Spiros Simitis, then the Hessian Data Protection Commissioner, stated that hundreds of citizens had called their office to complain over fears of government surveillance related to the proposed census. The Constitutional Court delayed census collection while it reviewed public privacy concerns. Judicial review also halted government plans on personal data collection with a second ruling on 15 December 1983. This time, the Constitutional Court ruled that in the instance of the collection of personal data about public housing,

[92] Netzeitung (2001).

[93] Netzeitung (2001).

[94] Flaherty (1989, pp. 30–32).

West Germans had a "constitutional right to self-determination about the use of their own personal information on the basis of articles 1 and 2 of the Constitution."[95] This ruling served as yet another critical juncture during which German citizens were protected during personal information gathering by a government agency. Meanwhile, actual public protests were held in 1983 and 1987 over the proposed collection of personal data during the upcoming census. In polls conducted near the protests, 25% of surveyed households admitted they were planning on not completing the census forms.[96] After adjustments to data management plans significantly strengthened the protection of census data after collection, the census was finally carried out in 1987.

Regarding the second political factor to shape compliance with the BDSG, the Data Protection Commission itself faced opposition to its oversight by the national security community. As mentioned in the domestic terrorism discussion, BKA head Dr. Herold Horst had adopted the PIOS data retrieval system to profile suspects during counter-terrorism investigations. The DPC felt this use of personal information was dangerous, as data surveillance could potentially involve collecting information of non-suspects, without their consent. Horst clashed with DPC Commissioner Bull regarding the control and use of this police data. Bull requested the BKA delete some fingerprint data in storage and offered a set of guidelines in 1981 that involved data collection best practices.[97] Later, in 1986, DPC Commissioner Baumann complained that security officials were not following Commission advice on limits to police power over personal data, according to a new Code of Criminal procedures. Minister of the Interior Zimmerman complained of DPC interference with security measures, but Baumann took the issue to the Interior Committee of the Bundestag in 1986 and won his case. Like his predecessor, Baumann had argued that security officials were still subject to constitutional law and must provide protection for personal and digitized information.[98] Security officials eventually complied.

[95] Flaherty (1989, p. 45) and Webb (2003, p. 1).

[96] International Herald Tribune survey, 28 March 1983, p. 2.

[97] Deutscher Bundestag/Federal Republic of Germany (1981), Flaherty (1989, pp. 71–72), and Third Activity Report of the BfD (1982).

[98] Flaherty (1989, p. 76).

To summarize, in the case of Germany, there is substantial support for the development of a digital human rights regime. The Hessian state developed its own data protection law and protection commission in 1970, under the influence of legal professional and human rights advocate Spiros Simitis. Simitis then went on to influence the national legislative debate in the early to mid-1970s, providing expert testimony to the Bundestag and various investigative bodies. In addition, the state was pressed to create national data protection legislation by the *Deutsche Juristentag*, a highly organized network of lawyers and jurists. After the BDSG law passed in 1977, the implementation of the law was challenged by the previously scheduled census collection order, and by security services seeking to deter terrorist activities. In both instances, the power of the law and the validity of DPC efforts were supported, and not weakened by judicial and parliamentary review.

Bibliography

2001. September 3. Accessed December 20, 2018. https://www.munzinger.de/search/portrait/Hans+Peter+Bull/0/15205.html.

Ahearn, Raymond J., and Paul Belkin. 2010. *The German Economy and U.S.-German Economic Relations*. CRS Report for Congress. Washington, DC: Congressional Research Service.

Anderson, Christina, and Alan Cowel. 2018. "Was the Killer of Sweden's Leader in 1986 Under Investigators' Noses All This Time?" May 24. Accessed September 16, 2018. https://www.nytimes.com/2018/05/24/world/europe/sweden-olof-palme-killing.html.

Anderson, Stanley V. 1973. "Public Access to Government Files in Sweden." *American Journal of Comparative Law* 21 (3): 419–473.

Aust, Stefan. 2008. *Baader-Meinhof: The Inside Story of the RAF*. Oxford: Oxford University Press.

Australian Financial Review. 1988. "Europe Poor Performer In High-Tech Stakes." *Australian Financial Review* 25.

BBC News. 2005. "On this Day—24 April". Accessed September 2016, 2018. http://news.bbc.co.uk/onthisday/hi/dates/stories/april/24/newsid_2523000/2523095.stm.

———. 2017. "Swedish 'Laser Man' Ausonius on Trial for 1992 German Murder". December 13. Accessed September 18, 2018. https://www.bbc.com/news/world-europe-42340711.

BBC World News. 2016. "Who Were Germany's Red Army Faction militants?" January 19. Accessed December 5, 2018. https://www.bbc.com/news/world-europe-35354812.

Becker, Jillian. 1977. *Hitler's Children: The Story of the Baader-Meinhof Terrorist Gang*. Philadelphia, PA: J.B. Lippincott Co.

Bennett, Colin J. 1992. *Regulating Privacy: Data Protection and Public Policy in Europe and the United States*. Ithaca, NY: Cornell University Press.

Berman, Sheri. 2006. *The Primacy of Politics: Social Democracy and the Making of Europe's Twentieth Century*. Cambridge, NJ: Cambridge University Press.

Bourn, Colin, and John Benyon. 1983. *Data Protection: Perspectives on Information Privacy*. Conference Proceedings. Leicester: University of Leicester.

Bull, Hans Peter. 1984. *Datenschutz oder die Angst vor dem Computer*. München, DE: Piper.

CBS Evening News. 2016. "September 6, 1972: World Learns of Munich Olympics Massacre". September 6. Accessed December 19, 2018. https://www.cbsnews.com/news/on-this-day-september-6-1972-world-learns-of-munich-olympics-massacre/.

Dammann, Ulrich. 1977. *Data protection Legislation: An International Documentation*. Frankfurt: Frankfurt am Main.

della Porta, Donatella. 1999. "Protest, Protesters, and Protest Policing: Public Discourses in Italy and Germany from the 1960s to the 1980s." In *How Social Movements Matter*, edited by Marco Giugni, Doug McAdam and Sidney Tarrow, 66–96. Minneapolis, MN: University of Minnesota Press.

Der Spiegel. 1977. November 14. Accessed December 19, 2018. http://www.spiegel.de/spiegel/print/d-40764083.html.

———. 1989. "Really, Honestly: A Confidential Test Report by the Bonn Data Protection Officer Reveals the Mania for Collecting Among the Police State Security." *Spiegal Politics*. Der Spiegel. February 12. Accessed April 2021. https://www.spiegel.de/politik/echt-so-ehrlich-a-e4aac248-0002-0001-0000-000013493728?context=issue.

———. 1992. "Blue Miracle: Citizens are Brazenly Spied On, Parliamentarians Are Provided with Secreit Dossiers: The Protection of the Constitution Interprets the New Data Protection Laws at Will." *Spiegel Politics*. April 5. Accessed April 2021. https://www.spiegel.de/politik/blaues-wunder-a-92ec1679-0002-0001-0000-000013679277?context=issue.

———. 2007. "Immer Radikaler: Interview mit Daniel Cohn-Bendit." *Der Spiegel*.

"Employee Spying in Retail." *Heise Online*. April 2, 2008. Accessed April 2021. https://www.heise.de/newsticker/meldung/Mitarbeiter-Bespitzelung-im-Handel-Auch-Edeka-und-Plus-im-Visier-195390.html.

Federal Republic of Germany. 1981, February 12. *Deutscher Bundestag*, 907–909. Bonn, FRG: Bundestag.

———. 1982. "Third Activity Report of the BfD." INPOL, Bonn, FRG.

Flaherty, David H. 1979. *Privacy and Government Databanks*. London: Mansell.

———. 1989. *Protecting Privacy in Surveillance Societies: The Federal Republic of Germany, Sweden, France, Canada, and the United States.* Chapel Hill, NC: University of North Carolina Press.

Fuster, Gloria González. 2016. *The Emergence of Personal Data Protection as a Fundamental Right of the EU.* Springer.

Hall, Peter A., and David Soskice. 2013. *Varities of Capitalism: The Institutional Foundations of Comparative Advantage.* Oxford: Oxford University Press.

Hancock, William L. 1994, October. *Counterterrorism in Great Britain, Germany, and France: 1968 to the Present*. Winnepeg, Manitoba: Department of Political Studies.

Hanshew, Karrin. 2010. "Daring More Democracy: Internal Security and the Social Democratic Fight against West German Terrorism." *Central European History* 43: 117–147.

Herold, Horst. 1968. "Organisatorische Grundzuge der elektronischen Datenverarbeitung im Bereich der Poizei." In *Taschenbuch fur Kriminalisten*, 240–254.

Hondius, Frits W. 1980. "Data Law in Europe." *Stanford Journal of International Law* 16: 87–111.

Katzenstein, Peter J. 1990. *West Germany's Internal Security Policy: State and Violence in the 1970s and 1980s.* Edited by Occasional Paper 28. Cornell Studies in International Affairs. Ithaca, NY: Cornell University Press.

———. 1998. "Left-Wing Violence and State Response: United States, Germany, Italy, and Japan, 1960s–1990s." Working Paper 98, Cornell University, Ithaca, NY: Institute for European Studies.

———. 2003. "Same War—Differnt Views: Germany, Japan, and Counterterrorism." *International Organization* 57: 731–760.

konkret. 2008. "Talar-Muffel von Hamburg, konkret 12/1967." *Go¨tz Aly: Unser Kampf. 1968 – ein irritierter Blick zuru¨ck.* Frankfurt: Fischer, December.

Liedtke, Werner. 1980. *Das Bunesdatenschutzgesetz: Eine Fallstudie zum Gesetzgebungsprozess*. Dusseldorf: Mannhold.

Mardellat, Patrick. 2011. "The Political (and also Economic) Consequences of the Euro: Lessons from the Crisis." Working Paper, Political Economy, Sciences Po, Lille, France.

Moghadam, Assaf. 2012. "Failure and Disengagement in the Red Army Faction." *Studies in Conflict & Terrorism* 35: 156–181.

Munzinger, Ludwig. 2019. https://www.cio.de/a/das-munzinger-archiv-in-zeiten-der-digitalisierung,3325416.

Musolff, Andreas. 2011. "Hitler's Children Revisited: West German Terrorism and the Problem of Coming to Terms with the Nazi Past." *Terrorism and Political Violence* 23: 60–71.

"Niemand hat mehr den Überblick." *NETZIETUNG.DE.* March 30, 2001. Accessed April 2021. http://www.netzeitung.de/deutschland/145655.html.

OECD. 1976. *Establishing Institutional Structures to Monitor and Enforce Data Protection*, 83–94. Policy Issues in Data Protection and Privacy, OECD Informatics Studies. Paris, France: Organization for Economic Cooperation and Development.

———. 2000. *A New Economy? The Changing Role of Innovation and Information Technology in Growth.* Information Society. Paris, France: Organisation for Co-operation and Economic Development.

———. 2020. *Roadmap Toward a Common Framework for Measuring the Digital Economy.* Paris, France: OECD.

———. 2021. ICT Investments. *OECD.*

Preece, Julian. 2010. "The lives of the RAF Revisited: The Biographical Turn." *Memory Studies* 3 (2): 151–163.

Riccardi, J. Lee. 1983. "The German Federal Data Protection Act of 1977: Protecting the Right to Privacy?" *Boston College International and Comparative Law Review* 6 (1): 243–271.

Schwartz, Paul M. 2002. "German and US Telecommunications Privacy law: Legal Regulation of Domestic Law Enforcement Surveillance." *Berkeley Law Scholarship Repository-Hastings Law Journal* 54: 751–801.

Siebert, Horst. 2005. *The Germany Economy: Beyond the Social Market.* Princeton, NJ: Princeton University Press.

Simitis, Spiros. 1971. "Chancen und Gefahren der elektronischen Datenverarbeitung." *Neue Juristische Wochenschrift.*

———. 1976. *Establishing Institutional Structures to Monitor and Enforce Data Protection.* Policy Issues in Data Protection and Privacy. Paris, France: Organization for Economic Cooperation and Development.

———. 1978. "Datenschutz Notwendigheit und Voraussetzungen einer gesetzlichen Regelung." In *Informatik - Fachberichte: Herausgegeben von W. Brauer im Auftrag Der Gesellschaft für Informatik (GI)*, by Wilhelm Steinmüller, Leonhard Ermer and Wolfgang Schimmel. Berlin: Springer-Verlag.

Tanner, Henry. 1977. "German Troops Free Hostages on Hijacked Plane in Somalia; Four Terrorists Killed in Raid". October 18. Accessed December 19, 2018. https://www.nytimes.com/1977/10/18/archives/german-troops-free-hostages-on-hijacked-plane-in-somalia-four.html.

University of Maryland. 2018. *Global Terrorism Database.* Accessed March 2019. https://www.start.umd.edu/data-tools/global-terrorism-database-gtd.

Webb, Philippa. 2003. "A Comparative Analysis of Data Protection Laws in Australia and Germany." The *Journal of Information, Law and Technology* 2.

World Bank. 2021. *World Development Indicators.* WDI.

CHAPTER 5

The United Kingdom: Business Aligns with Human Rights Advocacy

British governments repeatedly and often resisted domestic and international efforts to formalize any type of data legislation, only reluctantly passing data protections after compelled by a combination of domestic and international actors. Due to the earlier success of ICT sector growth in Britain, personal data was classified as a purely economic variable for many years, more so than in Sweden or Germany. Ironically, though Northern Ireland was a hotbed of civil unrest, security forces didn't have to push the government for data access, useful for counter-terrorism actions. Several factors created the necessary impetus for establishing digital human rights in the United Kingdom. International pressure by the economically minded OECD, the membership requirements of EU supranational law, plus human rights activism by MPs and civil society, together produced such a volume of pressure that the government finally passed data protection. With the Brexit vote in 2016 removing the need to harmonize British law with EU law, the fragility of digital human rights in Britain is likely to continue for the foreseeable future.

The United Kingdom was the last of my case states to adopt data protection legislation (Sweden in 1973, Germany in 1977, United Kingdom in 1984). A core barrier to developing data protection legislation in the United Kingdom lay in the lack of a written constitution with a bill rights protections. As a result, Britons experienced a more politicized process to achieve digital human rights, as political will regarding

R. Dowd, *The Birth of Digital Human Rights*, Information Technology and Global Governance,
https://doi.org/10.1007/978-3-030-82969-8_5

Table 5.1 UK Data Laws (Phase I: 1970–1999)

Year	*Name of law*	*Description*	*Net score*
1984	Data Protection Act	Regulates use of automatically processed personal data for individuals; designed for compliance with Council of Europe Convention 108	+49 Protect Data +9 Security Use +5 Economic Use
1998	Data Protection Act	Created new provisions for regulation of processing personal information; designed to ensure compliance with EU Directive 95/46/EC	+67 Protect Data +25 Security Use +18 Economic Use

Source www.legislation.gov/uk

data legislation waxed and waned across time, based upon whether the Conservative or Labour party held the majority in Parliament. To further complicate matters, the press vocalized opposition against any potential data law, fearing it would impinge upon freedom of the press. Security officials weighed in on the discussion as well, raising concerns over data privacy and the need for data surveillance during prolonged periods of domestic terrorism in Northern Ireland. Content analysis of British laws reveals an overall prioritization for digital human rights, beginning in 1984. Let's examine each of the contributing factors to data legislation to uncover the delayed, but eventual creation of data protection in Britain (Table 5.1).

The lack of a formal, written constitution raised one of the main hurdles for data protection legislation in Britain.[1] Unlike the countries of Sweden and Germany, both of whom had constitutions which established a base set of human rights, the United Kingdom had no such document. Without formal, legal protections for human rights in the United Kingdom, there was no existing framework on which to build digital human rights. The norms of privacy protection present in the German case due to a history of oppressive Nazi surveillance simply did not exist in Britain.[2] Compared to Sweden, the United Kingdom had no established history of government transparency about information collected on the

[1] Bennett (1992, p. 82).

[2] Flaherty (1989).

population. As a result, the process toward legislating data management was much more piecemeal, and driven by an odd combination of the legal community, academics, and the ICT sector itself.

Politicians were the last to support digital human rights legislation. It took a personal loss involving a Labour MP in 1982 to expose the lack of protections for personal data privacy, and motivate the government to consider data protection legislation. Prior to Phase I, there had been a few scattered attempts to bar data abuse by media or the government while collecting personal information during investigations involving private citizens. In the House of Lords, Lord Mancroft introduced an unsuccessful bill in 1961 to prohibit "… any unjustifiable publication relating to his private affairs and to give him rights at law in the vent of such publication."[3] On the House of Commons side, several attempts were made to introduce similar legislation. MP Alex Lyon advocated for a "Right of Privacy Bill" in 1967, but it failed to obtain general support. Mr. Brian Walden initiated his own version of the "Privacy Bill" in 1969, which also died. These were but the beginning of data legislation efforts.

Labour controlled the British government during the early years of ICT adoption and computer databank diffusion. While some MPs were interested in digital human rights, broad support for passing data legislation was non-existent. Despite the fact that Britain did not have a plan to develop centralized databanks for government use, individual MPs worried about the potential for abuse as computerized record-keeping grew in practice. These individuals pressured the Home Office to do something. The government responded with the Justice Report *Privacy and the Law*, released in 1970, which offered a draft proposal based upon Walden's Privacy Bill. The press opposed the report recommendations due to fears of serious restrictions to freedom of the press and speech.[4] Concerned parliamentarians continued to push the Home Office for a proactive plan regarding information privacy legislation, and asked for legislative options that would not impinge upon press freedoms. The Home office finally caved to the pressure and created an investigative committee to research the topic further.

The Younger Commission, headed by Sir Kenneth Younger, first met in May of 1970. The committee initially looked only at the issue of

[3] Parliament (1961).

[4] Dworkin (1973).

privacy as relates to public sector use of digitized personal data. (The Committee later added private sector data use in their assessment, after receiving feedback from various industries to expand the breadth of the evaluation.) The committee was told to "consider whether legislation is needed to give further protection to the individual citizen and to commercial and industrial interests against intrusions into privacy by private persons and organizations, or by companies, and to make recommendations."[5] Within their mandate, they conducted a series of public opinion polls to measure public support for privacy legislation. 38% of Britons considered privacy as important, 29% as very important, and 16% extremely important.[6] *The Younger Committee Report on Privacy* suggested a series of protection measures, but committee members disagreed, with fourteen members against, and two in support of a legislative bill protecting personal data. Thanks to the majority dissent, the committee did not propose a law codifying the right to privacy. Dissenters worried that legal cases could arise in which court officials would be forced to choose between an individual's right to privacy and "public interest."[7] The committee also feared that a bill to protect information privacy would unfairly restrain free speech, again reflecting the influence of press resistance. Rather, the Younger Committee asked that the Press Council institute a voluntary code of ethics, and it called for a new Complaints Commission to accept and examine public complaints regarding invasions of privacy during press investigations. Both instruments were subsequently rejected by the press.

In terms of positive mechanisms, the report offered ten principles, primarily focused on data treatment by the finance industry and those performing automatic data processing.[8]

- Collect personal information only for specified reasons
- Data access granted onto to those with authorization
- Store data for a limited, pre-set time period
- Anonymize statistical data[9]

[5] Younger Committee (1972, p. 1).

[6] *Report of the Committee on Privacy*, Cmnd. 5012.

[7] Parliament (1973).

[8] Bennett (1982, p. 86).

[9] Parliament (1973), Comments by Mr. Robert Carr.

- Financial institutions must receive consent from data subject to release credit information to others
- Data security measures to avoid abuse or misuse of information[10]
- Maintain data accuracy; make corrections when confronted

Lastly, the Younger Commission recommended a Standing Commission be appointed to "examine the use of computers, particularly for handling personal information." Heath's conservative government virtually ignored the committee's suggestions, but agreed to establish a standing committee. The only suggestions that did become law included credit information protections, enacted within the Consumer Credit Act of 1974.

Several data collection plans by the government increased public fears over data privacy. The format of the 1971 census in Britain resulted in the "biggest outpouring of public concern about privacy ever witnessed in that country."[11] As over 100,000 census-takers went throughout the country collecting data, people complained of the invasive nature of questions regarding details such as ethnicity and the number of persons living in each household. Some residents refused to participate altogether, several lawsuits were filed, and an official investigation was launched to address census procedures.[12] In other example, public outcry arose in 1970 over the centralization of 33 million records on British drivers for a new agency, the Driver and Vehicle Licensing Centre.[13] Mr. Leslie Huckfield complained during the House of Lords debate over the Control of Personal Information Bill that the licensing center was just the beginning of widespread privacy losses during computerization of public data files planned for several government agencies.[14] This digitization of data was the first of many such government efforts. The Department of Health and Social Security prepared to digitize social work records, the National Police compiled criminal history records in databanks, and the Department of Defence, Trade and Industry, as well as the Civil Service Department built their own databanks to house digitized personal data of

[10] Bourn and Benyon (1983, pp. 12, 13).

[11] Bennett (1982, p. 52).

[12] Magwick and Smythe (1974).

[13] Bennett (1982, p. 48) and Warner and Stone, p. 105.

[14] Parliament (1972).

those they served. Most troubling to members of the public and therefore to some MPs were plans to link many of these databases, heightening the risk of individuals' data being seen by persons unauthorized, yet working with other state agencies. (MPs regularly mentioned fears of a Nixon-like Watergate scandal, should data protection not be addressed by Her Majesty's government.)[15]

Public pressure came to head as the new Labour government took office in 1974. Individual MPs continued to call for action on the recommendations in the 1972 Younger Report, but the government responded with more "research" on the matter. The "Control of Personal Information Act" sponsored by Huckfield and Coombs in 1972 asked for the creation of a data bank tribunal to regulate and monitor personal information management. Their bill received a second reading in April of 1972, but was defeated in 1973.[16] As in the past, the government created yet another standing research committee on the topic, rather than actually craft data legislation.

The Lindop Committee, named after Chair Sir Norman Lindop, launched in July of 1976, and met over 50 times in the next two years. The majority of the committee's work concerned how to define terminology not addressed in the Younger report, as well as how to outline the needed scope of data protections. Data privacy was identified as, "the individual's claim to control the circulation of data about himself."[17] Their first report, released in 1978, called for legislation to establish a Data Protection Authority, who would then implement codes of behavior for data treatment, including "collecting, processing, and storing personal data on computers" based on "fair information principles."[18]

Unfortunately, the issue became politicized yet again, as the Labour government asked for additional input by the IT industry. The Lindop Committee generated a list of 250 organizations and asked them for feedback. While considering data governance, the Labour government lost a no-confidence vote in 1979. Thatcher's Conservatives were elected in 1979, and decided to delay data legislation again, finding the Lindop

[15] Younger Report (1972), Comments by Mr. Robert Carr, HC Deb 13 July 1973 vol. 859 cc1955–2058.

[16] Parliament (1972). See also Price (1984).

[17] Bourn and Benyon (1983, p. 14?).

[18] Bennett (1992, p. 90).

suggestions suspect, given that the committee was launched by a Labour initiative.

Though politicians delayed data legislative action multiple times, civil liberties groups pressured the Home Office throughout the 1970s to act.[19] However, as civil society pressure mounted, the rhetoric shifted from opposition based on a need to protect press freedoms, toward support based on unease about amounts of information surveillance conducted by national security authorities. In 1981, the Home Office Secretary indicated the government sought to balance the dual mandates of protecting privacy justice (Ministry of Justice) yet also protecting national security (Department of Interior).[20] Domestic actors had long pushed the government for or against certain types of data laws, and now the Council of Europe membership mandates and the OECD began lobbying for regional data policy convergence in order to benefit the member states' economies. It was the latter, international effort, which eventually convinced the Thatcher government to act on data legislation.

International Pressures Mount

In 1981, the Council of Europe held a meeting specifically to address data policy: *The Convention for the Protection of Individuals with regard to Automatic Processing of Data* ("Convention 108").[21] Convention 108 sought to mobilize data transport across state lines during business transactions, a high priority for the rapidly developing ICT sector of several Council of Europe and OECD member states. The treaty outlined several mandates on data protection during the automatic processing of personal data, and recommended national laws to protect storage and use of digitized data. If protections were uniform across the CoE membership, data commodification would be virtually limitless. All CoE members including the United Kingdom were encouraged to ratify the treaty to facilitate economic growth. This request contributed to the mounting pressures upon the recalcitrant UK government to create a DHR policy.

Why did a previously hesitant UK government suddenly commit to data protection legislation? Margaret Thatcher won the premiership of the UK Parliament in 1979, based on promises to resurrect the British economy; she had a campaign promise to deliver. British firms needed

[19] Bennett (1992), Bourn and Benyon (1983), and Fuster (2016).

[20] Bennett (1992), Bourne and Benyon, p. 25, and Cornford (1981).

[21] Council of Europe (2018).

an edge to compete against the more established US firms. If they could guarantee that any data imported into Britain or exported elsewhere by British firms would meet the standards of protection within Convention 108, it would set them apart from US firms, given that America had failed to pass any national data protection laws. Thus, a strange partnership was born between the British ICT sector and human rights activists in pushing the government to finally act on the issue. In reality, without joining the Convention, British tech firms feared profit losses if they were shut out of data access within the European market. In addition, other EU states had signed the treaty and were offering protected environments for EU citizens' data transport and use. Finally, the data protection was framed in a way that the trade-focused Thatcher government could embrace, as it matched their economic policy goals. The United Kingdom signed Convention 108 in 1981, and later ratified it in 1987. Timothy Raison, Secretary for the Home Office, announced a forthcoming White Paper which would explain the government's intended national data legislation. And, as a part of her economic growth efforts, Thatcher declared 1982 to be a "Technology Year," encouraging companies to play catch up with the US virtual monopoly over technology manufacturing, and to establish a firm hold for British ICT companies within European markets.

The White Paper of 1982 addressed data protections, but in reality followed none of the core suggestions made by either the Younger or Lindop Committees. Instead of creating a permanent agency to act as a Data Protection Authority (DPA), the paper suggested a registry to oversee the cataloguing of computers processing personal, non-anonymized data.[22] The watered-down bill was introduced by the Thatcher government in the House of Lords in December of 1982, and received a second reading in January of 1983, but was unable to pass through both sides of Parliament before the May break. It was again introduced and passed in the Lords in June/July of 1983, and was taken up by the Commons in January of 1984. The bill passed with a vote of 226 for 104 against, securing according to Gerald Kaufman, "... the absolute minimum the government can get away with."[23] The wording angered human rights groups, as it provided no protections for

[22] Bennett (1992, p. 92).

[23] Bennett (1992), Gerald Kaufman comments 1984.

manual (paper-based) data, and it allowed for cross-border data transfers. Despite these weaknesses, it was the first data protection law of the United Kingdom, and its success was due to a mixed alliance among the "... business community, the trades unions, the consumers' associations, the computer industry, the medical and other professions, and the civil liberties and human rights interests...".[24]

I now explain how each of the three major factors (economic commodification, domestic security threats, and human rights activism) contributed toward the 1984 law and the subsequent 1998 revision.

Data Commodification and the Economy

The role of ICT within Britain's economic history is best explained by examination of socioeconomic changes during the emergence of industrialization. Beginning in the late seventeenth and eighteenth centuries, Great Britain adopted machine-based textile processing, and British inventors invented steam engine power; mechanized production increased labor efficiency exponentially. By 1851, the country was one of the world's largest exporters of manufactured and commodified goods, including textiles, engineering products, steam engines, coal, and iron.[25] Unfortunately for Britain, it was unable to maintain this advantage. By the twentieth century, the United Kingdom obtained much of its advanced technology from other states, as the Fordist mechanisms adopted in the early 1900s were not as adaptable to the production of advanced technological goods.[26]

Trade conditions in an increasingly globalized marketplace shaped twentieth century British economic policy as well. During the interwar years, the country functioned as a "managed economy," whereby free trade preferences gradually shifted toward protectionist policies. After 1930, the government added general tariffs on manufacturing, tightened controls on cartels and foreign investment controls, and abandoned the gold standard in 1931. After World War II, during the "Golden Age of

[24] Bourn and Benyon, p. 32.

[25] Cambridge Economic History of Modern Britain (2014).

[26] Fordism is a principle of mass production marked by large-scale production of standardized, low-cost goods. It depends upon production volumes that reduce economies of scale such that even semi-skilled employees are able to afford the products they are making.

European economic growth," the United Kingdom diverged from the corporatist strategies used in the Scandinavian states such as Sweden, or Germany. Instead of using collective bargaining to facilitate wage restraints, British leaders subsidized ailing industries, incentivized technology invention (not tech diffusion as in Germany), and kept owners and industrial controls separate. Such interventions were not able to prevent economic recession; by the 1980s, the United Kingdom experienced unemployment levels similar to the depression years of the 1930s, matched with production levels dropping from 9.3% in 1963, to 1.2% by 1986. The Thatcher government strongly felt that reversing past policies was critical. She significantly reformed fiscal, economic, and trade policyes, privatized key industries, and reduced the "propping up" of outdated sectors to improve competitiveness in the global market.

British economic growth during the mid to latter twentieth century reveal mixed outputs from 1964 to 1979. Among primary indices, agriculture grew 30%, but mining contracted 58%.[27] In the secondary industries, manufacturing expanded by 25%, whereas construction increased by a mere 5%. Only the tertiary industries saw consistently positive growth: both telecommunications (95% growth) and financial and intermediate industries essentially doubled (115% growth). GDP remained positive—going from £58.7 to £76.5 million by 1979.

Adding complexity to the environment of mixed output growth, the exogenous shocks created by the OPEC output restrictions of 1973 and 1979 led to reductions in demand on car-related products. This motivated the United Kingdom to develop and expand its oil extraction capabilities in the North Sea. A "petrocurrency" environment emerged, whereby the value of the pound was correlated with oil prices. This was both good and bad; when oil prices rose, this added value to the pound for investors, but made British imports too pricey in the global marketplace. Even during times of economic change leading to job contraction such as in the early 1980s, aggregate decline in ICT fields fell much less (−7.7%) than it

[27] ONS *Annual Abstract of Statistics*, 2010, "UK Growth Across Time," Chapter 1, p. 4. Agriculture in constant prices grew from £55 to 71.93 million; mining contracted from £187 to 109.2, manufacturing grew from £72.6 to 90.6, construction from £65.9 to 69.4. The tertiary industries experienced positive growth; telecommunications doubled from £30.6 to 59.7, and financial and intermediate industries grew from 27.6 to 59.6. Production as a whole gained from £62.6 to 87.6.

Table 5.2 ICT services sector contribution, United Kingdom, 1970–1999

Years	*ICT services exports, % of services exports*	*Investment in ICT Supplies, % of total non-residential gross fixed capital formation*	*High-tech exports, % of manufactured exports*	*Insurance & financial services, % of commercial services exports*
1985–1989	4.7	13.95	9.99	14.02
1990–1994	20.52	18.51	24.7	16.31
1995–1999	28.68	24.94	27.88	20.71

Source World Bank, World Development Indicators Database; OECD

did traditional manufacturing (−27.7%) between 1979 and 1986).[28] The British tech sector was gaining ground on traditional manufacturing.

Growth in American technology industries began to cool through increased global competition, and British firms stood ready to fill some of the worldwide demand for ICT goods and services. Between 1977 and 1984, high-tech manufacturing expanded by 46% in the United Kingdom.[29] Within ICT, computer services increased by 48%, and electronic data and computer processing equipment grew by 23%.[30] This in turn created significant demand for high-skilled staff; the high-skilled work force rose by 24% to make up 55% of the total labor market between 1978 and 1984, while unskilled labor shrank 19% to comprise 22% of the work force in 1984.[31] Furthermore, 99% of net growth in employment between 1980 and 1984 occurred in companies formed after 1977, having fewer than 50 employees, many of which were newer, start-up ICT companies (Table 5.2).

I expected states with large-scale economic dependence on ICT firms to be more to likely pass data policies that empower economic commodification policies for use of personal and/or digitized data. There is considerable support for this prediction in the case of Britain. ICT goods and services were increasingly an important contributor to the UK economy. During Phase I, ICT services exports more than quadrupled,

[28] Keeble (1989, pp. 153–155).

[29] Butchart (1987).

[30] Keeble (1989, p. 155).

[31] Kelly and Keeble (1988).

investment in ICT supplies nearly doubled, and high-tech exports tripled in growth. Similar to the case of Sweden, insurance and financial services firms experienced the most volatility in growth; they contributed 20.88% in 1986, fell to 13.34% in 1991, then grew again to 24.65% by 1999. All four measures ended the period at levels higher than in 1985. While the primary and secondary indices continued to contract and/or plateau, ICT goods and services followed an overall growth pattern during Phase I.

In the countries of Sweden and Germany, though one domestic interest group exerted more influence over the policy outcomes in data legislation, the other influences were seen with varying respects. In Britain, the resulting legislation occurred due to heavy influence by the economic power of data. The conservative Thatcher government overcame its internal resistance to regulating data protection, once it was tied to the success of the growing technology sector. Also, within the United Kingdom, domestic terror attacks evolved into a major security threat, thanks to the Troubles Years of conflict in Northern Ireland. As you will see next, in addition to the importance of ICT growth, the volume and persistence of domestic terror attacks during Phase I informed British policy-makers decisions regarding the content of data legislation.

Security Concerns and Digitized Data

Among the cases in this book, the United Kingdom experienced the largest number of attacks upon domestic security, with ten years of violence attaining 100 deaths or more. The casualties were primarily attributed to the Troubles years (1968–1999) of violence within Northern Ireland, a conflict which shaped the national debate on domestic terrorism and national security not only during that time, but even to today. It is beyond the scope of this book to provide a full exploration of the causes and implications of the conflict, however, general patterns during the Troubles significantly contributed to British reticence to fully provide digital human rights. Let's explore how Northern Irish politics contributed to this decision.

The Troubles Years

The Troubles years are rooted in generations of hardened disagreements over the political control of Northern Ireland. One side consisted of

Catholic nationalists, who wished for Northern Ireland to be joined to the political unit of the independent Republic of Ireland.[32] To pacify the nationalists living in Northern Ireland, the British government granted them home rule from 1922 to 1972. Home ruled included some policy autonomy, with laws made by a Northern Irish parliament known as Stormont.[33] The opposite side of the political divide were the Protestant Unionist groups, loyal to the U.K. government. Though a minority of the population, Unionists often held the majority of seats and political power in Stormont. Once elected, gerrymandering assured disenfranchisement of the nationalist Catholic communities, through means such as housing discrimination and denial of various cultural rights.

The cumulative effect of years of discrimination bred resentment in the Catholic communities against the Protestant loyalists, gradually giving way to more violent action by those seeking to overthrow British governance. Ardent Irish nationalists joined the Irish Republican Army, a paramilitary organization bent on restoring Northern Ireland to the free and independent Republic of Ireland. Though IRA activists maintained loyalty to the cause of leaving the United Kingdom, splinter groups of the IRA chose to escalate aggression against UK authorities.[34] When the local constabulary was unable to manage the intensified violence between Catholics and Protestants, British troops were sent in to control the fighting.[35] What followed was over 30 years of prolonged civil conflict in Northern Ireland. Looking at the data in Table 5.3, for ten years, greater than 100 casualties took place per year, with peak casualties of >500 persons in the years of 1972, 1974, 1988, and 1992. The massive upsurge in violence drove the need for UK security and government officials to monitor the activities of the IRA.

[32] Irish nationalists are also known as Republicans.

[33] During the push for Irish independence, anti-British forces in the Irish Republican Army waged violent political opposition to British forces. Irish independence occurred in 1921, except for the section of Northern Ireland in which Protestants who were also British Loyalists lived. The territory of Northern Ireland remained under the political authority of the British government, as part of the UK. The government compromised with the nationalists living in Northern Ireland by creating a semi-independent parliament for the region, populated by officials who ran in regional elections.

[34] Bamford (2005).

[35] Bamford (2005).

Table 5.3 Select years of security incidents, United Kingdom, 1970–1999

Key years	*Fatalities*	*Injuries*	*Casualties*
1970	20	1	21
1972	368	223	591
1973	210	275	485
1974	235	329	564
1975	245	129	374
1976	264	19	283
1977	103	17	120
1979	133	146	279
1984	69	249	318
1988	372	276	648
1992	94	453	547
1993			0
1996	14	395	409
1998	46	259	305
1999	7	161	168
Total, All Years, Phase I	**3268**	**4718**	**7986**

Several factors explain the escalation of violence. First, the British army instituted counter-insurgency tactics following Bloody Sunday. On 30 January 1972, Catholics held a protest event in Londonderry, that turned deadly when the British army turned weapons on the demonstrators, killing 13 civilians, with dozens more injured. (This was the single most violent day in the early 1970s.) The UK government further retaliated against the independence efforts by dissolving the parliament in Stormont. Meanwhile, opposition forces splintered into several IRA factions, with some bent on achieving full island independence from Britain by forcing them into compliance by means of extreme violence. Third, during the 1980s, IRA leadership changed hands and tactics, resulting in attacks on high-value targets, including murdering the British Ambassador to Ireland, killing a high-ranking advisor to PM Thatcher, and bombing a boat on which Prince Charles' godfather Lord Mountbatten vacationed with his family. The IRA also bombed the Grand Hotel in which PM Thatcher was staying in October of 1984. Finally, a provisional ceasefire was declared unilaterally by the Provisional IRA in 1994, and brokered peace talks eventually resulted in the Good Friday, or "Belfast" Agreement of 1998. The terms have maintained an overall peace in

Northern Ireland ever since, although the conditions of Brexit threaten to shake the relative stability in Northern Ireland since 1998.

Data Accumulation by Law Enforcement

How did the rising violence in Northern Ireland shape the process of setting British data legislation? During the 1980s, MPs discussed the ramifications of proposed data legislation, in the context of prosecuting criminal activity related to the Troubles attacks and in context of more personal risks. In April of 1983, Mr. Whitelaw argued in the House of Commons that the Official Secrets Act cannot be skewed within the wording of the new data law to provide data access to criminals themselves, saying,

> ...a data subject with access to his file, where the file relates to police suspicions about his criminal activities, would be nonsense...we all believe in the protection of national security.[36]

Michael Meacher, who suffered personal embarrassment when his medical records were obtained and printed in a news story carried by *The Sun*, countered the idea that information access even by law enforcement is innocuous, saying,

> We all know that police information—after all, the police are fallible, like us all—can often be irrelevant, out of date, incomplete or inaccurate and that the unchecked circulation of such material can often be extremely damaging.

In other words, Meacher argued that individuals should have a measure of control over the data that police or law enforcement collected about them. In the House of Lords, Lord Gardiner raised objections to the free access to personal data, and discretionary use of such data invasion by security and law enforcement actors. Gardiner highlighted the breach of personal privacy taking place when law officials shared citizens' personal data with multiple actors, including those *not* associated with domestic security, stating in a July 1983 debate,

[36] Parliament (1983), Whitelaw and Meacher comments.

> … there was close contact with police officers at local stations and the practice of exchanging mutually useful information had developed on a quid pro quo basis. The police denied this statement categorically, and in a Home Office answer to a Parliamentary Question this denial was maintained: 'Any suggestion that the police give facilities to debt collectors and private investigators is quite without foundation.' We were assured by the police that the sources of information for private detectives were not police sources.[37]

To pacify the worried those about data distribution by security officials, the 1984 law included restrictions upon law enforcement's use of personal data. Compared to the other cases, use of digitized data by British security actors was still in fact quite generous, though the need for surveillance data had diminished after the de-escalation of violence in Northern Ireland during the mid-1980s, and peace solidified with the signing and keeping of the Good Friday Agreement in 1998. UK policymakers continued to prioritize a mixed set of data use privileges, with digital human rights being the primary norm, but by no means, the only goal behind data governance decisions. Digital human rights activists had to work long and hard in the United Kingdom to realize any measure of data protection success.

Digital Human Rights

In general, human rights advocates in Britain had a much lower level of influence upon data governance when compared to their counterparts in either Sweden or Germany. Plainly, the contributing factors in Sweden (government records access) and Germany (a totalitarian surveillance state under the Nazis and Stasi) didn't exist in the United Kingdom. As a result, the British population started out less concerned with data protection than were their Swedish or German peers as data computerization began in the 1970s.[38] The public salience of data protection did eventually increase across time; in 1972, only 16% of Brits felt that privacy issues were "extremely important," but by 1987, 73% of

[37] Parliament (1983), Lord Gardiner comments.

[38] In 1976, Swedes ranked privacy of the people in the top 3 issues of concern. See Bennett (1992, p. 42), and "Public Attitudes to Data-Processing in the Information Society", English Summary of the Report from the Swedish Central Bureau of Statistics, Stockholm: Data inspektionen, January, 1985.

Table 5.4 Data Protection Register/Information Commissioner's Office (ICO), UK[a]

Years served in ICO	*Name of registrar/commissioner*	*Professional background*
1984–1993	Eric Howe	BBC Journalist
1994–2001	Elizabeth France	Magistrate, Legal Expert

[a]Agency name was changed from the DPR to ICO in year 2000

the public described this as "very important."[39] Each time the public expressed reservations about increasing governmental data collection or data-sharing across agencies, the government established an investigative committee which then reported to Parliament any findings. Therefore, to trace the contribution of legal and academic elites to the outcome of British digital human rights, we'll take a second look at the activities and influence of the Younger and Lindop Committees.

Recall that after the failed efforts by various MPs to introduce and pass a bill protecting personal data privacy in the late 1960s, the government generated the Justice Committee report on *Privacy and Law* in 1970.[40] The report offered a draft bill built upon Brian Walden's failed bill of 1969. The draft argued that (Table 5.4),

> each human being needs to able to limit the area of his intercourse with others... Above all we need to be able to keep to ourselves, if we want to, those thoughts and feelings, beliefs and doubts, hopes, plans, fears and fantasies, which we call 'private' precisely because we wish to be able to choose freely with whom, and to what extent, we are willing to share them.[41]

In Sweden and Germany, the governments and national data protection agencies (DPAs) were directed by legal experts who borrowed from the norms of their professions, and using the scope of DPA authority,

[39] 1972 statistics from Great Britain, Home Office, *Report of the Committee on Privacy*, Cmnd. 5012 (The Younger Committee); 1987 statistics from Data Protection Registrar, *Third Report*, London, HMSO, 1987, pp. 40–45.

[40] Dworkin (1973).

[41] Younger Committee (1972).

advocated for digital human rights. Though the precise policy suggestions in *Privacy and Law* were ignored by the government, the door had been opened for further discussion on data protection by Parliament and the government.

Advocacy by Epistemic Professionals

In Britain, DHR advocacy occurred in multiple locations by a variety of actors. To pacify digital human rights advocates, the Home Office established the Younger Committee. The committee Chair, Sir Kenneth Younger, brought an incredible level of legal expertise to the data governance process. Younger joined Parliament as the winning Labour candidate from Grimsby in 1945, and later served in the Foreign Office under PM Bevin in 1950–1951. In the 1960s and 70s he advised the government on legal and penal matters. Under his leadership, the group set the pattern of input seen with subsequent committees tasked with pursuit of the areas of data privacy and governance.[42] In addition to his position on the Younger Committee, he acted as the chair of the privacy committee from 1970 to 76, during which he also directed Chatham House—the Royal Institute of International Affairs research body. In plain terms, he cast a wide and deep net of advocacy for digital human rights across multiple spaces of the British government and public debate space.[43]

Under Younger's leadership, the Committee delved deeper into privacy concerns than perhaps the Home Office had anticipated. Enhancing Younger's advocacy voice, the civil rights history of two of the Committee members also shaped the approach by the committee to the issue. Alex Lyon, a human rights advocate, had been the Labour MP from York from 1966, supported British entry into the European Economic Area in 1971, later being appointed by Wilson to serve as a minister of state regarding race and immigration issues in 1974. Another committee member, Lord Donald Ross, had served as a legal advocate since 1964, and held positions such as Sheriff of Ayre and Bute in the 1970s, Chairman of the

[42] Oxford Dictionary of National Biography, Sir Kenneth Gilmour Younger biography.

[43] Younger died prematurely in 1976, just as he had been appointed to serve as chairman for the second data privacy research committee set up by Parliament.

Judicial Studies committee in the 1990s, and eventually retired as Scotland's second most senior judge.[44] Both lobbied hard for (digital human rights) DHR legislation. During a Parliamentary speech, Ross maintained that major human rights conventions should inform British data policy: "from the point of view of principle..." the UK law "should now be brought into line with these important declarations."[45] Both Lyon and Ross signed the dissenting, minority opinion that the Committee should have put forward a powerful and comprehensive data protection law, rather than propose ongoing voluntary practices to protect personal data by the Press and others. Despite the fact that the majority opposed an actual law, the Younger Report released in 1974 built a foundation for digital human rights protections through a series of ongoing suggestions about informational security, anonymity of statistical data collections, and the importance of data accuracy and monitoring by the government.[46]

The Justice Committee built on these foundation with a White Paper given in response to the 1974 Younger Report. The 1975 report *Computers and Privacy* agreed with the Younger committee on the need for legislation to restrain some use of digitized personal data, and on the necessity of a permanent government agency responsible for database monitoring.[47] The last proposal was a critical step in the pathway toward data protection; the new "Data Protection Authority" could ensure that public and private sector computer users utilized safeguards to secure digitized personal data. Notably, MP Alex Lyon served on both the Justice Committee as well as the Younger Committee, as did Paul Sieghart, another influential jurist and human rights advocate that would shape British data policy in substantial ways during the 1980s and 1990s.

A third committee ramped up the volume of DHR rhetoric further still. Sir Norman Lindop chaired a Data Protection Committee of ten persons established in July of 1976 to once again, investigate possible data legislation. Unlike the earlier committees, this group wasn't drawn exclusively from lawyers or human rights activists. Lindop was not an attorney, but previously worked as a Lecturer in Chemistry at Queen Mary University in London. The ten committee members included a few from legal

[44] *The Herald* (1997).

[45] Kenyon (2016, p. 5).

[46] Bourn and Benyon (1983, p. 12, 13).

[47] Dworkin (1973).

or academic professions, IT industry representatives (the latters' participation being a point of contention for civil liberties groups), a statistics professor, an IBM executive, a public health expert, a researcher, a bank executive, several civil servants, and one member of the press.[48] Only one member—Paul Sieghart—had a background in privacy advocacy, but his voice was a unifying power within the committee. Despite the diverse nature of their professional backgrounds, the committee members successfully managed to focus on the narrow mandate they were given as compared to prior legislative committees: simply address the concerns over computerized data privacy. Sieghart's influence is clearly seen within the committee's focus upon a plan for digital human rights

Paul Sieghart's family fled Austria with the Jewish diaspora to live in England in 1939. After dropping out of a mathematics program at University College, London, he practiced law, then switched careers to become a human rights author and advocate. Seighart sat on the British section of the International Commission of Jurists, as well as the Justice and Lindop committees. He unsuccessfully pushed the Home Office to appoint him to the permanent Data Protection Committee established as a requirement within the 1984 Data Law. A prolific author, he wrote titles covering international human rights, as well as issues discussing computers, technology, and personal privacy. Within his various roles on committees and as an advisor to the UK government on data privacy, he diligently advocated for digital human rights. Sieghart's perspective on DHR can be summed up with a statement made in 1984:

> There are no harmless data. Or to put it another way, it is not the data that are harmless, it is what people do with them that is the problem.[49]

[48] *New Scientist* (1976). Professor James Durbin taught statistics at the London School of Economics between 1950 and 1988. John Hargreaves served as an IBM executive. Dr. Charles Florey, the son of Lord Howard Florey, the discoverer of penicillin, worked as a public health expert in his own right. Charles Read directed the Inter Bank Research Organization. Ken Potts held the Chief Executive post of the Leeds City Council. Professor F. M. Martin taught social administration at Glasgow University. Celia Goodhart and Bridget Paton worked in local government bodies. Sir David Pitblado was an auditor general. Hugo Young, a member of the press, wrote for the *Sunday Times*.

[49] Bennett (1992, p. 35), and Bourn and Benyon (1983). Sieghart made this statement at a 1984 conference on data protection, hosted by the University of Leicester.

His influence can certainly be seen within the Lindop *Report on Data Protection* of 1978. The report was based on surveys with over 300 organizations and individuals.[50] It called for an expanded scope of data governance to include public, and private sectors, and expressed particular frustration at the reticence of the police and secret services who "refused to answer any questions." Seven broad principles were introduced:

- Data subjects should be informed about data collected about them, the length of time it would be kept, and by whom it would be used.
- Personal data should only be used for reasons authorized by the data subject.
- Personal data accuracy must be maintained.
- Users should only handle personal data for use in lawful interests.
- Data subjects should be protected from prejudice resulting from data access.

Margaret Thatcher's government delayed action on data legislation, because she had campaigned on promises of business de-regulation. However, ICT industry executives interceded, specifically asking for some form of data legislation; tech firms wanted to reassure international business partners of at least minimal UK data protections. The 1984 Data Protection Act became law, a full 170 months after the first UK data legislation commission had been created regarding the issue of data protection.

In 1998, another Data Protection Act became law, updating the 1984 provisions. The 1998 law originated in response to EU adoption of Directive 95/46/EC which required member states to align their national laws with the Council of Europe Convention 108, as well as with the more stringent protection requirements set by the Commission.[51] States were given a three-year timeline for compliance. The United Kingdom balked at the demands of privacy being an actual "right" as this had not been codified within the 1984 British data protection law. In the 1998 law, the United Kingdom did agree to enforce the human rights principles in the European Court of Human Rights, including Article 8, which granted a right to respect for private life.

[50] Warren and Dearnley (2005).

[51] The UK ratified Convention 108 in 1987.

To complete our look at UK data governance, data protection became law due to crucial links which developed between non-state actors and international organizational pressure. Domestic rights activists such as Alex Lyon and Paul Sieghart, championed for digital human rights, and the Council of Europe applied international pressure, albeit more economically motivated. Domestically, British technology firms wanted DHR in order to remain globally competitive, and the European Union coerced UK compliance with human rights-based protections, based on EU membership requirements. Now let's spend some time uncovering more about the latter, as the top-down process of setting European Union data policy created a convergence point of digital human rights for data legislation across Europe.

Bibliography

Bamford, Bradley W. C. 2005. "The Role and Effectiveness of Intelligence in Northern Ireland." *Intelligence and National Security* 20 (4): 581–607.

BBC News. 2005. "On This Day—24 April". Accessed September 2016, 2018. http://news.bbc.co.uk/onthisday/hi/dates/stories/april/24/newsid_2523000/2523095.stm.

Bennett, Colin J. 1982. *The Concept of Open Government and Its Interpretation and Development in British Politics.* Cardiff: University College of Cardiff.

———. 1992. *Regulating Privacy: Data Protection and Public Policy in Europe and the United States.* Ithaca, NY: Cornell University Press.

Bourn, Colin, and John Benyon. 1983. *Data Protection: Perspectives on Information Privacy.* Conference Proceedings, Leicester: University of Leicester.

Butchart, R.L. 1987. "A new UK Definition of the High-Technology Industries." *Economic Trends* 400: 82–88.

Cornford, James. 1981. "The Prospects for Privacy." *The Political Quarterly.*

Council of Europe. 1985. "Details of Treaty No.108—Convention for the Protection of Individuals with Regard to Automatic Processing of Personal Data." *Council of Europe.* Accessed May 5, 2018. https://www.coe.int/en/web/conventions/full-list/-/conventions/treaty/108.

Dworkin, Gerald. 1973. "The Younger Committee Report on Privacy." *The Modern Law Review* 36 (4): 399–406.

Flaherty, David H. 1989. *Protecting Privacy in Surveillance Societies: The Federal Republic of Germany, Sweden, France, Canada, and the United States.* Chapel Hill, NC: University of North Carolina Press.

Floud, Roderick, Jane Humphries, and Paul Johnson. 2014. *The Cambridge Economic History of Modern Britain.* Vols. 1: 1700–1870. Cambridge: Cambridge University Press.

Fuster, Gloria González. 2016. *The Emergence of Personal Data Protection as a Fundamental Right of the EU*. Springer.

Government of the United Kingdom. 1987. *Third Report*, 40–45. Data Protection Registrar. London, UK: Her Majesty's Stationary Office (HMSO).

———. 2010. *UK Growth Across Time*. London, UK: ONS Annual Abstract of Statistics.

Hancock, William L. 1994, October. "Counterterrorism in Great Britain, Germany, and France: 1968 to the Present." Winnepeg, Manitoba: Department of Political Studies.

House of Lords. 1973. *HL Debate* . Vol. 343, cc104–178. London, UK.

Keeble, D. E. 1989. "High-Technology Industry and Regional Developmen in Britain: The Case of the Cambridge Phenomenon." *Environment and Planning C: Government and Policy* 7: 153–172.

Kelly, T., and D. Keeble. 1988. "Locational Change and Corporate Organisation in High-Tech Industry; Computer Elctronics in Great Britain." *Tijdschrift voor Economische en Sociale Geografie* 79: 2–15.

Kenyon, Andrew T. 2016. "Defamation and Privacy in an Era of 'More Speech'." In *Comparative Defamation and Privacy Law*, 1–16. Cambridge: Cambridge University Press.

Madgwick, Donald, and Tony Smythe. 1974. *The Invasion of Privacy*. London: Pitman.

New Scientist. 1976. "Protection for Whose Data?" *New Scientist*, July 1.

OECD. 1976. *Establishing Institutional Structures to Monitor and Enforce Data Protection*, 83–94. Policy Issues in Data Protection and Privacy, OECD Informatics Studies. Paris, France: Organization for Economic Cooperation and Development.

———. 2021. ICT Investments. *OECD*.

Office of National Statistics. 2010. *UK Growth Across Time*. Annual Abstract of Statistics. London: ONS.

ONS. n.d. *Office of National Statistics*.

Oxford Dictionary of National Biography. n.d. *Sir Kenneth Gilmour Younger*. Biography, Oxford, UK: Faculty of History, University of Oxford.

Parliament of the United Kingdom. 1984. "HC Debs." London, UK, Col. 43.

———. 1961. "Historic Hansard House of Lords." *Parliament.UK*. June 15. Accessed March 5, 2018. https://api.parliament.uk/historic-hansard/lords/1961/jun/15/right-of-privacy-bill-hl.

———. 1972. "Order for Second Reading, HC Deb 21 April 1972." Vol. 835, London, UK, cc967–1102.

———. 1973. "HL Deb 6 June 1973." Vol. 343, London, UK, cc104–178.

———. 1983. "HC Deb 11 April 1983." Vol. 40, London, UK, cc553–628.

Price, David. 1984. "The Emergence of a UK Data Protection Law." *Yearbook of Law Computers and Technology* 1: 131–135.

Report of the Committee on Privacy, 1972. Cmnd. 5012, Her Majesty's Government.
The Cambridge Economic History of Modern Britain, 2014. Vol. 2. Cambridge: Cambridge University Press.
The Herald. 1997. "Lord Ross Warns That Judges Should Stay Out of Politics; Unease Over Crime Speech". February 12. Accessed October 2018, 3. https://www.heraldscotland.com/news/12077997.Lord_Ross_warns_that_judges__should_stay_out_of_politics_Unease_over_crime_speech/ .
University of Maryland. 2018. *Global Terrorism Database*. Accessed March 2019. https://www.start.umd.edu/data-tools/global-terrorism-database-gtd.
Warren, Adam, and James Dearnley. 2005. "Data Protection Legislation in the United Kingdom." *Information, Communication & Society* 8 (2): 238–263.
World Bank. n.d. *World Development Indicators*. WDI.

PART III

Regional Policymaking and Digital Human Rights in the Global Sense

In the next four chapters, the focus shifts outward, I answer two questions. *Why did the EU settle upon a digital human rights framework as the convergence point for Community data policy?* And—*How has the EU managed enforcement of digital human rights, when parties from third country states violate the norm during utilization of EU citizens' data?*

The answers require a look at three processes. First, I examine legislative efforts to achieve policy congruence in Phase II (mid 1990s–2020). The structure and functionality of the EU policy-making procedures led to a back-and-forth negotiation between domestic interests of the member states, key actors, and the more powerful states' seeking to exert their influence inside the EU institutions. Second, I hone in on the activities taken by Working Party-29 (WP-29), a vital advisory body comprised of epistemic experts from across Europe. The normative framework of the legal profession from which WP representatives derived had a profound effect on shaping supranational policy in the EU for over twenty years. Lastly, I explore the ways in which the EU has effectively exported the norm of digital human rights. Although exporting DHR was not the primary goal of EU policymakers, it is evident through negotiated arrangements with diplomatic partners, such as the US. The EUhas also intensified DHR enforcement across time, utilizing the European Union's judicial system to sanction states and non-state actors for violating digitized data protection.

To conclude, I look at the implications for the findings in the book. The pathway to digital human rights involves a new policy space for governments—that of the intersection of technological innovation, the internet, and human rights. The role played by key elites and domestic interest groups upon data governance can illuminate policy-making in other areas of nascent technologies, such as artificial intelligence and robotics. Governments and international organizations alike cannot ignore the human rights impact of new technology adoption and diffusion. In addition, the firms creating these innovative products and services have shown themselves willing to push back against government attempts to control how technology is managed. Some governments, such as that of China, take a very different approach than that of the EU to technology governance, seeing it as threat not to individual human rights, but as a threat to collective social controls. It's this last approach that has the potential to limit the ability of EU members and similarly minded states to set a global pattern for digital human rights.

Let's now examine the coordination of data policy within the European Union, at a crucial time point for setting the framework for where we are today.

CHAPTER 6

EU Policy Convergence—Supranational Data Policies in the EU (Mid 1990s–2016)

Part II illustrated the origins of data governance, which began at the national level due to efforts by data profiteers, security officials, and human rights advocates. In Sweden, Germany, and the United Kingdom, different priorities among the three competing interests led to diverse national policies. Germany and Sweden chose significant levels of digital human rights, and the United Kingdom opted for minimal protections in order to maintain global competitiveness. By 1999, most EU states had created some type of data protection law. However, the complex web of national laws led to problems when states attempted to cooperate with one another—whether in matters of business, anti-terrorism efforts, or even in securing consistent digital human rights (DHR) provision across the EU Community. By the early 1990s, it was clear that the EU needed a blanket-policy for data governance. The challenge lay in reaching consensus on the type of data legislation for the region. This chapter addresses the evolution and outcome of the EU data legislative process. But what significance does EU data policy have for the rest of the world?

Through two pieces of EU legislation—Directive 95/46/EC, and the General Data Protection Regulation (2016), the European Union has established digital human rights across Europe. Since 1995, and particularly since 2016, the EU has enforced digital human rights protections not only among member states, but EU officials and institutions have

R. Dowd, *The Birth of Digital Human Rights*, Information Technology and Global Governance,
https://doi.org/10.1007/978-3-030-82969-8_6

worked diligently to hold non-EU states and non-state actors accountable for how they manage EU citizens' data. To better understand how and why the EU has taken such a firm stand on digital human rights, we need to uncover *why* and *how* the EU reached a point of policy convergence, despite the multiplicity of national preferences among the members. In this chapter, I'll reveal the two-level game in which policymakers make EU law, explain the process of making supranational policies, check the levels of exposure for data profiteering and security risks, and then, examine the national data institutions and key actors who influenced the process of data governance at the EU-level. Finally, we finish up the chapter with a look at the outcome: EU data legislation.

The Two-Level Game

In his classic "Diplomacy and domestic politics: the logic of two-level games" Robert Putnam proposed that national governments will work during diplomatic negotiations to preserve domestic interests, while simultaneously trying to avoid international losses.[1] The larger the "win-set," or the wider the number of domestic actors who are satisfied with an internationally proposed policy, the greater likelihood that the diplomat can agree to terms dictated by her diplomatic colleagues, or a membership in an international organization.[2] Helen Milner concurred with Putnam's proposal, in that international cooperation will be filtered through the policy preferences of domestic actors.[3] When an international organization makes a policy suggestion for member states, the likelihood of ratification and adoption of said policy is conditional upon how closely the suggested policy aligns with the preferences of the most influential domestic interest groups (Fig. 6.1).

Remember that the development of EU data governance is divided into two time periods with some overlap: Phase I (1970–1999) and Phase II (roughly the mid 1990s–2016). Data protection was legislated only at the national level during Phase I, but moved to the international level of policy coordination during Phase II. Thus, EU policy-makers have played a two-level game, with national representatives moving back and

[1] Putnam (1988).

[2] Putnam (1988, pp. 435–450).

[3] Milner (1997, pp. 9–15).

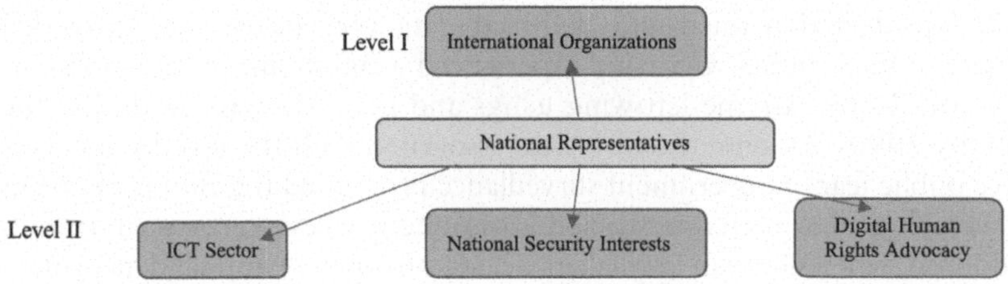

Fig. 6.1 Offers a graphic representation of the two-level game

forth between their domestic legislative environment and the international stage, seeking policy compromises that fulfill commitments in both arenas.[4] First, I take a quick look at the two levels of policy-making.

National Efforts in Phase I (1970–1999)

From the 1970s–present, data legislation in European states involved competition among domestic interests along the three main areas introduced in the national case chapters. ICT firms continually sought economic gains from data use, national security authorities increasingly tried to use digitized personal data during criminal investigations and anti-terrorism efforts, and human rights activists pushed back against the free use of such data, asking for human rights protections. As has been established in Chapters 3–5, when the three interest groups wanted different types of national data policy, states chose which interest(s) to prioritize above the other(s). Some states legalized data protection as a fundamental human right, an outcome I labeled as "digital human rights." Global digital human rights originated in Sweden and Germany and as you will see in the remainder of the book, have since diffused across Europe.

To recap the national policies chosen during Phase I, Sweden and Germany took the lead on digital human rights. Sweden experienced few domestic security problems during the 1970s–1990s, and the ICT sector was minimally influential upon economic growth. The country did, however, have a history of public access to government records, which raised public concerns about privacy loss during the computerization of public records in the 1970s. As a result, the *Datalagen* of

[4] Milner (1997) and Putnam (1988).

1973 protected manual and digitized data very heavily and provided digital human rights. Germany experienced a significant number of security attacks by extreme left-wing gangs and neo-Nazi groups during the 1970s–1990s. Despite the casualties associated with the attacks, a pervasive public fear of government surveillance prohibited the *Bundestag* from developing a law with unrestricted government access to personal data. In addition, when German lawmakers decided to create national data protection, regional data laws were already in place. The national government consulted with regional data protection authorities (DPAs), the majority of whom were legal professionals, and the DPAs suggested a policy with high levels of personal data protection. Combined with the lagging development of the German ICT sector compared to technology growth in other states, and Germany had the highest number of data protection laws passed among my cases during this period. Germany and German legal rights experts have continued to push for the internationalization of digital human rights norms.

By contrast, the United Kingdom reluctantly passed data protection legislation. Among the national cases in this book, the United Kingdom experienced the largest number of domestic terror attacks, centered in Northern Ireland during the Troubles Years. Though nearly 8000 people were hurt or killed from the 1960s–1990s, there is no evidence that security officials heavily pressured the government for specific types of access to personal data in the United Kingdom. Interestingly, ICT interests were the most aggressive seekers of data protection. Tech firms were very concerned about losing comparative advantage to the Americans and other European states within the global marketplace. This fear was predicated by the fact that Britain had not ratified Convention 108 of the Council of Europe, which outlined basic levels of personal data protection for all members, so that safe data mobility could occur throughout the OECD trade community. The Thatcher government eventually acquiesced to pressure from ICT firms, and passed the Data Protection Act in 1984.

Now I turn to the process of understanding data legislation at the EU level. Before looking at the chronology of events leading to EU data protection, it is essential to have a baseline understanding of how the *acquis communautaire*, or body of EU laws, is made.

Making Laws in the European Union

Making law for the EU is a very complex process, involving a mix of intergovernmentalism and supranationalism, depending on the issue under discussion. Intergovernmentalism is used for issues in which states' sovereignty is given priority. When intergovernmentalism is employed, every member state has an equal voice as policy recommendations are made. These matters typically allow a lot of leverage to individual member states on how much of an EU policy suggestion to implement within their own national law. Intergovernmental topics include domestic security, immigration, and agricultural policies. By contrast, supranationalism grants more policy autonomy and authority to EU institutions above the states. When supranational rules apply, member states are obliged to adopt EU law into national legislation with full compliance.[5] Using supranationalism, once a majority has decided in support for the new law, dissenting members must implement the law, despite being in disagreement. Supranational laws cover market integration, monetary policy for Eurozone states, and external border management.

One last thought on the history and transition from intergovernmentalism to supranationalism. The Treaty of Rome (1957) created the European Community, and "laws" as such really didn't exist; any areas of shared concern were addressed via intergovernmentalism. Gradually, the mission creep of the Community grew, expanding fully under the Treaty of the European Union, or Maastricht (1993). Under the terms of the Maastricht treaty, issues of concern were divided into three topical pillars. First Pillar topics consisted of core economic initiatives like the customs union, Single Market, and economic and monetary policy. The Second Pillar added in Common Foreign and Security Policy. The Third Pillar vastly expanded the scope of EU governance, to involve Justice and Home Affairs (JHA), and the Schengen zone for free movement of people, goods, and ideas. Until the Treaty of Lisbon in 2007, only First Pillar issues were decided in a supranational manner. The Treaty of Lisbon disbanded the pillar system, moved many former JHA issues into what used to be the first pillar (meaning supranational oversight), and eliminated pure intergovernmentalism in favor of the co-decision legislative process, which I explain in a moment. According to the European Parliament,

[5] Pollack (2015).

> The Treaty of Lisbon completes the absorption of the remaining third pillar aspects of the area of freedom, security and justice (FSJ), i.e., police and judicial cooperation in criminal matters, into the first pillar. The former intergovernmental structure ceases to exist, as the acts adopted in this area are now made subject to the ordinary legislative procedure (qualified majority and codecision), using the legal instruments of the Community method (regulations, directives and decisions) unless otherwise specified.[6]

Today, there are three main types of EU laws. Directives are binding legislation, but member states are granted some freedom on how to implement the directive into national law. Regulations are binding legislative acts applicable to all member states, with very specific guidelines on how to incorporate into national laws. Decisions apply to only specific countries or perhaps, even companies. The various EU institutions also generate recommendations and opinions, but these are non-binding.

Since the Treaty of Maastricht, EU laws are made by the institutional triangle of the Commission, the Council of Ministers, and Parliament, using the "Ordinary Legislative Procedure." Each institution has a unique role to play in the process, and can act as either a facilitator or stumbling block for potential policies. Under what is known as the "Community" method, the European Commission acts as the point of origination; the Commission will add a topic to the agenda, and ask the Council of Ministers to investigate the matter further. The Council of Ministers works in tandem with the EU Parliament to write the text of a proposed law; this begins the "co-decision" process. Though I am simplifying the process for ease of description, sub-committees are often created by either/or the Council and Parliament to craft the content of the law, with readings on both sides to consider the changes suggested by the other institution. Of note, when making Regulations, the Commission assembles a committee of technical experts. Their findings are shared with the Council, who shares the information with Parliament as they edit the proposal. After research and debate, the Council decides whether to pass or oppose the proposal, using the qualified-majority vote (QMV).[7] Parliament also holds a vote on whether to pass the proposal. If both sides agree, the

[6] Pavy (2020).

[7] Under QMV voting, laws are passed if 55% of member states vote in favor (15/27), and the proposal is affirmed by member states having at least 65% of the total EU population. QMV is also referred to as the "double majority" rule.

new law is adopted. Finally, if an issue is of particular importance to the entire EU, it is possible for the European Council to ask the Commission to initiate legislation. The European Council consists of the heads of government for all EU member states, and meets periodically to discuss matters of extreme importance to the entire Union membership.[8] Now I return to the investigation of setting data policy.

Agenda-Power, Hegemonic Preferences, and Technical Expertise

The structure of EU institutions and the role afforded to various participants when initiating a new law, have had a profound impact on whether an issue is considered for legislation at all, what type of content the law will include, and how the law will be implemented, overseen, and adjusted for changes across time. For the purposes of setting EU data legislation, I focus attention on four components which directly contributed to the birth of digital human rights in the EU: **pressure from outside the Union via international organizations** (IOs), the potentially **disproportionate power of certain states in setting the policy convergence point**, the use of **technical expertise from legally trained policy advisors, and the agenda-setting power of the EU Commission**. International organizations started the conversation about coordinating data policy across the region, in order to further economic growth. Without data legislation being added to the EU agenda by the Commission, digital human rights would have remained a purely national phenomenon. The only way the EU settled upon harmonization of national laws into a regional data protection scheme is because the more powerful states in the Union approved, or at least did not oppose, the suggested convergence point. Finally, if both national governments and EU officials had not used legal experts as the policy advisors and data protection overseers, data governance in Europe could have followed either a more private sector driven plan, as seen in the US, or remained a piecemeal patchwork of national plans without any shared understanding on the intertwined

[8] The European Council and the Council of Ministers are two separate entities and have entirely different roles in the EU institutional system. The Council of Ministers shares co-decision power with the European Parliament under the ordinary legislative method. The European Council has no legislative powers, and is comprised of elected heads of government.

nature of digitized data with personal identity. It's time to examine Level I of Putnam's Two-Level Game—the international environment for data governance.

External Pressures—Regime Complexity

Institutionalization is the formalization of a set of rules for behavior, otherwise known as norms. If norms are institutionalized at the international level, a regime is born. Regimes are formalized rules, rules established by members of an international organization (IO) wishing to ameliorate or solve a shared problem. States create a regime and willingly relinquish some of their policy sovereignty in order to solve the shared problem, or at least improve things beyond the power of one state when acting alone. Member states make commitments to the organizational norms and policies adopted by the group of states in the regime of the IO. Examples of regimes within the European Union include economic development programs,[9] nuclear non-proliferation,[10] and human rights sanctions.[11]

Placing the idea of regimes into the context of data policy, this book has shown that preferences around data treatment are driven by domestic and international interests. The theoretical argument in Chapter 2 posited that data governance in the EU occupies a space of *regime complexity.* A regime complex occurs when states occupy *multiple* policy spaces simultaneously. In other words, when a state is a member in multiple organizations, government policy-makers have to balance domestic preferences against the policy responsibilities attached to the obligations for states who are members in multiple intergovernmental or international organizations. EU states have joined multiple international organizations, with overlapping, nesting, or duplicative regimes, having policies that may compete or conflict with their domestic preferences on data legislation. Thus, important point one is: **personal and cyber data policies set by EU states were created in an environment of international regime membership and regime complexity. This activity occurred at what I classify as Level I of the Two-Level Game.**

[9] European Parliament (2020).

[10] NTI (2019).

[11] Europa (2020).

Level I: International Regime Memberships

Each organization has different goals which shape policy suggestions to their members. In the 1970s, personal data was moved from paper or manual form to computerized and automatically processed data. National laws in this period were designed to preserve the ability of companies to collect and store computer-based, or stationary, yet nationally networked data in the most secure manner possible. In the 1980s, international data protection regimes were formed. The OECD began to encourage policy convergence designed to protect data privacy, but also asked states to allow the movement of computerized data across national borders to facilitate economic growth and business transactions.[12] EU states generally agreed and many adopted legislation at the national level to free transnational data flows required by economies increasingly reliant upon service-based and technology industries. By the mid-1990s, data transmission via the internet was treated similarly to other data, and existing policies for computer data banks, and personal data treatment were applied to the management of this new type of data: cyber data. Thus, I show that the initiative behind the early days of EU data governance policies was rooted in **the economic commodification of data, the first potential EU regime for data governance**.

At the international level of regime complexity, EU policy-makers are influenced by pressures from international organizations to adopt certain policies. Being a member of an international organization (IO) can mean joining a regime, as the organization may set obligations or at least pressure members to pass laws that comply with treaties or international agreements. European states are members of multiple IOs, each capable of creating issue regimes, including the United Nations, NATO, the Council of Europe, the OECD, and the European Union (Table 6.1).

During the years under examination, neither NATO nor the United Nations had a highly developed data policy regime.[13] However, both the Council of Europe (CoE) and the Organisation for Cooperation and Development (OECD) produced data policy recommendations, which had significant influence upon data policy content in the EU.

[12] Fuster (2016) and OECD (2010).

[13] The United Nations Global Pulse project emerged following the 2008 financial crisis. The project includes data privacy recommendations, introduced from 2011 to 2014. Guardian 2011; United Nations 2019.

Table 6.1 EU states international organization memberships, by year joined

Country	*United Nations*	*NATO*	*Council of Europe*	*OECD*	*European Union*
Austria	1955	*	1956	1961	1995
Belgium	1945	1949	1949	1961	1958
Bulgaria	1955	2004	1992	*	2007
Croatia		2009	1996	*	2013
Republic of Cyprus	1960	*	1961	*	2004
Czech Republic	1993	1999	1993	1995	2004
Denmark	1945	1949	1949	1961	1973
Estonia	1991	2004	1993	2010	2004
Finland	1955	*	1989	1969	1995
France	1945	1949	1949	1961	1958
Germany	1973	1955	1950	1961	1958
Greece	1945	1952	1949	1961	1981
Hungary	1955	1999	1990	1996	2004
Ireland	1955	*	1949	1961	1973
Italy	1955	1949	1949	1962	1958
Latvia	1991	2004	1995	2016	2004
Lithuania	1991	2004	1993	*	2004
Luxembourg	1945	1949	1949	1961	1958
Malta	1964	*	1965	*	2004
Netherlands	1945	1949	1949	1961	1958
Poland	1945	1999	1991	1996	2004
Portugal	1955	1949	1976	1961	1986
Romania	1955	2004	1993	*	2007
Slovak Republic	1993	2004	1993	2000	2004
Slovenia	1992	2004	1993	2010	2004
Spain	1955	1982	1977	1961	1986
Sweden	1946	*	1949	1961	1995
United Kingdom	1945	1949	1949	1961	1973

Council of Europe—"Convention 108"

The Council of Europe's (CoE) foundational principles includes strong protections for human rights, encoded within the *Convention for the Protection of Human Rights and Fundamental Freedoms* (ECHR). Article 8 of the ECHR states that "Everyone has the right to respect for his private and family life, his home, and his correspondence..."[14] CoE data policy recommendations build upon the norm of privacy within general human rights. The Council first moved toward building a data protection regime in the late 1960s. The Legal Committee responded to two motions coming from the Consultative Assembly of 1967, requesting the Committee to examine the impact of technological developments upon privacy.[15] In 1973 the CoE adopted Resolution 73 (22) and suggested protection of individuals' informational privacy for data stored in private sector databanks. At the 236th meeting of the Ministers' Deputies, the CoE approved Resolution (74) 29, *On the Protection of Privacy of Individuals Vis-à-vis Electronic Data Banks in the Public Sector*. The resolution focused on government databanks, and requested privacy protections, stating:

> Considering that the aim of the Council of Europe is to achieve a greater unity between its Members; Desiring to contribute to public understanding and confidence with regard to new administrative techniques which public authorities in the member states are using in order to ensure the optimal performance of the tasks entrusted to them; Recognising that the use of electronic data banks by public authorities has given rise to increasing concern about the protection of the privacy of individuals;...

The report also advocated for national data laws requiring governments to:

- Inform the public of storage or automatic processing of personal information.
- Data banks to keep personal information current and use it only for pre-designated purposes
- Create data storage time limits
- Set precautions and codes of conduct to limit misuse of personal information
- Grant databank access only to authorized users with necessity of use
- Anonymize all statistical data[16]

[14] Council of Europe (1950).

[15] Fuster (2016, p. 83).

[16] Council of Europe (1974).

These recommendations were taken seriously, and the member states debated the content and necessity of an organizational treaty to solidify the measures on a more permanent basis. The treaty, the *Convention for the Protection of Individuals with regard to Automatic Processing of Personal Data*, thereafter known as Convention 108, was signed on 28 January 1981, creating the first truly international regime for digital human rights. Original signatory states from the EU included France, Germany, and Sweden. The CoE regime had much more impact upon the EU states that did the OECD Guidelines, for several reasons which I discuss momentarily. Convention 108 asked specifically for data protection, linked such protection to states' obligation to provide fundamental rights, and invited regional institutions such as the EU to promote implementation by their member states. The Convention asked states to protect data domestically and during transborder flows, framing protective policies as necessary to protect privacy rights. Full adoption of Convention 108 hinged on ratification at the "second level," or by domestic legislatures of CoE/EU member states.

The CoE Convention 108 treaty officially entered into force on 1 October 1985, following ratification by a required minimum of states; these included Sweden (1982), France (1983), Norway and Spain (1984), and Germany (1985). Note that Germany and Sweden are two of the national case states from Phase I, both of whom had stringent national data protection laws in place from the early 1970s. States that delayed ratification included the United Kingdom, which did not ratify the convention until 1987; this delayed ratification aligns with resistance by the British press and Conservative party to adopt DHR protections, as discussed in Chapter 5. In the United Kingdom, data protection was driven by the fear of reduced trade if the country did *not* adopt some form of data protection, rather than being motivated by human rights concerns about personal privacy. Concurrent to the work being done by the CoE on setting guidelines for data use, were actions taken by the OECD, also considering data protection measures.

OECD Data Policy Guidelines

The OECD originated the first international effort at harmonization of data processing protection for trade purposes; in actuality, it came into force one year before Convention 108. Why did the OECD tackle data governance? Member states and OECD economists sought to prevent disruption to economic growth tied to ICT expansion, given that so much of the tech industry was data-driven.[17] From the perspective of the OECD, the multiplicity of data privacy laws adopted by member states actually created barriers to data mobility, and were harmful to economic and social development, due to the conflicting content of national laws. The OECD conducted conferences in 1974 and 1977 which looked at privacy, citizens' access to data, and cross-border data mobility. The organization also called in legal experts to discuss possible policies; advisors included Peter Gassman (Germany, engineering and economics consultant), Louis Joinet (France, drafter of French *Informatique et Liberté* law), and Professor Peter Seipel (Sweden, Professor of Law).[18] The experts focused on concerns about "reconciling fundamental but competing values such as privacy and the free flow of information."[19] The *OECD Guidelines Governing the Protection of Privacy and Transborder Flows of Personal Data* were adopted on 23 September 1980. The Guidelines contained several core principles:

- Limit personal data collections to lawful means, preferably with data subject consent
- Collect personal data only for original uses, and limit use to these purposes
- Do not disclose personal data without either data subject consent OR the authority of the law
- Provide security measures against unauthorized data access or disclosure
- Provide a transparent policy concerning personal data
- Give data subjects rights, including information confirming the personal data held about the subject, and honor data subject requests for information correction or erasure

Member governments were encouraged to incorporate the Guidelines into national practices, but no formal enforcement mechanism existed. In the end, the suggestions were merely historical, and not successful. The

[17] Gassman (1976) and OECD (2011, p. 15). Multiple OECD member states had already adopted national legislation during the 1970s, including Sweden (1973), the US (1974), and Germany (1977).

[18] Gassman (1976) and OECD (2010, 2011).

[19] OECD (2011, p. 19).

Guidelines were historical, because they provided the first attempt at an international regime for digital human rights. However, given the voluntary nature of the Guidelines, and the fact that they were not written into a ratifiable treaty as was Convention 108, the suggestions didn't yield immediate national policy impact. The OECD's voice did add to the chorus of international organizations calling for data protection legislation, helping to intensify the salience of digital human rights. For EU states, this meant additional pressure to adopt a regional set of data policies that would harmonize the current legal discrepancies across the Union. The type of harmonization that would emerge remained to be seen, and would be decided during a somewhat arduous process.

Creating Policy Convergence and Hegemonic States

Creating EU legislation takes a clear, albeit lengthy route, with power divided between different institutions. By implication, making data legislation will be no different than policy-making around other topics. Therefore, we can use established political science knowledge to set our predictions on data policy convergence. In international relations, research shows that some states exhibit significantly more power and influence than do others—we call these states hegemonic powers.[20] Who qualifies as a hegemonic power relies upon measures such as military capacity and/or global economic power. In the European Union, given these factors, the United Kingdom, France, and Germany are the predominant hegemonic states in the EU. While designing EU data policy, the hegemonic states may attempt to drive convergence toward a policy that will benefit their domestic interests. Another IR principle—complex interdependence—contends that hegemonic states more readily create international organizations, *and* inside existing organizations, they pressure small and mid-sized states to follow the policy preferences of the more powerful states. After a policy regime is created, even if the capacity of the hegemonic state declines such that it is no longer a primary power in the international system, the prior policies it helped to established will

[20] Keohane (2005), Keohane and Nye (1989), Krasner (1983), and Morgenthau (1947).

persist, due to institutional rigidity.[21] Once created, we should expect data legislation to continue in the same direction, unless conditions change drastically.

This brings us to **important point two**, which we glean from applying the concept of hegemonic states with complex interdependence to the EU data policy space. We can predict that **as EU states coordinate policies, the hegemonic states** may have more power and influence than other members. They **might either attempt to drive policy convergence toward a shared policy that will benefit their domestic interests, or at the very least, try to avoid policies detrimental to their own domestic interests**. The question then remains—During EU data policy-making, did the United Kingdom, France, and Germany prefer policies enshrining data commodification, security access, or digital human rights? Duplicating my argument on national policy preferences, hegemonic states might not desire mutually exclusive policies (data capitalism OR data surveillance OR digital human rights). However, when the demands of these preferences are in conflict, priorities must be chosen.

To predict the specific types of data policies France, Germany, and the United Kingdom will seek, I return to look at Level II—national economic conditions, security threats, and legally trained policy advisors used within the United Kingdom, France, and Germany, this time, from the mid-1990s–2016. Chapters 3–5 examined these elements from 1970–1999 for Germany, and the United Kingdom, but not for France, it will therefore be necessary to spend time looking at French conditions during Phase I. Economic, security, and human rights conditions in our hegemonic states during Phase II determined the expected EU policy convergence point for data policies.[22] I start with an economic overview.

Level II: The First Institution and the Economic Seeds for an EU Data Regime

From the 1990s, ICT products and/or services were believed to hold latent potential for contributing to economic growth.[23] In time, cyber

[21] Keohane and Nye (1989).

[22] Data availability varies by state and variable being measured. ICT variables used conclude at 2016. Terrorist attacks were compared up to 2014.

[23] Meijers (2014).

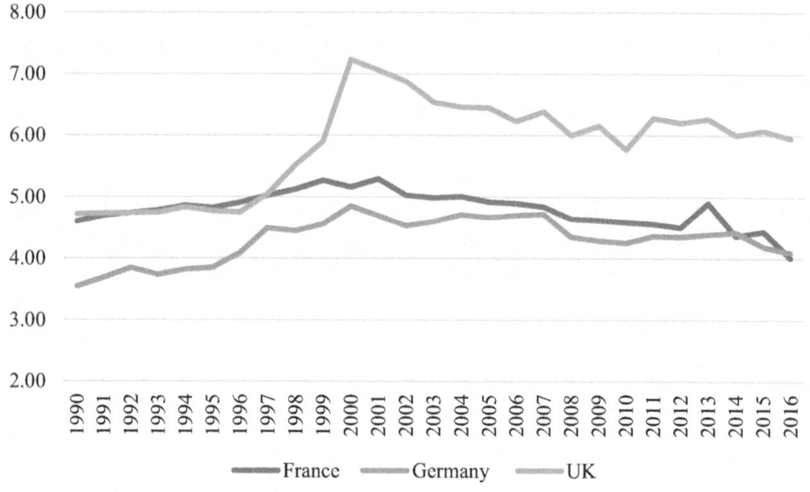

Chart 6.1 ICT value added, % of GDP, powerful EU states (Data: World Bank WDI Database, OECD, Eurostat)

data became economically commodified, or identified as a value-based commodity, within the ICT sector. As mentioned, cyber data was treated as an extension of general data, to be managed with the discretion of data processors and controllers, and policies were set to cover its use.[24] The links between internet access and economic growth, and later the role that cyber data could play in corporate growth was of great interest to ICT firms and to economic planners. To what extent did the powerful states rely upon the data-rich tech sector for economic growth from the 1990s forward? Two markers help answer this question—the level of value added by the ICT sector to the national economy, and how this value compares against tech growth dependence in the other two powerful states. Chart 6.1 represents the impact of data upon the digital economy using value added as a percentage of GDP. Both France and the United Kingdom started the 1990s with levels between 4.6 and 4.7%. The United Kingdom reached a high point of 7.23% in 2000, and although the sector retracted somewhat in the early 2000s, levels remained about 6%. French growth was relatively stable, hovering between 4 and 5% until a decline in

[24] Fuster (2016).

Fig. 6.2 Data technology export contribution (DTEC)

recent years. The German ICT sector grew the least, contributing from 3.5% to a maximum of 4.5% of GDP. The United Kingdom has benefited the most from growth in data-rich sectors, followed by France.

Unfortunately, the "Value Added" measure does not fully capture the economic value tied to data transfers *across borders*, which was the main goal cited by the OECD, Council of Europe, and EU Commission as a justification for creating data protection. Though measuring additional single variables is helpful to understand which areas of ICT may be growing faster than others, the use of separate variables does not reveal the *combined* effects of exported data tied to the growth of ICT business volume in the hegemonic states. To accomplish this, I created a composite measure which covers the additive effect of economic gains from exports made by technology-based firms, using a wider variety of variables.

The Data Technology Exports Contribution (DTEC)

The Data Technology Exports Contribution (DTEC) captures the explosive growth in industries which rely on profits from the *exports* of data. The DTEC contains the most commonly used measures by the OECD, IMF, and World Bank capable of depicting the export value of data: ICT goods exports, ICT services exports, high-tech exports, and insurance-financial services exports. The DTEC represents the percentage of contribution made by each variable to the national economy; annual figures were summed, standardized using Stata, then averaged for each 5-year period. See Fig. 6.2 and Table 6.2.[25]

Again, the United Kingdom experienced the most growth, when compared to the other two states. All time periods revealed positive DTEC exports for the country, even following the 2008 financial crisis. Although France and Germany made considerable gains across time, they still lagged behind the United Kingdom. This provides further economic

[25] Variables are standardized using STATA, then averaged for each 5-year period.

Table 6.2 Data technology export contribution (DTEC) composite

Country	*1985–1989*	*1990–1994*	*1995–1999*	*2000–2004*	*2005–2009*	*2010–2014*	*2015–2016*
France	−0.94	−0.90	−1.91	0.01	−0.90	0.34	1.44
Germany	−4.22	−3.49	−1.56	−0.15	−0.55	−0.41	0.01
U.K	0.36	0.36	1.73	5.42	3.54	1.89	1.98

Source Eurostat, OECD

evidence that the United Kingdom should prefer EU legislation that facilitates data mobility. Overall, all three states received positive economic benefits from ICT growth, with the United Kingdom and France gaining the most. It's possible that all three will support data commodification within EU data policies, but **the United Kingdom and France would benefit the most from an EU data commodification regime**.

Level II – The Second Institution and the Influence of Security Risks

In the mid-1970s and 1980s, several EU states experienced domestic terror attacks by radical leftist, separatist, or Palestinian sympathetic groups. These attacks diminished somewhat in the 1990s. However, law enforcement, criminal prosecutors, and national security officials expanded efforts to use personal data as information-gathering mechanisms to prevent, track, and prosecute domestic terrorists. Data collection and monitoring were also seen as an additional way to ensure border security from outside terrorists coming in.[26] Many legislatures argued for data collection privileges to be legalized for law enforcement during debates on data legislation. Such efforts intensified following the September 11, 2001 terrorist attack in the U.S., and the subsequent attacks to London and Madrid in 2004 and 2005. EU officials realized the expanded regional risk of threats to public spaces, as well as to important data and financial infrastructures.[27] Utilizing data as a surveillance tool became the new buzzword among governmental actors and researchers alike.[28] The heightened security concerns incentivized a desire for a security access

[26] Choucri (2012), Longo (2018), and Wallace et al. (2015).

[27] Franda (2001).

[28] Mueller (2010).

regime, in which personal and later cyber data could serve as a surveillance tool by state authorities.

Areas of security-based data legislation were broad. In early years it was as simple as giving law enforcement access to public databanks. From the 2000s, legislatures created policies to govern internet infrastructure, and internet practices, including those that generate finance-based data.[29] Access to the meta-data generated by internet or mobile phone use was another type of approaches used.[30] Further laws covered cyber space and telecom technology[31] and clamped down on online counter-narratives used in terrorist or anti-state propaganda flows.[32] Personal and cyber data received particular attention.[33] Table 6.3 data reveals the level to which hegemonic states were affected by increased global terror attacks in both Phases.

United Kingdom

Similar to the data for Phase I, the greatest number of security casualties occurred in the United Kingdom in the 1990s and 2000s. Notably, the volume of domestic attacks peaked from 1984–1989, and again between 2004 and 2009. As we know, the early UK figures are largely attributable to the civil conflict in Northern Ireland between 1968 and 1998. Recall that EU parliamentarians debating data legislation in the Commons during the Troubles years frequently noted the importance of information access to law enforcement and security officials. After 2000, the United Kingdom experienced another rise in domestic terrorism following the 2005 bombings in the London Underground. As domestic terror attacks have been an issue in the past and have risen to the forefront again more recently, Britain will likely prefer granting freedom of data access to security officials within EU data laws, but will have to balance that desire with a need to protect data profiteering by the technology sector.

[29] Lynn III (2010).

[30] Meta-data: "data about the data", Deibert (2013).

[31] Choucri (2012), and Rosecrance (1996).

[32] Goldsmith and Wu (2006).

[33] Cavelty (2013) and Mueller (2010, Chapter 8).

Table 6.3 Domestic terror casualties, 1970–2014, France/Germany/UK

Total Casualties	*1970–1974*	*1975–1979*	*1980–1984*	*1984–1989*	*1990–1994*	*1995–1999*	*2000–2004*	*2005–2009*	*2010–2014*	*Totals*
France	70	138	617	470	67	333	56	35	36	1823
Germany	97	74	346	436	371	119	58	8	4	1513
United Kingdom	1772	1250	1202	1494	1312	956	103	934	101	9124

Source Global Terrorism Database

France

The security history of France during Phase I shaped the security environment in subsequent years. In each decade, I'll cover a few examples of the types of security attacks the country faced in order to set the context of perceptions of security risk. Broadly speaking, after World War II, few immediate security threats remained, and Charles de Gaulle focused resources on nuclear deterrence development and acquiring security partnerships that limited the global hegemony of the United States.[34] France kept this externally focused security policy into the 1960s. After an increased number of domestic attacks by nationalist and fundamentalist terrorists in the 1970s and 1980s, preventive information gathering needs expanded. Throughout the 1980s, France underwent further attacks by a wide variety of groups and individuals motivated by ideological goals, expanding the need for data collection. Carlos the Jackal, a self-styed "professional revolutionary" carried out grenade, rocket, and bombing attacks, which killed and injured dozens.[35] The country endured attacks on the Turkish consulate, and on retail stores, airports, and public spaces (hotels, train, cafes, cinema, and offices). ASALA (Armenian Secret Army for the Liberation of Armenia), Hezbollah, and Action Directe were believed to be responsible for several of these violent events.[36] French security threats increased, driving demand for data surveillance.

In the 1990s and 2000s, France lived through the second largest number of domestic terror casualties, after the United Kingdom, further intensifying the need for data collection by law enforcement. In 1994, France suffered an Air France hijacking by the Armed Islamic Group (GIA), and in 2002, a bombing in Nice perpetrated by separatist militants in the National Liberation Front of Corsica (FLNC).[37] More recently, in 2015 Al-Qaeda adherents shot several Charlie Hebdo employees, ISIS members perpetrated the attacks on Paris entertainment venues in November of that same year, and the 2016 Bastille Day celebration in Nice was targeted by a Tunisian extremist.[38] The heightened numbers of

[34] Gordon (1993).

[35] NBC News (2017).

[36] Domingo (2010).

[37] Nundy (1994) and BBC News World Edition 2002.

[38] Rawlinson et al. (2016).

attacks drove home the necessity of data as a surveillance tool for proactive and prevention measures. Successive French governments have taken these threats seriously, adding more aggressive offense and defense mechanisms in attempts to restore social order and peace. Data has been a key weapon in their arsenal.

Since 2001, French white papers on government policy have linked domestic and international security together, highlighting the importance of information-gathering by national intelligence agents, and citing a need for data surveillance to protect industries and government assets.[39]

> Intelligence plays a central role in the knowledge and anticipation function. It irrigates each of the other strategic functions of our defence and national security strategy. It must be used both to guide political and strategic decision-making and to plan and conduct operations on the tactical level... A particular effort must therefore be devoted to it in the coming period, taking in both human resources and the technical capacities for gathering and exploiting data. Human intelligence (HUMINT), electronic intelligence (ELINT) and imagery intelligence (IMINT) are complementary and indivisible. The full value of intelligence is derived from combining the data gathered from these three channels.[40]

French authorities expanded the powers of law enforcement agencies responsible for counter-terrorism, and internal security.[41] In 2006, data collection powers were expanded to include traveler information, such that internet and telecom firms are required to grant police access to customers' data. In addition, Air France began administering a biometric data collection program during flights through the Roissy airport (*Programme d'Expérimentation d'une Gestion Automatisée et*

[39] Domingo (2010), République Française (2013), Defence and National Security Strategic Review, 2017, and Segell (2000).

[40] République Française (2013, p. 68).

[41] The Ministry of the Interior has the power to administer information databases on passengers and non-citizens entering the country. The new database was an expansion of the *Fichier National Transfrontière* database created in 1991, and grew the information gathering and data available to security officials. See Domingo (2010, p. 123).

Securisée).[42] Due to the intensification of domestic attacks by nationalist and fundamentalist terrorists, I expect France to support EU data legislation granting data access to security actors.

Germany

Germany endured a large number of bombings related to domestic terrorism during the 1980s and 1990s perpetrated by the Baader-Meinhof gang. Fortunately, the group was neutralized in the mid-1990s. During Phase II, Germany had the least number of domestic security attacks of the three countries. Right-wing extremist Ralf Spies allegedly committed attacks against Jewish immigrants in Dusseldorf in 2000. Though public attacks continued in the 1990s and 2000s, the German public remained skeptical of granting overarching surveillance power to the state. When these fears were combined with the fact that Germany had more personal data protection laws in place than the other states under consideration. Germany should support security access to information, as long as this access does *not* override the digital human rights imbedded in both regional and national laws.

To summarize: the United Kingdom received the most economic gains from the ICT sector, but it also had the largest number of security attacks. Therefore, British preferences will lean toward EU policies that sanction digitized data as both a commodity and a security tool. France followed the United Kingdom in ICT sector growth, but also experienced an increasing number of security attacks in Phase II. French officials should similarly support data commodification, but also prefer permission to use data for surveillance purposes. Finally, Germany lagged behind the other states for ICT exports and security attacks from the 1990s forward. It should be the least interested in data use by economic or security actors, preferring instead digital human rights as the primary data regime for the European Union. Now, to the final piece of the EU data legislation puzzle: the role played by legal professionals and policy advisors in the EU.

[42] Passenger participation was voluntary; Domingo (2010, p. 149–151).

The Power of Technical Expertise and Human Rights Advocacy

Lastly, I propose that a **third possibility exists in the European Union, in which fundamental human rights protections are extended over personal and cyber data to create a digital human rights regime.** At the national level, the case country studies revealed several EU states with histories of establishing privacy protection for personal data. Sweden adopted data protection legislation due to an extensive history of open access to government records. The German public insisted on data protection as a part of a larger effort to avoid government surveillance tendencies, as in the past. Finally, in the United Kingdom, human rights-minded advocates pushed for data legislation to no avail for over a decade. Following recommendations made by the Council of Europe, the United Kingdom signed but did not ratified Convention 108, which called for national data protection. Only when economic interests pushed PM Thatcher in the 1980s to either legalize personal data protection or risk business loss in a competitive global environment did the government pass such a law.

Level II: Normative Ethics and Legal Professionals as Indicators of Digital Human Rights

The intentional creation of digital human rights could potentially be seen in two ways within the EU policy space. First, if national and EU policy-makers specifically choose to use legally trained experts as policy advisors, this signals the intentional placement of data legislation within the human rights framework. Second, the content of national and EU laws will reflect a clear prioritization for digital human rights provisions, even when security access and/or data commodification is important.

When a policy-making environment includes uncertainty, and institutional coordination is required to create policy convergence around politicized issues, epistemic professionals serve as technical experts and information providers for policy-makers while designing a new law, and afterward when compliance monitoring is necessary.[43] Technical experts' advice reflects shared normative beliefs that may or may not involve

[43] Haas (1992).

systemic policy bias among the profession.[44] By choosing data policy advisors and bureaucratic agency leaders from legal professions, this signals a clear intent by legislative policy-makers to imbed values of human rights within data governance.

Haas points out that researchers looking to assess the power of epistemic actors can identify individuals based on their professional communities, trace normative beliefs commonly held within the profession, and then posit credible outcomes that would occur as a result of the consulting work for lawmakers.[45] In other words, an advisor's professional background is assumed to shape their advice, and it is understood that they will offer particular types of advice, based upon their professional ethics. If the hegemonic states choose policy advisors from legal professions as consultants on legislative content, or use legal professionals as data protection bureaucrats, this signals that a government sees data governance as a human rights matter. After all, policy-makers charged with legislating on behalf of an entire society do bring their own normative framework to the task of shaping national legislation. To choose legal experts for law advice and compliance oversight is implicative of intentionally imbedding human rights within data legislation.

As noted in the case chapters, Germany and Sweden used legal professionals, academic elites, and jurists as consultants for national parliaments when making domestic data laws. In this chapter, I outline the professional background of those leading each national data protection authority, draw out the content of national data protection laws, and highlight the role afforded to legal and human rights experts during the EU legislative process as evidence of human rights advocacy for EU-level digital human rights. As with the economic and security data, it will be necessary to do a deeper dive in the French case, given that it wasn't covered in earlier chapters.

Table 6.4 compares data legislation in the hegemonic states and outlines the percentages of content for each national data law that reflects the hierarchical priorities of data commodification, data as a security tool, or digital human rights protections.[46]

[44] Haas (1992, p. 25).

[45] Haas (1992, p. 34).

[46] See Table 6.1 for the coding scheme.

Table 6.4 Summary of national data law content—France, Germany, UK, 1970–1999

Country	*Total # of data laws, Phase 1*	*Provisions for security access (%)*	*Provisions for data protection (%)*	*Provisions for economic use (%)*
France	1	0	100	0
Germany	12	4.3	41.4	7.4
United Kingdom	3	5.2	52.4	2.5

There are clear differences in the data legislation produced within the three hegemonic states. Though the original French data law is much shorter than either the first UK or German laws, and France created only one data law in Phase I, it is devoted entirely to data protection rights, with no provision for security authorities to access personal, digitized data in a way that could potentially violate human rights, nor did the law have any content that allows for data commodification. Why and how did France choose a data law so exclusive to digital human rights?

France and Legal Epistemic Advisors

French personal data protection began with the 1978 French Data Protection Act, which incidentally, is the only data legislation France passed in Phase I. This law was in response to public outcry over a proposed government database to organize personal data used in all public records and databanks, known as SAFARI (*Système Automatise´ pour les Fichiers Administratifs et le Répertoire des Individus*).[47] The Minister of Justice appointed an investigative commission to determine the potential for rights violations; the "Tricot Commission" proposed the need for (Table 6.5),

> …measures to ensure that the development of data processing in the semi-public and private sectors will take place in the context of respect for private life, individual liberties, and public liberties.[48]

[47] Flaherty (1989, p. 166).

[48] P. 7, Council of Europe 1976 English translation of Tricot Report, Commission Informatique et Libertés (1975) and Flaherty (1989, p. 166).

Table 6.5 French data law, Phase I (1970–1999)

Year	*Name of law*	*Description*
1978	Law No. 78–17 (French Data Protection Act)	Initial data protection law, applying to "*informatique et libertés*" covering computer data processing, data files, and personal freedoms; created the *Commission nationale de l'informatique et des libertés* (CNIL), the national data protection authority

After much public concern, the government passed the *Loi no. 78–17 du 6 janvier 1978 relative à la informatique, aux fichiers et aux libertés*, or the "Law on Informatics, Data Banks and Freedoms" to guarantee personal data protection, such that "information technology should be at the service of every citizen."[49] Though the law was brief, it provided the foundation for digital human rights, created a national permanent agency to monitor data protections, and gave the body autonomous power, which it used to expand the scope of protections significantly.

The National Commission on Informatics and Freedoms (CNIL) oversees and regulates data protection, and is comprised of a college of 17 persons, drawn from a variety of political institutions in France. The mix includes two National Assembly deputies, two Senators, two members of the Economic and Social Council, two state attorneys from the General Assembly, individuals from the court system (Administrative Supreme Court, Financial Supreme Court, and French Judicial Court), as well as one individual appointed by the President of the National Assembly, one appointed by the President of the Senate, and three people chosen based on their expertise in the area of data protection.[50] The college itself votes to determine who will serve as CNIL President. Since its creation, some have argued that the functional structure of the CNIL not only keeps an exclusive and tight control over data privacy, it no longer submits to

[49] Loi no. 78–17 du 6 janvier 1978 relative à l'informatique, aux fichiers et aux libertés.

[50] Commission nationale de l'Informatique et des Libertés (CNIL) (1978) and Righettini (2011).

Table 6.6 French National Commission on informatics and freedoms

Presidents of the CNIL	*Term length*	*Professional background*
Pierre Bellet	1978–1979	Attorney, Jurist
Jacques Thyraud	1979–1983	Mayor, Politicians
Jean Rosenwald	1983–1984	President of the Court of Auditors
Jacques Fauvet	1984–1999	Former Director of *Le Monde*
Michel Gentot	1999–2004	State Councilor/Attorney
Alex Türk	2004–2011	Politician, Chairman of Schengen Committee, French Europol Supervisor
Isabelle Falque-Pierrotin	2011–2019	State Councilor, OECD Expert on Internet, Chair of EU Article 29 Working Party
Marie-Laure Denix	2019–2024	Administrative Court Auditor, Telecom Regulator

influence by the National Assembly, making it essentially independent of domestic political control.[51]

How true is this assertion? Those that make it onto the CNIL come from a variety of backgrounds, though some are politically appointed. However, once they join the CNIL their data policy suggestions and the amount of independent power wielded by the CNIL is significant. CNIL members have a great deal of autonomy and there are few obligations to accept input from any of the external stakeholders involved in the issue of personal data protection, including the National Assembly, civil society, human rights organizations, businesses, or the security segments of government. The diversity brought to the CNIL by the members is also reflected in the leadership of the organization itself (Table 6.6).

CNIL presidents have included legal experts, as well as politicians, and a journalist. This mix of professions contributed to the variety of missions pursued by the CNIL, as each president attempted to shape the mission in accordance with government goals as well as their own interpretation of the needs of the time. Regardless of the background of CNIL presidents, the 1978 law and the CNIL have set new boundaries for data treatment that differed from Swedish or German laws. France introduced the right to be forgotten, and prohibited large-scale data collection on data subjects, both of which have subsequently been added into EU data

[51] Flaherty (1989).

legislation.[52] The French law was amended in 2004 to protect personal data used during digital marketing purposes, and in 2011, regulations added on personal data trafficking when developing online content.

In the case of France, there is clear evidence of DHR protection within the bureaucracy. Though not are all legally trained, the CNIL itself has worked to enforce these rights. Lastly, while CNIL leaders came from mixed professional careers, the college has diligently protected digital human rights, and creatively expanded the rights afforded to data subjects.

Germany

As we saw in Chapter 4, German authorities struggled to define and protect personal data when computerization first began. The Data Protection Directors such as Spiros Simitis argued for a strong national, independent agency to oversee country-wide implementation after data protection was in place.[53] The first federal data legislation utilized and human rights protections within the Basic Constitution and regional data laws, and set up an independent national agency to safeguard compliance. The federal agency directors, known as Data Protection Commissioners (DPC), all came from legal careers and had extensive experience working with the Ministry of the Interior or other civil service branches (Table 6.7).

German legal officials advocated for digital human rights within Germany, in Europe, and elsewhere. DPC leaders, agency staff, and regional Data Protection Commissioners served as internal and external consultants for various international organizations when these IOs considered data policy suggestions for their members. For example, Interior Ministry officials consulted with Spiros Simitis, the Data Protection Commissioner for Hesse since 1970, regarding the new federal oversight agency design.[54] Simitis also served as legal consultant for data policy in the OECD treaty of 1980, and he was an advisor during European Union policy debates in the 1990s. German human data rights experts

[52] In Europe, the right to be forgotten applies to various aspects of personal information, including having a history of criminal convictions and participation in pornographic media.

[53] OECD (1976).

[54] Der Spiegel (1977).

Table 6.7 Selection of German data protection laws, Phase 1: 1970–1999

Year	*Name of law*	*Description*
1977	BDSG—Data Protection Law	First national data protection law, protecting against misuse during automatic processing
1983	Census Act	Discusses protections required by the Basic Law, regarding personal data collected during the census; Regulates the use of data collected for statistical and public administration purposes
1990	Data Protection Law Bundesdatenschutzgesetz (BDSG)	Revision of 1977 law; Adds responsibilities of federal Data Protection Officer, mandates on data secrecy and transmission provisions, and rights afforded to data subjects
1997	Digital Signature Act	Regulation of digital signature keys, including security measures and monitoring capability
1997	Act on the Protection of Personal Data Used in Teleservices	Charges tele-services providers with protection of personal data during telecom service provision

had a profound impact not only within their own country, but in outside states as well (Table 6.8).

Compared to the United Kingdom and France, German law provided the most extensive level of digital human rights at the regional and national levels. Germany also used legal experts as bureaucratic managers of the Data Protection Commission. The DP were given data protection oversight more than in the other powerful states and gave them

Table 6.8 German data protection commissioners, federal level

Name of commissioner	*Term length*	*Professional background*
Hans Peter Bull	1978–1983	Lawyer, Academic
Reinhold Baumann	1983–1988	Lawyer, Civil Servant with Minister of Interior
Alfred Einwag	1988–1993	Doctorate in Law, Federal Border Police Career
Joachim Jacob	1993–2003	Doctorate in Law, Deputy to Federal Data Protection Commission

Table 6.9 UK data laws, Phase 1: 1970–1999

Year	*Name of law*	*Description*
1974	Consumer Credit Act	Individuals granted right of access to credit source information for correction purposes
1984	Data Protection Act	Regulates use of automatically processed personal data regarding individuals; designed to ensure compliance with Council of Europe Convention 1981
1998	Data Protection Act	Created new provisions for regulation of processing personal information; designed to ensure compliance with EU Directive 95/46/EC

more power for investigating data protection violations. In the case of Germany, DHR are firmly entrenched and data protection will continue to be framed as a legal and human rights matter for the foreseeable future.

United Kingdom

The United Kingdom was the last of the hegemonic states to adopt data protection legislation (Germany 1977, France 1978, UK 1984). As noted in Chapter 5, the United Kingdom lacked both a written constitution and a bill of rights. Britain also experienced a very politicized struggle for data protection, with political support cycling up and down based on which party held the majority in Parliament. Conservatives were very resistant to data protection and ignored repeated efforts by other parties to introduce data protection legislation. Human rights advocates like Paul Sieghart and MEPs outside the Tory party proposed multiple data protection bills in the late 1960s and the 1970s, each of which were unsuccessful until the ICT sector pressured Margaret Thatcher to pass data protection legislation in 1984.[55] Unlike the initial German and French data laws, the first British specific data protection law (1984) did not design a national oversight agency (Table 6.9).

Data protection and monitoring procedures in Britain evolved and grew across time. In 1998, the Data Protection Act replaced the 1984 law, broadened the protections for digitized data, and established a Data Protection Registrar (DPR) as an oversight body. This was done in order to bring British law into conformity with EU Directive 95. The agency

[55] Bennett (1992).

Table 6.10 Data protection register/information commissioner's office (ICO)

Registrar/commissioner	*Dates of term*	*Professional background*
Eric Howe	1984–1993	BBC Journalist
Elizabeth France	1994–2001	Magistrate, Legal Expert
Richard Thomas	2002–2008	Civil Service
Christopher Graham	2009–2015	Politician, BBC Secretary, Advertising Standard Agency Head
Elizabeth Denham	2016–present	Human rights advocate, Privacy Commissioner in British Columbia

[a]Agency name was changed from the DPR to ICO in year 2000

was to be led by an individual appointed by the Crown, serve a five-year term, and answer to the Justice Committee.[56]

The authority and scope of the DPR has been less than that of its peer agencies in Germany or France. DPR leaders have come from a variety of professional backgrounds, similar to that seen with the French CNIL. Though some have had training in law or human rights, others moved to the agency from careers in politics or media. In 2000, Parliament passed the Freedom of Information Act, granting all British citizens rights of access to certain types of information held by the Government. The Act also changed the name of the DPR to the Information Commissioner's Office (ICO), and widened its scope of authority beyond personal data protection[57] (Table 6.10).

Though the United Kingdom has a full-time agency to guard data protection, by giving the organization multiple responsibilities, the government has effectively watered down the focus on digital human rights. The design of the agency, choosing staff from a varied set of professional backgrounds, and stacking in additional areas of oversight indicates the UK government had less intent on making digital human rights a separate and respected division of protections. The British government has not internalized the belief that digitized data is an identity-based product, thereby deserving of protection as a fundamental human right.

56 Hopping (2019) and UK Parliament (2009).

57 ICO is also responsible for compliance with the Environmental Regulation Act of 2004.

This lack of internalization to a very basic set of protections for digitized content in the United Kingdom as compared to either Germany or France.

Given the findings in the areas of ICT growth, security threats, and legal advisement, France, Germany, and the United Kingdom will favor different goals for convergence on EU data governance. The United Kingdom will desire data protections that do not restrict data use or movement, so as not to threaten ICT sector growth, with a secondary goal of using data as a security surveillance tool. German authorities will want to align EU data legislation with their own extensive levels of digital human rights protections. French authorities will look for a mix of data policies: stringent data protections, but also levels of national sovereignty over using data as instrument to combat domestic terror.

Now that we've assessed the second level of our two-level policy game for influence by the three interests—economic value of data, security need for digitized data surveillance, and the presence (or not) of legally trained epistemic advisors, we're ready to look at creation of EU data legislation.

Agenda-Setting Power: The EU Commission

Legislative agenda power is held exclusively by elites serving as national representatives within the main EU institutions, particularly those serving in the Commission and Council, which I expound on in a moment. In the early years of the European Community, intergovernmentalism reigned, and no legislation moved forward unless all member states agreed. Once supranationalism came into play, majority preferences could be adopted when setting joint policy. As the Commission is the point of origin for putting topics on the EU legislative agenda, I looked at the calls for data legislation during Phase I made by the EU Commission, indicative of a new political opportunity opening for personal data protection.[58] Keep in mind, that the Commission is led by a President, who serves a five-year, renewable term. The European Council nominates candidates for the Commission presidency, after which the EU Parliament votes to select the next president. Winning the presidency for five years gives a country significant control for setting the policy goals of the Commission under her/his tenure. Since IR theory proposes that hegemonic states utilize

[58] Garrett and Tsebelis (1996), Kassim et al. (2001), Moravcsik (1998), Nugent (2002), and Peters (1994).

international organizations to achieve their personal policy goals, it may be particularly telling if data protection makes it onto the EU legislative agenda when Germany, France, or the United Kingdom hold the Commission presidency.[59]

The Commission initiated data legislation once data computerization began. Initial efforts emphasized the importance of data commodification, with human rights protections being an indirect by-product of utility-based protections to facilitate data mobility and diffusion. The first calls for data legislation occurred in 1973, under Commission president François-Xavier Ortoli of France. His narrative singularly focused on economics, with no mention of human rights or data as a security tool. Ortoli asked the Council of Ministers and EU Parliament to take up the issue of data governance, contextually framing the issue as relevant for the growing economic potential in the data processing industry.[60] In 1974, the Commission requested the formation of a study group comprised of "governmental experts" to offer advice on data legislation.[61] This was followed by a motion submitted by a mixed coalition of Members of the European Parliament (MEPs) in 1976, who added a human rights element, asking the Commission for legislation regarding "protection of the rights of the individual, aware of the legitimate concern of the public at the risks of misuse or abuse of information stored in regional, national or international data banks."[62] The Commission agreed to opening the legislative discussion, but in a non-binding recommendation released on 29 July 1981, continued to marry the need for protecting privacy to the importance of data within the trade sphere, citing that,

> "data-protection is a necessary part of the protection of the individual. It is quite fundamental..." and that having, "... an approximated and assured level of data protection in the Member States will help to break down the

[59] Commission presidents, Phase I: Sicco Mansholt (Netherlands, 1972–1973), François-Xavier Ortoli (France, 1973–1977), Roy Jenkins (UK, 1977–1981), Gaston Thornton (Luxembourg, 1981–1985), Jacques Delors (France, 1985–1995).

[60] Commission (1973, p. 2). Also, Council of Europe (1974).

[61] Commission (1975). This study group is later referred to as the "Steering Committee."

[62] European Communities (1976).

> reserve that exists in regard to data processing and to the data-processing industry."[63]

The Commission completed the statement, with a formal recommendation, asking,

> "... those Member States of the Community which have not already done so to sign, during the course of 1981, the Council of Europe convention for the protection of individuals with regard to automatic processing of personal data, and to ratify it before the end of 1982."

The rhetoric used by subsequent Commission Presidents and the Commission as a unit outlined data legislation as an economic matter first and foremost, with privacy rights necessary to facilitate market goals. The president after Ortoli, Roy Jenkins (UK), did not promote data legislation in any way.[64] Following Jenkins, Gaston Thorn (Luxembourg) tied data protection to the need for a "common commercial policy, to the progressive abolition of restrictions on international trade."[65] Again, related to the goal of promoting cross-border business transactions, the Commission consistently pressured member states to ratify the CoE Convention 108 in the early 1980s, yet few did. By March of 1983, two members of the European Parliament (Sieglerschmidt of West Germany, and Glinne of Belgium) submitted a Working Document on behalf of the Socialist Group of political parties, asking exactly when the Commission would follow-up with a draft proposal for a Directive "to ensure a uniform level of data protection within the European Community."[66] Though this effort by MEPs certainly heightened the awareness of the need for data legislation, it didn't lead to an immediate response.

Only under the Delors Commission (France) did EU data protection legislation cross the tipping point of momentum toward becoming real law. Jacques Delors' goals for the Commission of 1985–89 largely revolved around the successful completion of the Single Market Programme by 1992.[67] Under the Single Market scheme, EU states

[63] Commission (1981).

[64] Ludlow (2016).

[65] EU Parliament (1983a) and Thorn (1984).

[66] EU Parliament (1983a, 1983b) (Oral Question 0–173/82).

[67] Endo (1999).

became one territory for the purposes of free movement of goods and services, without internal borders for border controls such as inspections or tariff assessments. The main goal of the Single Market Programme was to stimulate trade. Though he was keen to promote single market integrations, Delors had no specific initiatives that involved data processing industries nor personal data protection. The work of the Delors Commission on data protection came under the umbrella of promoting tech sector growth. It took several more years for the Commission to issue a proposal for a Directive specifically protecting individuals' personal data.[68]

Outside of calls for legislation by the Commission, the only other way data legislation could have been added to the EU policy agenda, would have been through a request made to the Commission by either the European Council, or the Council of Ministers, asking for data legislation. In reality, the European Council contributed very little to data policy efforts. In the mid to late 1980s, the Council presidency was held by the United Kingdom (Margaret Thatcher, 1981), West Germany (Helmut Kohl, 1983), France (Francois Mitterrand, 1984), back again to the United Kingdom (Margaret Thatcher, 1986), then again to France (Francois Mitterrand, 1989). Under their leadership, the European Council included data processing or personal data protection legislation within their overall agenda. The Council of Ministers passed resolutions asking the Commission to investigate the role of data within the tech sector, and sought measures to improve growth within the common market for telecommunications[69] See Table 6.11 for the summary of Commission leadership when held by the hegemonic states.

Though the focus was on data privacy protections only as a support for data processing industries, the door had been opened for EU data legislation. What type of legislation would the Union choose? Recall that many states had already set national data legislation; this was true not only in Sweden, Germany, and the United Kingdom, which I examined in Chapters 3–5, but also for other European states. EU policy-makers needed to somehow harmonize diverse policy preferences into one supranational law. As with national legislators, EU officials faced decisions about which interests to prioritize: categorize data as an economic commodity, allow data as a surveillance tool by security officials, or protect data as a

68 EU Commission (1990).

69 Council of the European Union (1988).

Table 6.11 Efforts by commission presidents to shape EU data laws

Country	*Predicted policy preference*	*Actions taken*
France	1. Digital human rights 2. Security Access	Delors Commission opened the door for digital human rights. France also pushed for national controls and security access post 9/11
Germany	Digital human rights	Didn't hold presidency; generally supported Commission efforts for digital human rights
United Kingdom	1. Data commodification 2. Security Access	Opposed digital human rights multiple times. Less pressure to achieve security access

fundamental human right? Or, include elements of all three possibilities, through some sort of prioritization framework?

The Outcome: EU Legislation and Digital Human Rights

Reaching a convergence at a point which established an EU digital human rights regime was by no means a certainty, if one looks at the early years of debate over data governance. By 1990, the EU had been externally pressured by the OECD and CoE data regimes to adopt a regional data policy. MEPs had consistently lobbied the Commission for data privacy protections. In addition, Commission presidents emphasized the economically damaging nature of competing and conflicting national data legislation among EU members. The stage was set for concrete action.

From 1990–1995, all of the major EU institutions intensified activity toward building a cohesive and comprehensive data law. In April 1990, consultants to the Commission advised that since "information is considered more and more as a tradeable commodity…[a] resource of great value which is sold at high prices by specialized companies" within Europe, the Community should develop policy for this issue area.[70] In July 1990, the Commission presented a new proposal to the Council asking for a Directive on data governance.[71] The Economic and Social

[70] EU Commission (1992, 24 final—SYN 393, pp. 4–5).

[71] EU Commission (1995, 375 final-COD287).

Committee reviewed the request in 1991, and the Delors Commission formally presented the proposal for a Directive covering the legal protection of databases to the Council of Ministers on 13 May 1992.[72] The Commission worked for several months alongside Parliament to craft the proposed policy, which became the first piece of supranational EU law dealing exclusively with data governance, afterward know as Directive 95. The Council of Ministers adopted an amended position on data governance in 1992, and accepted Parliament's revisions on the common position in June of 1995. Directive 95/46/EC came into effect on 24 October 1995.

Though it started as an economic initiative, the final wording of Directive 95 became the premier regional framework for a digital human rights regime in the European Union.[73] This Directive provides a critical juncture for EU data legislation; **after Directive 95, digital human rights became an accepted community norm.** As a Directive, it set mandatory regulations on data treatment by ALL Community members. Note that the directive also prohibited restrictions on cross-border data transmission, thus **still protecting data commodification**. Directive 95:

- Provided definitions for personal data, data processing, data controllers and processors, third party data recipients
- Applied the scope of protection to automatically processed data, above provisions in national laws
- Restricted personal data use to legitimate uses, for originally collected purposes, with corrections during use, and anonymization post use
- Prohibited personal data use which revealed race, ethnicity, political/religious/philosophical opinions, trade union membership, health, or sex life

[72] EU Commission (1992, 24 final—SYN 393).

[73] Directive 95 was not the only piece of EU legislation covering data practices in Phase II. The Amsterdam Treaty (1997) guaranteed personal data protection, but allowed data transfers without data subject consent during police cooperation. The Charter of Fundamental Rights of the EU (2000) incorporated data protection as a fundamental human right; despite protest by the UK against the expanding scope of EU human rights, the Charter of Fundamental Rights of the EU became EU law on 7 December 2000 through adoption of the treaty of Nice.

- Required consent for use by the data subject, who is to be informed on data changes or change to use
- Mandated that Member States create (if not already in existence) a national office for personal data projection, led by a designated officer to monitor compliance

Exemptions built into the Directive allowed for personal data use in matters of domestic security, **preserving national sovereignty on security matters, which was of particular importance to France and the United Kingdom, as predicted** earlier in this chapter. In addition to the specified mandates on data protection, the greatest impact of the Directive occurred around the establishment of a permanent advisory committee—Working Party 29 (WP 29). WP 29 was comprised entirely of legal rights experts, and wielded tremendous influence over the EU digital human rights regime for over 20 years, a power I'll explore in the next chapter.

2000–2010—Expanding the Scope of Digital Human Rights

Shifts in EU data governance after Directive 95 resulted from many factors, not the least of which was newly developed technology. In 2001 the EU Parliament and Council passed Regulation (EC) No 45/2001, requiring additional protections during cross-border data movement.[74] In 2000, the US-EU Safe Harbor framework allowed data transfers to the US, though it would later be replaced due to inconsistencies in the nature of compliance by US companies.[75] The EU-US data arrangements would be contentious at best, and lead to a series of legal cases to be discussed in Chapter 8. The Nice Treaty (2001) established a new EU oversight body—the regional European Data Protection Supervisor authority — whose authority would continue to legitimize the norm of digital human rights, despite growing pressures to securitize data for anti-terrorist purposes. This latter need would come up again and again, shaping the debate on limits to DHR.

The early 2000s were a period of intense international terror attacks, including attacks in London and Madrid. Terrorist attacks across Europe

[74] EU Parliament (2000).

[75] See Chapter 8 for more details.

heightened the need for data surveillance and cross-national counter-terrorism cooperation. EU Commission President Manuel Barroso (Portugal, 2004–2005), linked data collections and protection to anti-terrorism efforts, arguing that,

> "Preventing radicalisation and protecting our critical infrastructure are of pivotal importance...the implementation of the policies and legislative proposals...[may compromise] data protection and access to the Visa Information System."[76]

Barroso also acknowledged the ongoing and important role of expert advisors, who would continue to "reinforce and update [Commission] knowledge."[77]

For their part, Members of the European Parliament wanted data legislation to be moved completely out of third pillar competencies (under the control of national governments) and into the first pillar (supranational policy), in the jurisdiction of EU bodies, just so the EU could more directly coordinate regional security.[78] After two years of "reflection," the Lisbon Treaty reworked the EU pillar structure; the treaty moved cooperation on issues of freedom, security, and justice (FSJ) among member states' police and judicial authorities out of the third pillar into first pillar governance. These changes applied to data protection legislation.[79] **Thus the limits of data protection were redefined in a post 9/11 world: data protection would be a fundamental human right, but this right could be overridden due to national or regional security threats.**[80]

Directive 95 had inherent weaknesses along with strengths which became increasingly apparent as time passed. These necessitated its eventual replacement by the General Data Protection Regulation (GDPR),

[76] EU Commission (2005, p. 8).

[77] EU Commission (2005, p. 3).

[78] European Parliament (2005, p. 6).

[79] Panizza (2018).

[80] Articles 6a and 7, Lisbon Treaty 2007/C 306/02, C 306/186, C306/190, 191. Note that within the Lisbon framework, Denmark, Ireland, and the United Kingdom had exclusion clauses to reduce mandatory participation with rules on personal data sharing during judicial or police cooperation, again an instance of resistance against EU supranational data policy from the UK.

effective in 2018.[81] Between 2009 and 2011, national data authorities, Working Party 29, and the European Data Protection Supervisor met to discuss the ongoing need for data cooperation by security officials. In January of 2012, the Barroso Commission released *Safeguarding Privacy in a Connected World: A European Data Protection Framework for the 21st Century*. The report asked for a new Regulation to replace Directive 95, and it requested rules for data use during criminal investigations and judicial processes. The law should preserve individuals' "right to be forgotten" and set parameters for data breach notifications- an indication of continued actions by human rights advocates to preserve digital human rights despite the demand for security access to digitized data. The new data law should continue to encourage the growth of the Digital Single Market plan by keeping the burden placed on businesses as least cumbersome as possible. Finally, it should help security authorities in all Member States with the fight against terrorism by permitting the free flow of data during police cooperation. Notably, in *Safeguarding Privacy*, there was no further mention of the responsibility to adhere to CoE Convention 108, which had been included in prior discussions on data protection and had served as the foundational motive for EU data initiatives during the 1980s–2000s. From this point forward, EU policy-makers and institutions "owned" the digital human rights regime, essentially asking EU member states to initiate data protection legislation solely on their obligations to the EU, rather than on their obligations to other IOs like the Council of Europe or the OECD. With this view, supranationalism reigned over national data policy-making.

General Data Protection Regulation (GDPR)

In 2014, Jean-Claude Juncker (Luxembourg), the new EU Commission President, announced a series of actions to strengthen the norm of data privacy. His agenda further entrenched digital human rights in the EU, but did so based upon internet-based data, or cyber data. On 15 July 2014, Jean-Claude Juncker released his "Agenda for Jobs, Growth, Fairness and Democratic Change" which listed "A Connected Digital Single Market" as his first priority. Juncker wished to complete the data legislation overhaul within his first six months, because, "Information and

[81] EU Commission (2012, p. 3).

Communications Technology (ICT) is no longer a specific sector but the foundation of all modern innovative economic systems."[82] Digital economic growth required data protection legislation that reduced the continued fragmentation within national legislation. Crafting such a law challenged regional cooperation within the European Union *and* set up barriers with outside EU business relationships.

The GDPR replaced the outdated Directive 95 and extended digital human rights in three key ways. First, the law harmonized EU data protection to "protect people" *and* "ensure free data movement."[83] By providing for data mobility, GDPR kept intact the goals of the OECD Convention 108, without explicitly mentioning it. Additionally, special provisions were made for the protection requirements set on small and mid-sized businesses in order to reduce the financial burden of firms that employ <250 persons, and for whom providing data protection may be disproportionately expensive. (This helped to address concerns raised by French representatives.) Next, national authorities must cooperate on matters of data exchange, such as during security investigations and judicial proceedings (Articles 23, 45 and 50).[84] Finally, third countries outside the EU are required to meet the standards of intra-EU protections if the data of EU citizens will be collected by firms from third party states and/or if EU citizens data will be transferred outside the Union.[85] Growing resentment by EU ICT firms against US tech giants like Google motivated the latter provision, in combination with a series of violations by US firms against existing EU data protection laws. This will be explored further in Chapter 8.

Overall, beginning with Directive 95 and continuing to the GDPR, data protection originated in the EU in 1995, and has been preserved as a digital human rights regime ever since. This is rather amazing given the increased need for data surveillance, and of course, the ever-present desire to preserve data's economic value. EU lawmakers were initially pressured to create data legislation that could harmonize the diverse types of national laws passed in the 1970s and 1980s, mainly to further trade goals for the EU. While DHR was a by-product of these goals, once initiated,

[82] EU Commission (2015).

[83] EU Parliament (2016)—GDPR points 3, 53, and 150.

[84] EU Parliament (2016)—GDPR point 5, Article 50, Article 61, point 73, point 104.

[85] EU Parliament (2016)—GDPR point 6.

Table 6.12 Auto-code search terms

Data protection search terms	*Security search terms*	*Economic commodification search terms*
Processing or protection of personal data; Right to privacy; Fundamental right/rights and freedoms; Consent	Security, police, judicial, court, defense	Economic; business; marketing; Free movement of data

the regime took on a life of its own, as predicted by complex interdependence theory. To examine the outcome, and determine whether the preferences of France, Germany, and the United Kingdom became the convergence point EU data policies, I used a similar a priori coding scheme to that used in the national cases to evaluate all EU laws discussing data governance[86] (See Tables 6.12 and 6.13).

Digital human rights has maintained importance in EU law across time since it first emerged in 1995. Security terms can indicate positive or negative permission for access to personal or cyber data. Economic concerns are also worded as to promote or constrain data commodification. However, **all of the data protection terms concern positive provision of digital human rights**. EU laws creating harmonization in multiple areas of data treatment have also grown since 1995. What began as data protection for economic cooperation purposes, has spread into data protection during information exchanges as a part of police cooperation as well as data protection for the sake of human rights alone. The EU established a digital human rights regime.

Last Thoughts

Following the moves of a two-level game, the EU created a **digital human rights regime through a combination of national, regional, and international influences.** From the 1970s, EU states legislated data governance with policies that rivaled or competed with those of neighbor

[86] Using the EUR-LEX database, the following terms provided a lexigraphy for locating any binding laws mentioning data governance. After locating documents with the key terms, I then used MaxQDA software of the documents matching the search terms, and performed content analysis to measure and categorize the content of EU laws according to economic, security, and human rights provisions.

Table 6.13 Select EU data laws, auto-coded content

Year	*Legislation*	*Source/description*	*Data-based content*
1995	Directive 95/46/EC, Article 1	Established fundamental rights during processing of personal data; forbids restriction of free flow of personal data between Member States	Security 10% Economics 6% Data Protection 19%
1997	Amsterdam Treaty	Incorporated protection for personal data during automatic processing; free movement of data	Security 63% Economics 32% Data Protection 2%
2000	Charter of Fundamental Rights	Included the right to protection of personal data;	Security 45% Economics 35% Data Protection 20%
2001	Regulation No. 45/2001	Provisions for processing personal data; created European Data Protection Supervisor (EDPS)	Security 8% Economics 3% Data Protection 17%
2006	Directive 2006/24/EC	Required traffic data retention for 6 mos-2 yrs. for prosecution of serious crimes	Security 9% Economics 4% Data Protection 4%
2007	Lisbon Treaty	Abolished pillar structure, including past Treaty Provisions for protection of personal data; established data protection as a fundamental right	Security 70% Economics 25% Data Protection 4%
2012	Code of EU Online Rights, Chapter 4	Established basic rights for EU citizens when using online networks and services	Security 4% Economics 18% Data Protection 24%
2016	General Data Protection Regulation 2016/679	Extended protection of personal data as a fundamental human right; preserves free flow of data; mandates third country compliance	Security 10% Economics 3% Data Protection 20%
2016	EU-US Privacy Shield	Establishes minimal standards of protection for EU citizens' when personal data is transferred to US during use of digital marketplace or social media	Security 80% Economics 12% Data Protection 8%

(continued)

Table 6.13 (continued)

Year	*Legislation*	*Source/description*	*Data-based content*
N = 3804 sentences			Security 33% Economics 14% Data Protection 13%

states. International organizations pushed the EU for policy convergence in the 1980s, to simplify and expedite data mobility, thereby encouraging regional economic growth, though the harmonization of policies might impinge upon national preferences.[87] In the 1990s, Jacques Delors, the Commission President from France, opened the door for EU data legislation tied to the Single Market Programme. In addition, multiple MEPS from a variety of parties asked the Commission to attach privacy rights to such legislation, a move which expanded the scope of data protection to include a wider variety of digital human rights. National laws, EU level data regulations, and the recommendations by the OECD and Council of Europe regarding data protection generated a data regime complex.

EU data legislation has evolved across time. Initial policies were motivated by pressure from the Council of Europe Convention 108 to establish data protection premised upon technological growth and the growing economic value of data. These laws matched up with the preferences of EU states who already had powerful data protection legislation, such as Germany and Sweden, and to a lesser extent, France. Directive 95 and the Charter of Fundamental Human Rights both codified digital human rights as an area of supranational EU competence, despite frequent opposition by the United Kingdom. Today, the GDPR has expanded data protection further still by setting obligations for third party states such as the US to comply when using EU citizens' data. One could argue that this last component is an effort by the EU to globalize the norm of digital human rights.

Digital human rights are likely here to stay, but these rights do have limits. Preserving national security in a post 9/11 world has led member

[87] Drezner (2007).

states to open digitized data access not only to national law enforcement authorities, but also for use by outside security authorities across state lines. Combined with the ongoing financial value of the digital economy, and the question must be asked as to whether digital human rights legislation provides the extent of coverage that policy-makers and governments claim to provide. As things exist, data continues to be seen as an economic commodity and as a tool for preserving national security. Ultimately, states remain sovereign over all that concern citizens, including data tied to their personal identities. The rights of individual data subjects are protected only in so far as these individuals are able to understand and adjudicate for protection and control over their own personal and cyber data. Maintaining digital human rights in a world of governments constantly under stress from economic pressure and security threats will be difficult. As with data protection initiation, it will be up to well-placed policy advisors versed in human rights to ensure these protections endure. In the next chapter, we explore the role of epistemic elites in growing digital human rights in the EU.

Bibliography

BBC News World Edition. 2002. October 19. Accessed February 5, 2019. http://news.bbc.co.uk/2/hi/europe/2341659.stm.

Bennett, Colin J. 1992. *Regulating Privacy: Data Protection and Public Policy in Europe and the United States.* Ithaca, NY: Cornell University Press.

Cavelty, Myriam Dunn. 2013. "From Cyber-Bombs to Political Fallout: Threat Representations with an Impact in the Cyber-Security Discource." *International Studies Review* 15: 105–122.

Choucri, Nazli. 2012. *Cyberpolitics in International Relations.* Cambridge, MA: Massachusetts Institute of Technology.

CNIL. 1978. "Loi n° 78–17 du 6 janvier 1978 relative à l'informatique, aux fichiers et aux libertés." Paris, January 6.

Commission Informatique et Libertés. 1975. "Rapport de la Commission Informatique et Libertés, 'Tricot Report'." Paris.

Council of Europe. 1950. *Convention for the Protection of Human Rights and Fundamental Freedoms.* Rome, 4.XI.1950, Amended 2010. Rome, Italy: Council of Europe.

———. 1974. "Council of Europe Committee of Ministers." *Council of Europe.* September 20. Accessed April 27, 2018. https://rm.coe.int/16804d1c51.

Council of the European Union. 1988. "Council Resolution of 30 June 1988 on the Development of the Common Market for Telecommunications Services and Equipment up to 1992." *Publications Office of the EU.* June 30. Accessed June 18, 2018. https://op.europa.eu/en/publication-detail/-/publication/a3777ddf-2084-4d57-9df7-d2fa471619ea/language-en/format-PDFA1B.

———. 2020. "EU Adopts a Global Human Rights Sanctions Regime." December 7. Accessed May 15, 2021. https://www.consilium.europa.eu/en/press/press-releases/2020/12/07/eu-adopts-a-global-human-rights-sanctions-regime/.

Deibert, Ronald J. 2013. *Black Code: Surveillance, Privacy, and the Dark Side of the Internet.* McClelland & Stewart.

Der Spiegel. 1977. "Professor Spiros Simitis." November 14. Accessed April 27, 2018. https://www.spiegel.de/politik/professor-spiros-simitis-a-6cc32cf0-0002-0001-0000-000040764083?context=issue.

Domingo, Bruno. 2010. "National Borders, Surveillance, and Counter-Terrorism Tools in France Before and After 9/11." In *Border Security in the Al-Qaeda Era*, edited by John A. Winterdyk and Kelly W. Sundberg, 121–158. Boca Raton, FL: Taylor & Francis Group.

Drezner, Daniel W. 2007. *All Politics is Global: Explaining International Regulatory Regimes.* Princeton, NJ: Princeton University Press.

Endo, Ken. 1999. *The Presidency of the European Commission Under Jacques Delors: The Politics of Shared Leadership.* London, UK: Macmillan Press Ltd.

European Commission. 1973. "Communication by the Commission of the European Communities Concerning a Community Policy for Data Processing. Information Memo P-63/73, November 1973." *Archieve of European Integration.* November. Accessed June 20, 2018. http://aei.pitt.edu/31928/.

———. 1975. "Information Memo P-55/75, September 1975." *Archive of European Integration.* September. Accessed June 18, 2018. http://aei.pitt.edu/30369/.

———. 1981. "Commission Recommendation of 29 July 1981 Relating to the Council of Europe Convention for the Protection of Individuals with Regard to Automatic Processing of Personal Data." *81/679/EEC No L 246/31.* Brussels: Official Journal of the European Communities, July 29.

———. 1990. "Commission Communication on the Protection of Individuals in Relation to the Processing of Personal Data in the Community and Information Security." *Archive of European Integration.* September 13. Accessed May 16, 2021. http://aei.pitt.edu/3768/1/3768.pdf?

———. 1992. "Proposal for a Council Directive on the Legal Protection of Databases." *COM (92) 24 final—SYN 393.* Brussels: Commission of the European Communities, May 13.

———. 1995. "Opinion of the Commission Pursuant to Article 189 b (2) (d) of the EC Treaty, on the European Parliament's Amendments to the Council's Common Positions Regarding the Proposal for a European Parliament and

Council Directive." *COM (95) 375 final-COD287.* Brussels: Commission of the European Communities, July 18.
———. 2005. "Communication from the Commission to The Council and The European Parliament Interim Report on the Follow Up to the Informal Meeting of Heads of State and Government at Hampton Court." December 7. Accessed June 17, 2018. https://eur-lex.europa.eu/LexUriServ/LexUriServ.do?uri=COM:2005:0645:FIN:EN:PDF.
———. 2012. "Communication from the Commission to the European Parliament, the Council, the European Economic and Social Committee and the Committee of the Regions." *Safeguarding Privacy in a Connected World: A European Data Protection Framework for the 21st Century.*
———. 2015. *Why We Need a Digital Single Market.* Brussels: EU Commission.
European Communities. 1976. "European Parliament Working Documents 1976–1977." *Document 46/76 Motion for a Resolution.* April 6.
European Parliament. 1983a. "European Parliament Working Documents 1983–1984 Oral Question 0–173/82." March. Accessed May 16, 2021. http://aei.pitt.edu/59917/1/EPWD-2_B3_52.pdf.
———. 1983b. "European Parliament Working Documents 1983–1984." *Archive of European Integration.* March. Accessed May 16, 2021. http://aei.pitt.edu/59917/1/EPWD-2_B3_52.pdf.
———. 2000. "Regulation (EC) No 45/2001 of the European Parliament and of the Council of 18 December 2000 on the Protection of Individuals with Regard to the Processing of Personal Data by the Community Institutions and Bodies and on the Free Movement of Such Data." *Official Journal of the European Communities*, December 18.
———. 2005. "Commission Legislative and Work Programme (2005) European Parliament Resolution on the Commission's Legislative and Work Programme for 2005." *P6_TA (2005) 0053.* Official Journal of the European Union, February 24.
———. 2016. "Regulation (EU) 2016/679 of the European Parliament and of The Council of 27 April 2016 on the Protection of Natural Persons with Regard to the Processing of Personal Data and on the Free Movement of Such Data, and Repealing Directive 95/46/EC (General Da)." *EUR-LEX.* April 27. Accessed June 5, 2018. https://eur-lex.europa.eu/legal-content/EN/TXT/PDF/?uri=CELEX:32016R0679&from=EN.
———. 2020. *Trade regimes Applicable to Developing Countries.* December. Accessed May 16, 2021. https://www.europarl.europa.eu/factsheets/en/sheet/162/trade-regimes-applicable-to-developing-countries.
European Union. 2007. "Final Act: Treaty of Lisbon." *2007/C 306/02.* Brussels, BE: Official Journal of the European Union, December 17.
Flaherty, David H. 1979. *Privacy and Government Databanks.* London: Mansell.

———. 1989. *Protecting Privacy in Surveillance Societies: The Federal Republic of Germany, Sweden, France, Canada, and the United States*. Chapel Hill, NC: University of North Carolina Press.

Franda, Marcus. 2001. *Governing the Internet: The Emergence of an International Regime*. Boulder, CO: Lynne Rienner Publishers, Inc.

Fuster, Gloria González. 2016. *The Emergence of Personal Data Protection as a Fundamental Right of the EU*. Springer.

Garrett, Geoffrey, and George Tsebelis. 1996. "An Institutional Critique of Intergovernmentalism." *International Organization* 50 (2): 269–299.

Gassman, H. P. 1976. "OECD Guidelines Governing the Protection of Privacy and Transborder Flows of Personal Data." *Computer Networks* 5 (2): 127–141.

Goldsmith, Jack L., and Tim Wu. 2006. *Who Controls the Internet?: Illusions of Control in a Borderless World*. New York, NY: Oxford University Press.

Gordon, Philip H. 1993. *A Certain Idea of France: French Security Policy and the Gaullist Legacy*. Princeton, NJ, USA: Princeton Press.

Haas, Peter M. 1992. "Epistemic Communities and International Policy Coordination." *International Organization* 46 (1): 1–35.

Hopping, Clare. 2019. "Who Is the Information Commissioner, What Powers Do They Have, and How Will the ICO Enforce GDPR?" January 4. https://www.itpro.co.uk/information-commissioner/31751/what-is-the-information-commissioner-s-office-ico.

ICT Investments. *OECD, OECD ICT-Investments (2021)*.

Kassim, Hussein, Anand Menon, B. Guy Peters, and Vincent Wright. 2001. *The National Co-ordination of EU Policy: The European Level*. Oxford: Oxford University Press.

Keohane, Robert O. 2005. *After Hegemony: Cooperation and Discord in the World Political Economy*. Princeton, NJ: Princeton University Press.

Keohane, Robert O., and Joseph S. Nye. 1989. *Power and Interdependence*. Glenview, IL: Foresman Scott.

Krasner, Stephen. 1983. *International Regimes*. Ithaca, NY: Cornell University Press.

"Loi no. 78–17 du 6 janvier 1978 relative à la informatique, aux fichiers et aux libertés," January 6, 1978. Paris, France: Journal Officiel de la Republique Francaise.

Longo, Matthew. 2018. *The Politics of Borders: Sovereignty, Security, and the Citizen after 9/11*. Cambridge: Cambridge University Press.

Ludlow, N. Piers. 2016. *Roy Jenkins and the European Commission Presidency, 1976–1980: At the Heart of Europe*. London, UK: Palgrave Macmillan.

Lynn III, William J. 2010. "Defending a New Domain: The Pentagon's Cyberstrategy." *Foreign Affairs* 89 (5): 97–108.

Meijers, Huub. 2014. "Does the Internet Generate Economic Growth, International Trade, or Both?" *International Economics & Economic Policy* 11: 137–163.

Milner, Helen. 1997. *Interests, Institutions, and Information*. Princeton, NJ: Princeton University Press.

Moravcsik, Andrew. 1998. *The Choice for Europe: Social Purpose and State Power from Messina to Maastricht*. London: University College London Press.

Morgenthau, Hans. 1948. *Politics Among Nations: The Struggle for Power and Peace*. New York: Alfred A. Knopf Publishing.

Mueller, Milton L. 2010. *Networks and States: The Global Politics of Internet Governance*. Cambridge, MA: Massachusetts Institute of Technology Press.

NBC News. 2017. "'Carlos the Jackal' Goes on Trial Over 1974 Paris Grenade Attack." March 13. Accessed May 7, 2018. https://www.nbcnews.com/news/world/carlos-jackal-faces-paris-trial-over-1974-grenade-attack-n732591.

Nuclear Threat Initiative. 2019. "European Union (EU)." July 30. Accessed May 10, 2021. https://www.nti.org/learn/treaties-and-regimes/european-union-eu/.

Nugent, Neill, ed. 2002. *At the Heart of the Union: Studies of the European Commission*. Second. Basingstoke: MacMillan Press Ltd.

Nundy, Julian. 1994. "Jet Hijackers Die as 170 Are Freed." December 27. Accessed February 5, 2019. https://www.independent.co.uk/news/uk/jet-hijackers-die-as-170-are-freed-1390663.html.

NY Times. 1986. "France Arrests 9 in Paris Bombings." September 26. Accessed February 5, 2019. https://www.nytimes.com/1986/09/26/world/france-arrests-9-in-paris-bombings.html.

OECD. 1976. *Establishing Institutional Structures to Monitor and Enforce Data Protection*. Policy Issues in Data Protection and Privacy, OECD Informatics Studies, Paris: Organization for Economic Cooperation and Development, 83–94.

———. 2010. *Joint Roundtable of the Committee for Information, Computer and Communications Policy (ICCP) and its Working Party on Information Security and Privacy (WPISP)*. Address by Hans Peter Gassman. Paris: Organisation for Economic Cooperation and Development.

———. 2011. *Thirty Years After the OECD Privacy Guidelines*. Paris, France: Organisation for Economic Cooperation and Development.

———. 2018. *ICT Total, % of value added, 2011 (indicator)*. ICT Database. Paris: Organisation for Economic Cooperation and Development.

Panizza, Roberta. 2018. "The Treaty of Lisbon, Fact Sheets on the European Union." October. Accessed February 26, 2019. http://www.europarl.europa.eu/factsheets/en/sheet/5/the-treaty-of-lisbon.

Pavy, Eeva. 2020. *The Treaty of Lisbon*. November. Accessed May 1, 2021. https://www.europarl.europa.eu/factsheets/en/sheet/5/the-treaty-of-lisbon.

Peters, B. Guy. 1994. "Agenda-setting in the European Community." *Journal of European Public Policy* 1 (1): 9–26.

Pollack, Mark A. 2010. In *Policy-Making in the European Union*, by Mark A. Pollack, and Alasdair R. Young, edited by Helen Wallace, 15–44. Oxford: Oxford University Press.

———. 2015. "Theorizing EU Policy-Making." In *Policy-Making in the European Union*, by Helen Wallace, Mark A. Pollack, and Alasdair Young, 12–45. Oxford: Oxford University Press.

Putnam, Robert. 1988. "Diplomacy and Domestic Politics: The Logic of Two-Level Games." *International Organization* 42 (3): 427–460.

Rawlinson, Kevin, Angelique Chrisafis, and Vikaram Dodd. 2016. "From Charlie Hebdo to Bastille Day: France Reels After New Deadly Attack." July 14. Accessed February 5, 2019. https://www.theguardian.com/world/2016/jul/15/charlie-hebdo-bastille-day-france-reels-after-deadly-nice-attack.

République Française. 2013. "French White Paper: Defence and National Security 2013." Paris, France.

République Française. n.d. "Defence and National Security Strategic Review."

Righettini, Maria Stella. 2011. "Institutionalization, Leadership, and Regulative Policy Style: A France/Italy Comparison of Data Protection Authorities." *Journal of Comparative Policy Analysis*, 143–164.

Rosecrance, Richard. 1996. "The Rise of the Virtual State." *Foreign Affairs* 75 (4): 45–61.

Segell, Glen M. 2000. "French Cryptography Policy: The Turnabout of 1999." *International Journal of Intelligence and Counterintelligence* 13: 345–358.

The Guardian. 2011. "Activate 2011: Robert Kirkpatrick, director, UN Global Pulse." April 26. Accessed March 10, 2018. https://www.theguardian.com/activate/video/activate-robert-kirkpatrick.

Thorn, Gaston. 1984 (15 February). *Address by Mr. Gaston Thorn, President of the Commission of the European Communities, to the European Parliament*. Strasbourg: European Union.

UK Parliament. 2009. "The Role of the Information Commissioner." Accessed May 5, 2021. https://publications.parliament.uk/pa/cm200809/cmselect/cmjust/146/14604.htm.

United Nations. 2019. "About Global Pulse." Accessed March 10, 2019. https://www.unglobalpulse.org/about-new.

University of Maryland. 2018. "Global Terrorism Database." Accessed March 2019. https://www.start.umd.edu/data-tools/global-terrorism-database.gtd.

Wallace, Helen, Mark A. Pollack, and Alasdair R. Young. 2015. *Policy-Making in the European Union*. Oxford: Oxford University Press.

CHAPTER 7

Digital Human Rights Expansion by Epistemic Actors, and the Role of Working Party 29

Chapter 6 outlined how the Commission effectively opened the door for digital human rights. It also explained the dilemma faced by policy-makers, when creating new legislation in an environment fraught with varied states' interests. This chapter builds on the findings in Chapter 6, by looking past the point of policy creation to examine EU data policy adaptation across time. In effect, I ask, *how and why did key policy advisors take the new norm of data privacy protection and expand it to encapsulate several types of data use*? Of equal importance…*how did EU advisors apply constraints on multiple data practices, thereby altering the activities of state and non-state actors across the international system*?

In fact, three key findings emerge during the evolution of EU data governance. Epistemic advisors from within the legal profession have been the primary consultants used by the EU institutions since the advent of Directive 95. Though these individuals did not create digital human rights per se—such policies originated at the national level—they have nevertheless acted as norm entrepreneurs for expanding data privacy protection into multiple types of digital human rights. This was accomplished using the normative beliefs of their profession to frame different data practices as potentially infringing upon human rights, thereby inferring these actions were salient and worthy of scrutiny by EU policy-makers. Lastly, through their advising work and the status given to their suggestions as technical policy elites, legal professionals proactively grew the scope and

R. Dowd, *The Birth of Digital Human Rights*, Information Technology and Global Governance,
https://doi.org/10.1007/978-3-030-82969-8_7

breadth of digital human rights in profound ways. To lay the ground work for these claims, I begin with an explanation of norm entrepreneurship. Then, I discuss who qualifies as epistemic professionals, and how these individuals can become norm entrepreneurs. Finally, I explain how they fulfill their assigned role as advisors, and utilized this role to advocate for expanded digital human rights within the EU and the international system.

Norm Entrepreneurs

Constructivists within international relations have long maintained that new norms emerge due to human rights advocacy by individuals and groups, known as norm entrepreneurs, who intentionally strategize to promote adoption of the new norm.[1] Norm entrepreneurs (NEs) accomplish the acceptance of a new norm using mechanisms of transnational "moral proselytism."[2] NEs call attention to existing behaviors and policies as logically inappropriate with the human rights standards a state or group of states has endorsed. Through their networking activity and strategic placement within the international system, they successfully promote adoption and diffusion of a variety of new norms, including an international ban on land mine use and the global responsibility to protect targeted populations during genocide attempts.[3]

Creating normative change is not easy. Norm entrepreneurs come from a variety of social groups, and use multiple tactics to promote norm adoption. NEs include NGOs, members of the mass public, i.e., civil society, and professionals and their membership organizations. NE's know what has worked in past campaigns, and repeat successful actions during new missions. "Naming and shaming" human rights violators through media-based information campaigns is a common tactic of NGOs operating as norm entrepreneurs.[4] Transborder networking may be required to fully change outcomes, if the offending behavior is non-bounded. The latter action—constructing transnational networks—builds power through increased numbers, allowing NEs to combine resources,

[1] Keck and Sikkink (1998).

[2] Nadelmann (1990).

[3] Keck and Sikkink (1998) and Madokoro (2019).

[4] Hafner-Burton (2008).

strategize together, and magnify their voices by focusing pressure on multiple states simultaneously. In these instances, international organizations provide a platform for socialization to promote new norms, strengthen existing norms, or adapt norms as necessary.[5]

In transnational settings, norm entrepreneurs, particularly those who are technical professionals, draw upon their principle-motivated knowledge to shape international practices. They come from individual states, meet with their colleagues within international organizations, and together influence multi-national adoption of the new norm, through acting as consultants with topical expertise.[6] The European Union plays a part as a transnational networking space, providing a platform of access for NEs to influence multiple states simultaneously, enabling "transnational moral entrepreneurship."[7] It is one of many locations in which norm entrepreneurs can "ply their trade," to promote the norm of digital human rights, and to disseminate the expanded conceptualization of the norm.

Diving down into the internal workings of international organizations, norm entrepreneurs have realized mission success by policy activism within the commissions of IOs. A commissions is, "an ad-hoc committee of officials appointed by state governments or international organisations for the task of dealing with specific global issues."[8] Madokoro notes that such groups are uniquely capable of generating normative ideas. If commission members are technical experts, they bring a reputation of "cosmopolitan values and liberal internationalism…." casting their policy suggestions as innately logical, and therefore worthy of acceptance.[9] By means of investigative power and reporting responsibilities, commissions can act as norm entrepreneurs.

Clearly, there is enormous potential for impact by norm entrepreneurs upon the digital human rights landscape of the EU, given the right political opportunities. Yet norm entrepreneurship is but one piece of the puzzle when explaining expanding DHR. The next explanatory variable is that of epistemic communities, who, when combined with the activism of

[5] Keck and Sikkink (1998).

[6] Risse-Kappen (1995).

[7] Risse-Kappen (1995, p. 32).

[8] Madokoro (2019, p. 15).

[9] Madokoro (2019, p. 57).

norm entrepreneurs, bring a weight of legitimacy to push DHR expansion into not only the realm of possibility, but into the realm of probability.

Epistemic Communities

Peter Haas's excellent work on epistemic actors provides a clear explanation for the function of epistemic communities, defined as,

> … a network of professionals with recognized expertise and competence in a particular domain and an authoritative claim to policy-relevant knowledge within that domain or issue-area.[10]

With the elevation of scientific reasoning since the Enlightenment, public governance is now very technical. When a new issue presents itself to governing officials and it is of a specialized nature, if the officials don't possess knowledge of the issue field, informational uncertainty is particularly high. Epistemic professionals can be crucially important to policy-makers as they try to understand a new problem. Adding technical experts to the process of making laws or to bureaucratic oversight agencies provides a level of professionalization to the actions of a government, as technocrats are seen as less partisan. The need for epistemic experts is ever increasing, thanks to globalization and deepening levels of economic interdependence. Today, there is rarely a clear separation between domestic and international levels of socioeconomic policy-making. Both levels of policy-makers utilize epistemic professionals to guide their decisions by means of technical information provision. As a result, an institution stocked with experts is more respected and policy output perceived as more likely to reduce future risks to domestic and international relationships.

One other thing sets epistemic experts apart from general advisors. Though all professional groups own technical knowledge unique to their training, epistemic communities possess a strong set of shared normative beliefs. Epistemic advisors will generate a common preferred set of policies, based on what they believe will be in the best interest of general society. They weigh potential outcomes through the filter of professional community norms. Haas outlines a few key actions that epistemic communities perform, such as,

[10] Haas (1992, p. 3).

1. Provide technical information to reduce uncertainty
2. Utilize normative preferences when formulating policy advice
3. Identify salient government interests
4. Design policies based on issue saliency
5. Create projection scenarios of cause and effect, for policies under consideration
6. Serve as legitimizers of government policy, due to their status as highly respected experts.[11]

The more of these actions a group displays, the more likely it will fulfill the role of epistemic advisors.

Whereas Haas's work incorporated a state-centric focus on how epistemic advisors serve to identify domestic interests, his tests can be applied to the regional or international environments for data protection. Multiple EU treaties specified a role for investigatory committees and several treaties in the *acquis communautaire* created committees charged with giving socioeconomic policy input.[12] As noted within Chapter 6, before, during, and after a new piece of legislation comes to life, the Commission and Council of Ministers rely upon a research committee to provide technical information, offer policy content suggestions, and occasionally, give feedback on compliance.[13] In many cases, the meetings of high level officials such as the Commission or Council are entirely coordinated by committees, who design the meeting calendar, determine which topics are most-pressing, and collect and distribute any necessary information prior to the meeting.[14] Importantly, not all committees are created nor perform with equal amounts of authority, a point to which I return shortly.

The evidence and scholars have demonstrated the importance of the participation of epistemic professional within the international and domestic policy environments. If epistemic professionals are involved in the EU data legislation process, they could directly contribute to expanding digital human rights, depending upon the career background

[11] Haas (1992).

[12] Examples include the Economic and Social Committee (ESC) and the Committee of the Regions (CoR); see Wallace and Reh (2015).

[13] Pollack (2000, pp. 116–117).

[14] Wallace and Reh (2015, pp. 79–81).

of the individuals, and therefore, their normative framework. This impact can be accomplished via their participation within advisory committees, as technical advisors to the EU legislative institutions. For this to be true, we need to answer two questions which encapsulate norm entrepreneurship and Haas's description of epistemic communities:

1. Was there a group of legal epistemic advisors utilized by the EU Commission, Council of Ministers, and Parliament assigned to investigate data legislation?
2. If so, is there evidence that they used their professional norms to influence data governance and expand DHR?

As you will see, epistemic communities were highly involved as committee members, tasked with EU data governance matters. This claim is borne out by the professional credentials of the Article 29 Working Party representatives, an investigatory body created in 1995 for the purpose of data governance support.

The Article 29 Working Party (WP 29)

Article 29 of Directive 95 (WP 29) established a permanent and independent Working Party solely focused on the protection of personal data during automatic processing. The group was charged with providing direct information to the Commission on any matters related to the protections mandated within the Directive. WP 29 met from 1997–2016; it was replaced in 2018 by a new oversight agency (the European Data Protection Board, or EPDB), created by the General Data Protection Regulation (GDPR).

In terms of the design of WP 29, it duplicated much of the framework of the national data protection agencies. Similar to the patterns seen in the German and Swedish offices for data protection, WP 29 members were the directors or top officials of the national DPAs, often drawn from legal or academic professions noted for human rights-based preferences on socioeconomic policies. WP 29 had an enormously wide scope of competencies, including abilities to:

- Oversee national application of Directive 95
- Give the Commission opinions on data protection in third countries

- Advise the Commission on proposed amendments that would "safeguard the rights and freedoms of natural persons ... regarding ... the processing of personal data, and on any other proposed Community measures affecting such rights and freedoms."[15]
- Search for diverse levels of protection among Member States' practices
- Make independent, and un-requested recommendations via reporting to the Commission on "all matters" relating to personal data protection; the Commission was obliged to respond with any actions taken
- Issue annual reports to the Commission, Parliament, and Council of Ministers on the status of personal data protection within the Community and in third countries.

WP 29 released hundreds of guidelines, letters, official opinions, annual reports, and press releases over its twenty-year tenure. Included in the content of each annual report was a full list of current year members of WP 29. These reports provided the necessary information to investigate the members' professional backgrounds for epistemic qualifications. To answer the question on whether the key EU institutions used legal epistemic consultants, each WP 29 member was categorized into one of four career typologies: legally trained persons, academics, bureaucrats, and "other."[16] If a person previously worked in multiple or overlapping careers, they were placed into the category in which they had served the longest. Chart 7.1 offers the results. Legally trained professionals comprised the majority of WP 29 members, outpacing the next nearest categories of academia and bureaucracy by almost 3 to 1. One could arguably consider combining the legal and academic data into one category, as a majority of faculty members taught law or criminal justice. This would further increase the probability that a human rights-based perspective would guide the advice given by WP 29.

One additional thought on the functional behavior of the committee membership: WP 29 replicated the insularity against direct involvement by legislators or by civil society as seen within the French CNIL. This

[15] *Competences*, pg. 4, Directive 95/46/EC.

[16] Career history was established using online biographies, Linked In profiles, government data for the representative's training and positions held, and personal websites.

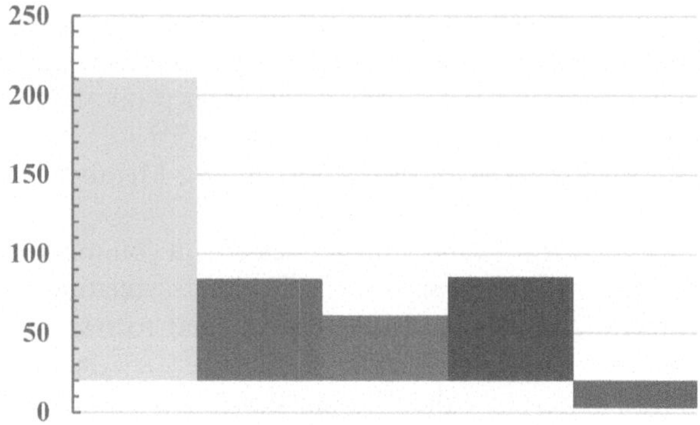

Legal = 211 Academic = 84, Other = 60, Bureaucrat = 85, No data = 3

Chart 7.1 Members' Career History, Working Party 29

functional behavior of the committee membership enabled WP 29 to perform independent research while not conducting interviews or receive direct input from members of the EU Parliament, ICT industry representatives, national or EU security officers, nor members of civil society. The European Union's reliance upon legally trained epistemic professionals within the data advice committee, the Article 29 Working Party, meets Haas's first test criterion, that of providing technical expertise.

Haas's second test criterion requires evidence that WP 29 made use of the norms of the legal profession when giving their advice. To locate application of legal/human rights norms, I examined the content of documents released during their 20 year tenure as data policy advisors. Using the same EUR-LEX search referenced in Chapters 3–5, I performed content analysis testing on 58 documents, including the recommendations, opinions, and annual reports of WP 29. Using MaxQDA software, a word frequency search identified the 100 most common phrases in the documents. Overwhelmingly, the most common terms discussed data protection during automatic processing. These terms became the core words for my auto-coding scheme, along with the key search words representing the three main structural factors used throughout this book—data protection, security needs, and ICT-based economic interests. The results of the content analysis are seen in Table 7.1.[17]

Table 7.1 Communications content of Article 29 Working Party, 1997–2016

Topics discussed	*Percentage of mentions*
Security terms (security, policy, court, judicial)	49.05
Protection terms (processing of personal data, protection of personal data, consent, right to privacy, fundamental rights and freedoms)	37.96
Economic terms (business, marketing, economic)	12.96
Free movement of data	0.03
Total	100
N = 6334 sentences coded	

While security terms comprised the largest number of mentions, in reality, the content had both positive and negative framing. For example, some sentences with the word "security" referenced the Common Foreign and Security Policy instituted in the Maastricht treaty, but did not actually discuss data treatment at all. In other sentences, the security terms gave permission for restrictions to data access by security actors. In contrast, the protection and economic terms generally reflected positive mentions. Quite interestingly, the free movement of data was mentioned only a tiny amount, despite the fact that it was the primary motivator for the Commission to create the original EU data legislation in the 1980s. Clearly, the priorities of WP 29 differed significantly from the initial aims of EU data governance.

WP 29 consistently framed new areas of data protection saliency as data utilization expanded. Reports tied advances in technology and data processing to growing risks of privacy loss for data subjects. The committee often questioned the ongoing effectiveness of existing data protection and did not hesitate to discuss data use by governmental and non-governmental actors. The committee also diligently monitored ongoing efforts to harmonize data policies within the EU, pointing out any discrepancies between states. Throughout its entire tenure, WP 29 regularly promoted an expansion of digital human rights, and no content released by the group asked for any reduction in data protection.

Content released by WP 29 revealed proactive statements promoting data protection rights reflected their epistemic training and highlighted a

[17] This method was a "blunt" auto-coding of content. Each sentence with one of the key frequently used terms was auto-coded (0,1) for presence of the word/phrase.

clear intention to expand the content and application of digital human rights. In their first annual report, the party confirmed both Haas's and Madokoro's predictions about norm entrepreneurship by epistemic communities. The report emphasized their role as expert advisors, with a clear and unified set of policy suggestions for the Commission, stating,

> Pooling the **collective expertise** of the national authorities, the Working Party will foster a **coherent approach in the application** of the broad principles of the directive and advise the Commission on data protection matters.[18]

Annual reports gave updates on member states' compliance efforts, as well the actions of third party states potentially in violation of the principles of Directive 95. They also offered clear corrections for poor data protection outcomes. For instance, the second annual report discussed the desire of Dutch data authorities for greater levels of protection on internet-transmitted health data, noting,

> The Commissioner expressed the opinion that for sensitive information on a patient to be transmitted through the Internet between public authorities in the health sector, this **information must be encrypted**, and that this should result in the necessary high level of protection.[19]

Though WP 29 took a strong and positive stance for more types of data protection, following the terrorist attack in the United States on September 11, 2001, security-based concerns shifted the focus even more to third party states' data treatment. Even as they recognized counter-terror needs, WP 29 framed the recognition with a reminder to continue provisions of digital human rights.

> Reacting to certain initiatives in the aftermath of 11 September, the group adopted an opinion on the need for a balanced approach in the fight against terrorism in December 2001. While recognising the need for an efficient fight against terrorism, the group points in this opinion to the basic conditions that have to be respected by recalling the commitment of our democratic societies to grant the respect of the individuals' liberties and fundamental rights (including the right to data protection) **underlining**

[18] EU Commission (1997, p. 6).

[19] EU Commission (1998, p. 9).

> **that the measures for the fight against terrorism should not and do not need to reduce the level of protection of fundamental rights.** A key element in the **fight against terrorism should consist in the preservation of fundamental rights** that form the **basis of our democratic societies - the same values** that those in favour of violent action seek to destroy.[20]

The sixth annual report acknowledged the crisis yet stood unified on upholding DHR. Comments such as these exemplified the normative objectives of WP 29.

Along with feedback on exogenous shocks to digital protections, the group tackled new areas of data use due to technological change, as well as the increased utilization of borderless data practices. The 11th annual report questioned the thin levels of protection under cross-border data transfers permitted by Binding Corporate Rules. In their Recommendation dated 1/2007, and in the 11th report, WP 29 complained,

> The Data Protection Directive 95/46/EC allows personal data to be transferred outside the EEA only when the third country provides an "adequate level of protection" for the data (Art. 25) or when the controller adduces adequate safeguards with respect to the protection of privacy (Art. 26). Binding Corporate Rules (BCRs) are one of the ways in which such adequate safeguards (Art. 26) may be demonstrated "by a group of companies in respect of intra group transfers" although the BCRs are not a tool expressly listed and set forth in the Data Protection Directive 95/46/EC. The use of BCRs to provide a legal basis for international data transfers from the EEA requires the approval of each of the EEA data protection authorities (DPAs) from whose country the data are to be transferred.[21]

WP 29 did not hesitate to question the validity of existing EU legislation to protect citizens' data. Binding Corporate Rules later became the center of debate between the EU and United States to the extent that data transfers by American firms would be threatened with legal sanctions by the EU judicial system, something I discuss further in the next chapter.

Later reports focused on ever-widening area of topics. Reports listed efforts by EU institutions to involve more digitized data stakeholders in the dialogue on data practices. The 2007 Conference on "Public Security, Privacy and Technology," brought together persons from public and

[20] EU Commission (2003, p. 25).

[21] EU Commission (2008, p. 11).

private sectors interested in the transfer of data, particularly in the presence of overlapping demands for privacy and security access.[22] Additional comments praised the Commission for the ePrivacy initiative, with new requirements after data breaches have taken place.

> Privacy and protection of individuals' data will be strengthened by the new rules introducing mandatory notifications for personal data breaches – the first law of its kind in the EU. This means that communications providers will be obliged to inform the authorities and their customers about security breaches affecting their personal data. This will increase the incentives for better protection of personal data by providers of communications networks and services.[23]

The Commission was also lauded for their awareness and policy developments to accommodate the invasive practices of cookies to track internet users' activities.

> In addition, the rules concerning privacy and data protection are strengthened, e.g., on the use of "cookies" and similar devices. Internet users will be better informed about cookies and about what happens to their personal data, and they will find it easier to exercise control over their personal information in practice. Furthermore, internet service providers will also gain the right to protect their business and their customers through legal action against spammers. The revised ePrivacy Directive has to be transposed into national laws by May 2011.[24]

The latter matter—tracking practices of EU citizens' online activities—occupied significant space among EU institutions in the ongoing debate around data use from the 2010s forward. WP 29, the EU Commission, and Parliament, and the Court of Justice for the European Union (CJEU) discussed the content and treatment of personal data. They also worried over how meta-data, or "data about data," was increasingly used in the capitalist surveillance efforts by US firms, who profited from the online behavior of EU citizens.

For two decades, WP 29 expanded the type of digital human rights afforded to EU citizens, both inside and outside the European Union.

[22] EU Commission (2008, p. 113).

[23] EU Commission (2010, p. 109).

[24] EU Commission (2010, p. 109).

Along with the Commission, WP 29 reached the conclusion that Directive 95 was no longer adequate for providing digital protection, due to the enlarged application of data use, and growing technological challenges to maintaining data security. Final reports lamented the lack of clarity on cloud computing protections and the missing global cooperation in setting international standards of protection on cloud-based data.

> Despite the acknowledged benefits of cloud computing, the Opinion outlines how the wide scale deployment of cloud computing services can create data protection risks, mainly a lack of control over personal data as well as insufficient information with regard to how, where and by whom the data is being processed/sub-processed. These risks need to be carefully assessed by public bodies and private enterprises when they are considering engaging the services of a cloud provider.
>
> This Opinion examines issues associated with the sharing of resources with other parties, the lack of transparency of an outsourcing chain consisting of multiple processors and sub-contractors, the unavailability of a common global data portability framework and uncertainty with regard to the admissibility of the transfer of personal data to cloud providers established outside of the EEA... Data subjects must be informed about who processes their data for what purposes and to be able to exercise the rights afforded to them in this respect.[25]

The General Data Protection Regulation (GDPR) became law in 2016, replacing Directive 95. WP 29 ceased to exist, and the functions it performed as protector of EU digital human rights became the mandate of the European Data Protection Board as of 2018. Over the lifetime of WP 29, it profoundly grew digital human rights in Europe, and as seen in the next chapter, the world.

Last Thoughts

The Article 29 Working Party became one of the most, if not **the most, powerful EU committee created to date**. The national data protection representatives serving on Working Party 29 acted as "norm entrepreneurs" when functioning as epistemic advisors on data governance to the EU. Through the makeup of committee membership, and normative-driven policy opinions produced by the group, epistemic elites

[25] EU Commission (2014, p. 6).

operating within WP 29 increased the range of digital human rights far beyond the initial framework set out in Directive 95. The various documents released by WP 29 from 1997–2016 supplied the majority of information on data practices for the Commission during the entire period in which Directive 95 was the primary EU data law. Supplying exclusive information and technical expertise around one issue gave the committee a large amount of power over the framing of data governance. They used this power to shift the narrative away from initial economic-based concerns toward human rights expansion for EU data legislation. Even after regional security problems mounted with increased terror attacks, WP 29 was able to keep the focus of EU data legislation as one of fundamental human rights, despite the competition from security concerns.

Before leaving the topic of epistemic communities and digital human rights, it's necessary to address the implications of WP 29's power to the larger debate regarding a democratic deficit in the European Union. Advisory bodies such as Working Party 29 are not elected by EU citizens. All the members of WP 29 were and are the heads of national data agencies. Their positions as national DPAs are appointed, often by the executive branch of each country or the Ministries of Justice or Interior. Though the official documents of WP 29 were publicly available online, the committee deliberations were not open to the public, nor were minutes released of the meetings. Though their communications referenced conferences held by other EU actors on the topic of data practices, there is no indication that they consulted directly with any of the multiple stakeholders involved in the process of data use, such as ICT firms, members of the public, or law enforcement officials. The advisory perspective they brought to the EU Commission was driven by legal community norms. While this was good for human rights protections, it did not contribute in a meaningful way to the demand for increased accountability and accessibility of EU institutions and bureaucracy. The ongoing complaints about a disconnect between Brussels bureaucrats and the public is fed by just such levels of disassociation between the legislative process and EU citizens. The process and people that worked seemingly well for EU data policy-making could exacerbate feelings of democratic deficit by European Union citizens, despite the large amount of digital human rights they enjoy.

Bibliography

EU Commission. 1997. *First Annual Report Working Party on the Protection of Individuals with regard to the Processing of Personal Data*. Brussels: European Union.

———. 1998. *Second Annual Report - Working Party on the Protection of Individuals with Regard to the Processing of Personal Data*. Brussels: European Union.

———. 2001. *Fourth Annual Report on the Situation Regarding the Protection of Individuals with Regard to the Processing of Personal Data and Privacy in the Community and in Third Countries Covering the Year 1999*. Brussels: European Union.

———. 2003. *Sixth Annual Report on the Situation Regarding the Protection of Individuals with Regard to the Processing of Personal Data and Privacy in the European Union and in Third Countries*. Brussels: European Union.

———. 2008. *Eleventh Annual Report on the Situation Regarding the Protection of Individuals with Regard to the Processing of Personal Data and Privacy in the European Union and in Third Countries*. Brussels: European Union.

———. 2010. *Thirteenth Annual Report on the Situation Regarding the Protection of Individuals with Regard to the Processing of Personal Data and Privacy in the European Union and in Third Countries*. Brussels: European Union.

———. 2013. *Sixteenth Report of the Article 29 Working Party on Data Protection*. Brussels: European Union.

———. 2014. *Sixteenth Report of the Article 29 Working Party on Data Protection*. Brussels: European Union.

Haas, P. M. 1992. "Epistemic Communities and International Policy Coordination." *International Organization* 46 (1) (Winter): 1–35.

Hafner-Burton, E. M. 2008. "Sticks and Stones: Naming and Shaming the Human Rights Enforcement Problem." *International Organization* 62: 689–716.

Keck, M. E., and K. Sikkink. 1998. *Activists beyond Borders: Advocacy Networks in Transnational Politics*. Ithaca, NY, USA: Cornell University Press.

Madokoro, D. 2019. "International Commissions as Norm Entrepreneurs: Creating the Normative Idea of the Responsibility to Protect." *Review of International Studies* 45 (1) (January): 100–119.

Nadelmann, E. A. 1990. "Global Prohibition Regimes: The Evolution of Norms in International Society." *International Organization* 44 (4) (Autumn): 479–526.

Pollack, Mark A. 2000. "The Commission as an Agent." In *At The Heart of the Union: Studies of the European Commission*, edited by Neill Nugent. New York: St. Martin's Press.

Poullet, Y., and S. Gutwirth. 2008. "The Contribution of the Article 29 Working Party to the Construction of a Harmonised European Data Protection System:

An Illustration of 'Reflexive Governance'?" In *Défis du droit à la protection de la vie privée - Challenges of Privacy and Data Protection Law—Challenges of Privacy and Data Protection law*, edited by M. V. Perez Asinari and P. Palazzi, 570–610. Brussels, BE: Bruylant.

Risse-Kappen, T. (Ed.). 1995. *Bringing Transnational Relations Back in: Non-state Actors, Domestic Structures and International Institutions.* Cambridge, UK: Cambridge University Press.

Wallace, H., and C. Reh. 2015. "Chapter 4: An Institutional Anatomy and Five Policy Modes." In *Policy-Making in the European Union*, edited by H. Wallace and M. A. Pollack, 72–112. Oxford, UK: Oxford University Press.

CHAPTER 8

Exporting the Digital Human Rights Norm

As seen in prior chapters, digital human rights (DHR) originated at the national level with Sweden and Germany, and diffused across the European Union member states, encouraged by the activism of epistemic professionals who utilized norm entrepreneurship. In this chapter, you will learn that the EU has not only held firm on the required behavior of member states, but has also expected others outside the EU to provide similar protections for the digitized data of EU citizens. Once DHR were adopted at the supranational level, the EU made these rights a priority for international dispersion, largely as a part of the shared identity of the EU as a provider and protector of human rights. The EU has become an exporter of digital human rights across the globe, by requiring third-party states and third-party actors, including MNCs (multinational corporations), to adopt DHR practices when working with EU citizens' digitized data. As EU institutions acted as external norm entrepreneurs and enforcers, this created policy conflicts with the United States and generated a series of lawsuits and sanctions against third-party firms such as Facebook and Google. In spite of the strain to the US relationship, EU institutions and member states held steady on the intent to protect and police others' misbehavior over digital human rights provisions. Let's delve into the process of externalizing the norm of digital human rights, and ask, *In what ways did the EU respond when digital human rights were violated by a variety of state and non-state actors*? To answer this

R. Dowd, *The Birth of Digital Human Rights*, Information Technology and Global Governance,
https://doi.org/10.1007/978-3-030-82969-8_8

question, we'll look at the pathway EU actors and institutions have taken when exporting the DHR norm across the globe.

EU Digital Human Rights Entrepreneurship: An Example of International Diffusion

Human rights norms diffuse through the international system using a variety of modalities along with multiple levels of activity. The pattern of DHR diffusion from the EU outward follows more of a cross-wise pattern, moving through economic and security-based international relationships. The EU is an international organization (IO). It diffuses human rights norms and values not just to member states through their commitments to the *acquis communautaire*, but it also attempts to diffuse these values throughout the global system of states. As a regionally based IO, the EU has nevertheless powerfully shaped global governance of digitized data through its requirement that outside actors comply with EU data legislation. Despite the uniqueness of this horizontal dispersion, the process still replicated some norm diffusion experiences of other newly introduced human rights norms. Digital human rights exportation relied upon basing the norm upon identity factors, use of socialization within treaties and long-standing international relationships, and in this case, proactive EU institutional mechanisms. Let's look at each contributing factor in turn.

International Norm Diffusion—The Importance of Identity

What factors shape norm choices? World society theory proposes that global institutions are sociologically constructed entities, based on universalized concepts of citizenship, human development, and rationalized identities. States intentionally craft identities, and these identities have direct impact upon the domestic and international behaviors of states.[1] In this case, I propose that the European Union has worked to maintain its identity as a human rights champion, and has backed up this reputation with policies and enforcement practices. This matters to global affairs, because both material and socially constructive practices change

[1] Hopf (1998).

human rights norms, leading to behavioral change at the state and substate levels. In fact, human rights adoption and cooperation often hinges upon agreed upon shared identities. The regional identity of the EU bloc of member states is also an example of a constructed and maintained identity. The EU identity has altered the European regional environment and now, the global environment, to make it more cooperative toward adoption of the new norm of digital human rights.[2]

Not all human rights norms are suitable for taking a global stance. Norms with a wider scope of appeal are more exportable,[3] as are those with the endorsement of crucial, or more powerful states.[4] Even if some treaty members don't fully internalize the norm, states will weigh any potential sanctions for noncompliance against any potential gains earned by violating the norm. Norms which align with "foundational metanorms (universality, equality, and individual rights).." have higher rates of influence.[5] Digital human rights are compatible with the "nine substantive" values the EU has consistently supported across time: "sustainable peace, freedom, democracy, human rights, rule of law, equality, social solidarity, sustainable development, and good governance."[6] In the instance of the European Union, norms involving the protection of digital human rights have aligned with the global reputation the organization has sought to cultivate—that of a liberal, human rights norm promoter.

Beginning in 1970, the European Political Cooperation (EPC) signaled the beginning of a crafted collective identity for the European Union which included human rights elements, and according to Laffan, "... implies that the EU defines this identity and interacts with the international system and other actors in the projection of this identity."[7] The clarification of and scope of EU human rights principles and practices increased as human rights were added to the Common Foreign and Security Policy (CFSP) in the Treaty on European Union in 1991. Though the attempt at a Constitutional Treaty with imbedded human rights elements failed in 2005, the human rights expansion efforts were

[2] Hopf (1998, pp. 188–190).

[3] Sandholtz and Stiles (2009).

[4] Finnemore and Sikkink (1998).

[5] Sandholtz and Stiles (2009, p. 18).

[6] Manners (2002, p. 66).

[7] Laffan (2004, p. 80); also, Manners and Whitman (1998, pp. 231–249).

not abandoned. Instead, the rights of the Constitutional Treaty were folded into the Treaty of Lisbon, which did pass in 2007. Lisbon included "universal" human rights principles based on the United Nations Charter and the larger body of international human rights laws. Lest one think that support for these efforts was elite-exclusive, opinion polls showed that EU citizens themselves identified the EU as a better promoter of global human rights, than that of the individual member states themselves, implicative of attitudes of support for the external promotion of human rights now done by the EU institutions and representatives.[8]

The EU intentionally chooses to cultivate international relationships beyond Union membership to magnify the pooled sovereignty of the membership in multiple issue areas. These relationships amplify the EU's soft power, or sociopolitical influence, beyond that of its internal borders, enabling its aim toward a global diffusion of cosmopolitan-based human rights for individuals and collective groups. This goal is a key element of EU foreign policy. Promotion of human rights within the EU institutions is simply not sufficient; it must be matched with external promotion as a "defining element of their political identity."[9] The aggressive stance of the EU to protect the digitized data-based identities of EU citizens has certainly evolved and grown across time. The EU's willingness to externally defend these rights provides an example of intentionality on the international diffusion of the digital human rights of EU citizens.

International Norm Diffusion and Enforcement—Common Mechanisms

International organizations including the EU have been purposive actors when it comes to which policies they promote externally.[10] Once a commitment to a normative identity around digital human rights was reached, and appropriate human rights practices linked to the identity of the EU as a champion of DHR, the EU has shown a commitment to export the digital human rights norm outside the community. The EU chose three main ways to support the goal of DHR exportation. Since 2009 when Lisbon went into effect, we have witnessed heightened

[8] Balfour (2008, p. 166); see also Eurobarometer (2005–2006).

[9] Balfour (2008, pp. 160–161).

[10] Barnett and Finnemore (1999).

levels of activity to externalize EU human rights values, including, but not limited to socialization with the EU's closest allies, using the EU Court of Justice as enforcer general, and via punitive sanctions against non-state actors, even those outside the EU.[11] Let's examine the components of norm diffusion and enforcement, one by one.

The Role of Close International Relationships

Treaty commitments, organizational memberships, and signature agreements require states to fulfill hard law obligations, be they related to trade, human rights, environmental protection, or security mechanisms. Crafted narratives inside treaties and conventions provide, "naming or labelling the social context [which] establishes the parameters, the very boundaries of acceptable action."[12] Controlling the discourse around the issue area and any required behaviors leads to legitimization of any actions taken by the IO to intervene in the human rights behaviors of signatory parties. Additionally, after organizations choose a norm-based mission, they often form a bureaucracy tasked with compliance oversight to insure the agreement partners keep to their commitments. IOs act like "modern missionaries" using their technocrats to model and diffuse what they think should be global norms in a specific issue area. Therefore, once an identity is chosen, it can be enforced, and indeed, exported using the socialized aspects of the relationship itself.

The EU has utilized human rights missionary activities internally, in the near neighborhood, and outside the region at the global level.[13] By example of intersections of norm proselyting between internal members and near neighborhood efforts, potential EU members faced human rights provision requirements present within the Copenhagen criteria (1973) and the wording of the Treaty of Amsterdam (1997), which set standards for "liberty, democracy, respect for human rights, and fundamental freedoms, and the rule of law, principles which must be upheld

[11] Cao et al. (2012) and de Búrca (2011).

[12] Barnett and Finnemore (1999, p. 711).

[13] Chapters 3–5 covered the internal efforts of individual member states and Chapter 6 outlined the ways in which national data protections were harmonized into a regional digital human rights regime.

by existing Member States and any potential Union members."[14] Outside the EU, eight different partnership agreements signed with Eastern European states after 1997 required compliance with the Copenhagen criteria, even if EU membership was not the end goal. Compliance has been encouraged through financial support and guidance on various political and administrative reforms.[15]

As one moves further away from Europe, additional agreements set expected goals to increase political stability, including human rights conditionality. Examples include the EU-Mediterranean Partnership preferential trade agreements (PTA) signed bilaterally with Latin American states including Mexico (1997) and Chile (2002), and the Lomé IV agreement, later replaced with Cotonou, made between the EU and African, Caribbean, and Pacific states (2000).[16] Most importantly, there are some states with whom the EU has *not* tied treaty deals to specific types of general human rights promotion include deals with Asian states, notably those with China.[17] I discuss China more specifically in Chapter 9, but it's useful to take an in-depth look at the EU-US relationship regarding data governance, as this relationship provides a key example of how the EU utilizes existing partnerships to export the DHR norm.

EU-US Relations—Exporting Digital Human Rights Through Socialization

The US-EU transatlantic alliance is complex and has shifted in several ways since World War II.[18] First of all, the relationship with the United States crossed into several bounded spaces—especially trade and security. Significant changes occurred within the EU-NATO relationship, impacting US-European multilateralism, as the EU began to seek more regional security autonomy.[19] The EU and the United States often shared

[14] Copenhagen Summit Declaration (1973) and Treaty of Amsterdam (1997), Article F(1).

[15] Börzel and Risse (2004, p. 15).

[16] Börzel and Risse (2004) and Hafner-Burton (2008).

[17] Börzel and Risse (2004, p. 19).

[18] Börzel and Risse (2004), Cao et al. (2012), Laffan (2004), and Riddervold and Newsome (2018).

[19] Riddervold and Newsome (2018) and Smith (2018).

in trade relations, and both partners rely heavily upon the volume of trade traffic between the two zones, but must protect domestic producers against high levels of competition or face ire back home.[20] Generally speaking, since 2001, US global hegemony has gradually declined, certainly in terms of a willingness to serve as the main security protector for Europe and indeed for many regions. Domestic tensions with rising terrorism and gun violence, economic woes brought about by the 2008 global financial crisis, and the increase of nationalistic populism on both sides of the Atlantic have presented challenges to the policies and practices of US and EU states' governments. For the purpose of this assessment, I focus upon the trade connections, as this is where data governance originated in the EU, and where the relationship with the United States has received the most attention in terms of bespoke agreements. Let's now put this in the context of DHR exportation, using the bilateral relationship between the EU and the US, which gives particular insight into the priorities chosen by the EU regarding where and when to target the effort on diffusing DHR.

Domestic data legislation commitments by states reveal fundamentally different ways of externalizing human rights values.[21] From 1990–2006 (during Phase II), 30 non-EU states adopted some form of comprehensive data protection regulations.[22] Yet comparing US to EU data governance, there are clear differences. The US relied upon the private sector to self-police and adhere to data governance practices within numerous other laws. Unfortunately, the United States has yet to create one comprehensive and overarching piece of federal legislation which mandates data protection or digital human rights. At present, there are hundreds of state level-laws that apply to digitized data, driven by sector-specific use. By contrast, the EU based data governance upon a specific data legislation, framed within a larger foundation of democracy and human rights, and backed this up by agencies and actors specifically and solely tasked with compliance oversight. Chronologically speaking, the United States took up data privacy concerns about the same time

[20] Börzel and Risse (2004), Burghardt (2015), Cooper (2009), and Herrmann et al. (2015).

[21] Börzel and Risse (2004).

[22] Newman (2008, p. 36).

as the Swedish and German cases.[23] Recall that the OECD Data Bank panel (1972) and export group drafted guidelines for privacy protections and transborder data flows (1978). The United States and multiple EU member states were and are OECD members, thus all received the same external pressure to adopt data privacy protections while also avoiding extreme "data protectionism."[24] The EU and the United States have thus taken very divergent pathways regarding data governance. These differences have complicated data movement during trade and security exchanges between the two zones. To understand how and why this occurred, let's briefly consider the US data governance framework.

The nearest thing to a national American digital human rights law is the Privacy Act of 1974, which deals directly with the privacy protections afforded during the automatic processing of data.[25] The 1974 act passed despite business resistance, largely because of the timing of the Watergate Scandal, which left invasive government practices foremost in the minds of many Americans. In 1977, the US Privacy Protection Study Commission recommended expanding federal personal data privacy measures beyond the content of the 1974 law. US President Jimmy Carter pushed for acceptance of the OECD recommendations in his 1980 State of the Union address. Yet no single comprehensive digital human rights law has been forthcoming. Essentially, the United States instead opted for a private-sector-driven model. In the United States, individual firms are responsible for insuring data protections, with oversight by the Federal Trade Commission who can take action if consumer protections aren't provided, such as failure to protect personal privacy, provide data security, or using digitized data in deceptive marketing campaigns. It is this distinct policy choice—to allow the private sector to control data management—that resulted in attempted agreements, and resulting clashes between the United States and EU over digital human rights.

From the EU perspective, US firms were asked to apply data protection on EU citizens' data, based upon concepts within Directive 95/46/EC. After American firms failed to self-police and provide DHR to EU citizens, more concrete action was needed to facilitate safe cross-Atlantic data transfers. The resulting policy was known as the Safe Harbour Privacy

[23] See Chapter 3.

[24] Fuster (2016, pp. 75–80).

[25] US Department of Justice (2021).

Principles, and lasted from 2000–2017. The agreement allowed the free transfer of digitized data between the two spaces as long as the American firms utilizing the data adhere to the EU protections built into Directive 94/46/EC. The US State Department kept a list of companies agreeing to the measures; each firm was responsible for self-regulating and keeping records of their actions. Alternatively, they could "self-certify" by registration with national EU data protection agencies (DPAs), and allow compliance to be managed on the EU-side, rather than the loose oversight by US authorities. Nearly 4000 US firms signed up to participate in Safe Harbour by the time the agreement had ended, including Apple, Coca-Cola, Facebook, Ford, Twitter, and Yahoo. Safe Harbour was later replaced with the Privacy Shield Framework, which will be discussed more shortly.

Unfortunately, Safe Harbour and its provisions were not stringent enough and levels of compliance were questionable to many in Europe, including to the EU states' data protection agencies (DPAs) in the frontline of oversight. In 2010, a working committee comprised of 16 regional German DPAs ("Dusseldorfer Kreis") issued a joint statement to German data exporters indicating a lack of faith in the US protections in place. Basically, this called into question the validity of any form of "self-certification." They recommended a series of quality measures whereby German data exporters could attempt to verify the digital protection practices of US companies. Their complaint about questionable American firms' compliance was matched with concerns raised by Working Party 29 in the "Opinion on Cloud Computing" released in 2012.

Matters came to a head in June of 2013, when the news outlets, The Guardian and The Washington Post, revealed a clandestine surveillance program of the US government, known as PRISM, information about which was tied to leaked US security info released by Edward Snowden. Using PRISM, EU citizens' digitized data on servers held by Microsoft, Google, Facebook, or any other company could be harvested for use by the National Security Agency (NSA) in the United States. The EU Parliament requested that the Commission order an investigation into the ways in which EU citizens' data could be compromised via PRISM and other US security practices. Suddenly the two realms—security and trade—were inexorably linked, and not necessarily in a peaceful way.

The Commission conducted an audit of US practices in 2013 which found significant violations. The alleged violations regarding the US PRISM program were eventually taken to the Court of Justice, which found Safe Harbour invalid as a protection tool in 2015. In 2016, the GDPR replaced Directive 95, and the EU-Privacy Shield replaced Safe Harbour. Both policies represented larger efforts to solidify the expanded DHR protections. The significance of this process was particularly telling as a method of change in regards to human rights norm evolution between the EU and United States. The developments of a more aggressive stance by the EU in the 2010s offer an example of the EU as norm exporter, by way of using a social relationship. Responding to violations by actors in the United States, and directly pushing for additional digital human rights provisions by US firms and by the US government, the EU made it clear that the expectations on DHR provisions for EU citizens applied to a close trade and security ally. I now turn to the role of the Court of Justice of the European Union (CJEU) as a digital human rights norm enforcer.

Proactive EU Institutions: CJEU and EDPS as Norm Enforcers

Previously known as the EU Court of Justice (ECJ), the CJEU creation in 1973 set a "new legal order" for the community, premised on the rule of law, democratic justice, and universal human rights in a way that strengthened the narrative for liberal values, and supported it with a judicial system. The values imbedded in the EU membership criteria were now directly enforceable, with a more objective adjudication process. When states in eastern and central Europe expressed interest in joining the Union, they faced meeting the criteria formalized in the Copenhagen conditions and therefore enforceable as a part of the *acquis communautaire*. In other words, the behaviors linked to identity-based liberal democracy were bound into EU hard law. Proof of formal, identity-based values is found in the wording of Article 6(3) of the Treaty of Amsterdam, and the Millennium Declaration of 1999, both of which emphasize equality, diversity, and member states' identities.[26] Accumulatively, there is a vast body of EU law which substantiates identity-based human rights provisions for EU member states. Creating such laws implicitly gave the EU judicial system the authority to enforce liberal and human rights values tied to digital data.

[26] Laffan (2004).

As such, the CJEU took on an increasing number of cases which required the use of international and comparative law to determine rulings based on extraterritoriality of human rights broadly.[27] This included cases with infringements upon DHR. Extraterritoriality extends jurisdiction beyond traditional state borders. The Court cases taken and rulings made reflected a reliance upon the Charter of Fundamental Human Rights, as binding within the Lisbon Treaty. Actions by the CJEU were indicative of the power of EU institutions post-agenda setting, as a powerful enforcer and indeed expander of the scope of authority to the extent that compliance can be "beyond governments' original intentions when delegating supervisory competences."[28] For the European Union, extraterritoriality of DHR meant exporting these rights beyond national borders of individual member states, and even beyond the collective borders of the Schengen Zone, to the furthest reaches of the international system in which EU citizens' data can be transported. In 2011, an independent panel of international experts in law and human rights found that since Maastricht became effective in 1993, the EU had shown itself willing to apply EU law to outside actors across multiple issue areas, including but not limited to social and cultural rights. In Principal 3 of their Joint Commentary to the Maastricht Principles reads,

> …states may have …extraterritorial obligations arise when a state exercises control, power, or authority over people or situations located outside its sovereign territory in a way that could have an impact on the enjoyment of human rights by those people or in such situations. All states are bound to these obligations in respect to human rights.[29]

In fact, Maastricht, the founding document of the modern European Union, essentially set states' responsibilities toward human rights to go so far as to **oblige** EU member states to respect and extend human rights protections "… both within their territories and extraterritorially."[30]

As a case example of CJEU willingness to appropriate DHR beyond EU borders, we can once again look at the EU-US relationship. The context for replacing Safe Harbour was tied to the institutional oversight

[27] de Búrca (2011).

[28] Tallberg (2000, p. 104).

[29] De Schutter et al. (2012, p. 1090).

[30] De Schutter et al. (2012, p. 1090).

power the court had over digital human rights. Directive 95/46/EC set the initial legal parameters for these rights, and set up Working Party 29 as a permanent oversight committee with the power to monitor member states compliance, non-member states behaviors, and the overall landscape of technological innovation that would impact data use. In addition, in 2001, after feedback from WP 29, and the Economic and Social Committee, Parliament and the Council passed a new binding law, Regulation (EC) No. 45/2001, that established an "independent supervisory body responsible for monitoring the application of such Community acts.." as relates to personal data protection and free movement of data.[31] The new EU supervisory authority, known as the European Data Protection Supervisor (EDPS) would work in tandem with WP 29, the national data protection authorities (DPAs), and the CJEU to insure that digital human rights were afforded to EU citizens over their digitized data. The EDPS was granted both supervisory and enforcement powers, based upon the various mandates issued to it by Parliament, the Council, and the Commission. From 2004–2018, the EDPS issued over 1,500 case opinions on data practices.[32] Use of coercion via means of legal enforcement can be a powerful tool to promote social change within the international system.[33] Together, the WP 29, the EDPS, and the EU judicial system enforced the norm of digital human rights, not only inside the EU system, but most importantly, outside it.

Punitive Actions: Case Evidence of Institutional Norm Enforcement

From 2000–2015, the CJEU reached 31 case decisions, eight general court decisions, and gave two civil service tribunal rulings related to data protection, providing evidence of the seriousness with which the EU institutions take the norm of DHR.[34] The earliest investigations began in 2001; infringement charges hinged on violations of Direction 94/46/EC, Directive 2002/58, Directive 2006/24, the EU Charter of Fundamental Rights (CFR), and Regulations 45/2001 and 1049/2001. Litigants included member states (Luxembourg, Ireland,

[31] Parliament 2000.

[32] https://edps.europa.eu/data-protection/our-role-supervisor/register_en.

[33] Risse et al. (2013, p. 13).

[34] Laudati (2016).

Germany, Austria, Hungary, Netherlands), non-EU states (US), and non-state actors—individuals (Lindquist, Huber, Schecke), corporations (Promusicae, Satakunnan, Tele2, Bavarian Lager, SABAM, Bonnier, Google), some non-governmental entities (Digital Rights Ireland), and even other EU institutions (European Central Bank, European Parliament).[35] The variety of alleged data mismanagement actions included failure to implement EU data protections within national laws, publicizing personal and digitized data, an inability or lack of willingness to secure digitized data, incorrect or blocking the release of data when permitted, and transfer of data despite known poor protections at the destination site. Examining each of these cases in turn is beyond the scope of this book, but focusing on a key case is very useful to understand the critical junctures in time when actions by EU institutions such as the CJEU revealed a clear intent to strongly support DHR, even to the point of taking consistent and strong legal action. Such is the example of Schrems v. Ireland and its impact upon the replacement to the Safe Harbour agreement, known as Privacy Shield.

Two things occurred which drew EU attention toward the need for additional legal action. First, WP 29 and the German regional DPAs raised fundamental concerns regarding the questionable level of protections for EU citizens' data when used by American firms. The EU Commission issued two official statements in 2013, calling for an extensive review of Safe Harbour.[36] The EU-US Privacy Contact Group and the EU-US Working Group conducted the investigation, the results of which were referenced by the Commission in a list of thirteen recommendations on how to strengthen the implementation of Safe Harbour. Carrying out the suggested changes was premised in a belief that the existing agreement could remain intact, albeit with revisions, given in a formal Commission Decision known as 2000/520.[37] However, this was not the end of the matter.

[35] This list is not comprehensive, but a sample of the cases taken from 2000–2015. See Laudati (2016) and the CJEU website for information on additional cases.

[36] See COM (2013) 846 final and COM (2013) 847 final, of 27 November 2013.

[37] See C (2016) 4176, 12 July 2016.

Schrems I Ruling

Second and perhaps of most importance, was the legal case brought by an Austrian data activist, Maximillian Schrems, against Facebook Ireland, the results of which altered the plan of simply revising the Safe Harbour principles.[38] As a college student, Schrems had requested a copy from Facebook Ireland of the data collected about him while using his personal account. He was shocked to discover over 1200 pages of content, recording everything from simple likes, to every message he'd ever sent. He subsequently placed a complaint of data privacy loss with the Irish Data Protection Commissioner (DPC), asking Irish authorities to block this data transfer to the US as a violation of EU data legislation. The Irish DPC declined to investigate, citing EU Commission Decision 2000/520 as providing proof of adequate protections to EU citizens' data when moved to America. Schrems challenged this decision in the Irish High Court, and asked the CJEU to take up the investigation.[39] The CJEU agreed; their subsequent ruling pushed the scope and responsibility over DHR provision further than it had gone before, stating that the Commission,

> ….may adopt a decision stating that a third country ensures an adequate level of protection. This decision is binding on the Member States and all their organs.[40]

The Court took the matter further still, in terms of expanding their own authority of oversight, stating that,

> …it alone has the jurisdiction to review the compatibility of Union institutions acts, including Commission decisions. (paras. 60–61)[41]

At its core, the 6 October 2015, CJEU ruling C-362-14 found Safe Harbour as inadequate to provide protection to EU citizens' data in

[38] This was not the only CJEU ruling to invalidate data sharing between the United States and an Atlantic trade partner. In 2006, the court annulled the 2004 Passenger Name Record Agreement (PNA), and released an objection opinion against a similar policy, the EU-Canada PNR Agreement, in 2017.

[39] Schrems was joined by Digital Rights Ireland as a joint litigant in the 2015 case.

[40] EDPS (2016).

[41] See COM C-362-14.

America, as measured by the standards of Directive 95. Commission Decision 2000/520 no longer stood as legal precedent, effectively killing the Safe Harbour Agreement, and threatening data transfers outside the EU.

In the 2015 Schrems I case, the CJEU found fault with the lack of equivalent data privacy and data protection measures in the United States. It also cited a lack of judicial outlets for citizens seeking legal options to make complaints about the insufficiencies.[42] EU officials and the US Department of Commerce went back to the drawing board, determined to design a new, clearer, and more stringent data sharing agreement which would meet the basic standards of digital human rights. The EU-US and Swiss-US Privacy Shield Frameworks went into effect upon adoption by the EU Commission on 12 July 2016. The goal of the new agreements remained, "to facilitate trade and commerce between the United States and the European Union."[43] American users of EU citizens' data were to voluntarily self-certify with the US Department of Commerce, declaring a commitment to the principles of data privacy protections within the agreements. The US Federal Trade Commission held responsibility to teach compliance efforts. Firms' commitments to the US oversight process were void if the firm alternatively chose to submit to compliance oversight with the European data protection authorities (DPAs).

Schrems II Ruling

Schrems responded to the October ruling and invalidation of the Safe Harbour agreement with a new case, filed on 1 December 2015. Recall the timing of the new case as relates to other EU efforts to increase the clarity and scope of digital human rights within EU law. Directive 95 had grown increasingly obsolete, and would be replaced in 2016 with a more specific and expanded scope of protections in the GDPR. In the new CJEU case, Schrems alleged that the element left intact from the Safe Harbour ruling—that of SCCs—could not ensure data privacy protection for EU citizens. The 2015 Schrems I case had left an opening for firms currently using EU data to continue to import such data via the standard contractual clauses (SCCs) issued by the Commission. SCCs required national DPAs to allow export of EU citizens' if data importers had previously met data security measures, protected sensitive data, erased

[42] Monteleone and Puccio (2017).

[43] https://www.privacyshield.gov/article?id=OVERVIEW.

or corrected personal data upon request, and gave notification of any requests for access by law enforcement agents in third-party states. The Schrems II case proposed that SCCs were defective in that US surveillance programs could violate data privacy, without any judicial recourse available to EU data subjects. On 16 July 2020, the CJEU ruled that the Commissions Privacy Shield Agreement did indeed violate EU law. A SCC Decision made by the Commission in 2010, had allowed data mobility to third-party states, but protections were not "essentially equivalent," particularly in the case of data transfers to the United States.[44] The ruling negated the transfer power granted under Privacy Shield, citing a failure to provide the core digital human rights guaranteed within the new GDPR and the EU Charter of Fundamental Human Rights. US businesses and national security interests would now be required to adhere fully to the GDPR, or face sanctions by EU authorities. Violators could be fined up to 4% of global volume, or up to €20 million.

Non-State Targets: EU as Norm Enforcer to the Private Sector

While international law is typically designed to curb the behavior of states, other actors are also subject to aspects of hard and even soft law. Non-state actors now face codes of conduct imposed by intergovernmental organizations (IGOs) and states. The EU's willingness to adopt extraterritoriality measures when it comes to human rights enforcement is part of a larger set of principles within international organizations to set global ethics around the human rights behaviors of non-state actors.[45] The EU has been joined its efforts to promote human rights within a variety of settings by the most powerful IO on the planet to date, the United Nations. On 16 June 2011, the UN Human Rights Council released the "Guiding Principles on Business and Human Rights: Implementing the United Nations 'Protect, Respect, and Remedy' Framework" designed by Professor John Ruggie and his team of human rights experts.[46] Individuals, MNCs, and domestic firms are held to task for human rights provisions in multiple countries and across multiple production sites and

[44] Monteleone and Puccio (2017).

[45] Bernaz (2013).

[46] Bernaz (2013).

along supply chains from start to finish.[47] Punishment comes during shareholder meetings, in national courts, with media attention by naming-and-shaming NGOs, and of course, in EU courts and by EU institutions. As Bernaz argues, "corporate accountability" can be very loosely defined, and exists along a continuum of the degree of both provision and disciplinary action for failure to provide. Typically, individual states are the actors obliged to "prevent and punish corporate human rights violations…"[48] As with other types of human rights, digital human rights offenders now face extensive and stronger reporting requirements; failure to provide and failure to document reap some very negative punishments. States are obliged to protect people living in their jurisdictions, and can "adopt measures against organizations or corporate entities which commit such acts… would constitute a violation by the State of its international obligations."[49]

EU institutions have a proven track record of holding non-state actors accountable for DHR provision, using EU legal framework. Arguably, less is known about maintaining state control of data, or giving domestic ICT firms a competitive advantage as among the occasional side effects of applying EU data legislation to non-state actors. Regardless of the side benefits, forcing non-state actors, both within and without the EU, to provide and protect DHR is ample evidence of the presence of the new norm and the firm commitment by the EU to uphold and diffuse the norm in the international system. I propose that there are two ways the EU does this: taking non-state actors to task and enforcing the norm, under Directive 95 and the GDPR. First, these laws allow EU member states and institutions to "name and shame" violators within a very large, globally public spotlight, via court cases or public statements of accusation.[50] Second, it also allows the EU to administer pain to the offending actor(s) via financial and/or legal sanctions. Let's look at some sample cases which substantiate the norm enforcement as applied to non-state actors using these two actions.

[47] Hyde (2011).

[48] Bernaz (2013, p. 503).

[49] De Schutter (2004, p. 6).

[50] Hafner-Burton (2008).

Google Spain SL v APED & Mario Costeja Gonzalez

In 2010, Mario Costeja González filed suit against Google Spain for failure to erase personal financial information related to a prior news notice about attempts to recover funds on a debt he owed for social security overpayments. At stake was whether search engines such as Google were subject to jurisdictional provisions of DHR at all, if search engines were responsible only if the engine held a subsidiary in an EU member state (or not), and whether data subjects had the "right to be forgotten." The CJEU accepted the case and ruled in favor of González. Search engines could be categorized as "data controllers" involved in the "processing of personal data." Furthermore, as Google had a subsidiary in Spain, it operated as a business within the EU, and became legally responsible to the EU Directives and other data legislation. Lastly, the "right to be forgotten" was a real and recognizable component of digital human rights, as given in Article 12 (b) of Directive 95, which granted data subjects the right to "rectification, erasure or blocking of data the processing of which does not comply with the provisions of [the] Directive." Article 6 indicated that data must be held "no longer than necessary."[51] Google was effectively "named and shamed" and subsequently ordered to remove González's outdated personal information.

GDPR Fines

The terms of the GDPR require specific ways to punish those who violate rights indicated within the Regulation. Two tiers of fines exist for violations. Lesser fines against controlling and processing and certification of monitoring include €10 million, or 2% of the firm's worldwide annual revenue from the most recent year. Higher fines of €20 million, or 4% of the firm's worldwide annual revenue result from violations on basic data processing, consent procedures, and transfers to third-party states. Several non-state actors have been fined for data handling violations by either national DPAs, or have been sanctioned by the EDPB/EDPS since the GDPR went into effect in 2018. I will highlight the top three cases, in terms of financial sanctions, as of January 2021.[52] The French DPA, the

[51] See Directive 95/46/EC.

[52] See https://www.enforcementtracker.com for further fines.

CNIL (*Commission nationale de l'informatique et des libertés*), levied the largest fine as of this publication; €50 million, against Google. Google was found guilty of lawless processing and violating the principles of processing with a failure to provide information on where personal data was and was not harvested from the data subject. The German Hamburg regional DPA, or BfDI (Der Bundesbeauftragte für den Datenschutz und die Informationsfreiheit) issued a €35,3 million fine against H& M after a data network drive was invertedly made open to anyone in the company, exposing employees' sensitive personal information. Last in the recent top three, the Italian DPA "Garante" authorities (Garante per la protezione dei dati personali) fined an Italian telecom firm, TIM, over €27,8 million for over 150 violations. Millions of their customers faced hyper-marketing campaigns based on data breaches and violations of GDPR prohibitions against personal information acquisition and use. Altogether, the willingness to financially fine MNCs, combined with the various CJEU court cases substantiate the claim that the EU shows a complete willingness to enforce the provision of global digital human rights against a variety of offenders.

Last Thoughts

This chapter has shown ample evidence of the EU as a global norm enforcer. This role is a present and active role taken by the institution, as a part of a desire to maintain its intentional identity and international reputation as a human rights provider and protector. Using this cultivated identity, the EU has and continues to utilize international relationships and proactive institutions to socialize and coerce other states and non-state actors to accept and diffuse the norm of digital human rights (DHR). Trade relationship agreements, court rulings, and fines give evidence of the serious commitment the EU has made to DHR. Next, in Chapter 9, I conclude the book by looking at the anticipated changes brought by today's technology, as well as the increasing willingness of non-democracies such as China, to push back against digital human rights, and instead to set themselves as the creator of a counter-narrative to global DHR.

Bibliography

Börzel, Tanja A., and Thomas Risse. 2004. *One Size Fits All! EU Policies for the Promotion of Human Rights, Democracy, and the Rule of Law*. Stanford, CA: Workshop on Democracy Promotion, Stanford University.

Balfour, Rosa. 2008. "Human Rights Promotion." In *The Search for a European Identity: Values, Policies and Legitimacy of the European Union*, edited by Furio Cerutti and Sonia Lucarelli, 159–175. Abingdon, OX, UK: Routledge.

Barnett, Michael N., and Martha Finnemore. 1999. "The Politics, Power, and Pathologies of International Organizations." *International Organization* 53 (4): 699–732.

Bernaz, Nadia. 2013. "Enhancing Corporate Accountability for Human Rights Violations: Is Extraterritoriality the Magic Potion?" *Journal of Business Ethics* 117 (3): 493–511.

Burghardt, Günter. 2015. "The EU/US Transatlantic Relationship - the Indispensible Partnership." In *Trade Policy Between Law, Diplomacy and Scholarship*, edited by Christoph Herrmann, Bruno Simma and Rudolf Streinz. Springer.

Cao, Xun, Brian Greenhill, and Aseem Prakash. 2012. "Where is the Tipping Point? Bilateral Trade and the Diffusion of Human Rights." *British Journal of Political Science* 43: 133–156.

Cooper, William H. 2009. *EU-US Economic Ties: Framework, Scope, and Magnitude*. CRS Report for Congress, Congressional Research Service.

de Búrca, Gráinne. 2011. "The Road Not Taken: The European Union as a Global Human Rights Actor." *The American Journal of International Law* 105 (4): 649–693.

De Schutter, Olivier. 2004. The Accountability of Multinationals for Human Rights Violations for European Law. Working Paper 01/04, Center for Human Rights and Global Justice, New York, NY.

De Schutter, Oliver, Asbjørn Eide, Ashfaq Khalfan, Marcos Orellana, Margot Salomon, and Ian Seiderman. 2012. "Commentary to the Maaschrict principles on extra territorial obligations of states in the area of economic, social, and cultural rights." *Human Rights Quarterly*. 34: 1084–1169.

European Commission. n.d. "Commission Directive 94/46/EC of 13 October 1994 Amending Directive 88/301/EEC and Directive 90/388/EEC in Particular with Regard to Satellite Communications."

European Commission. 1995. *Commission Directive 94/46/EC of 13 October 1994 amending Directive 88/301/EEC and Directive 90/388/EEC in Particular with Regard to Satellite Communications*. Brussels, BE: Official Journal of the European Communities.

European Commission. n.d. *Commission Implementing Decision (EU) 2016/1250 of 12 July 2016 Pursuant to Directive 95/46/EC of the European Parliament and of the Council on the Adequacy of the Protection Provided by the EU-U.S.*

Privacy Shield (Notified Under Document C(2016) 4176) (T. C/2016/4176). Brussels, BE: European Commission.

European Commission. 2013. *Communication from the Commission to the European Parliament and the Council on the Functioning of the Safe Harbour from the Perspective of EU Citizens and Companies Established in the EU.* COM (2013) 847 final. Brussels, BE: European Commission.

European Commission. 2013. *Communication from the Commission to the European Parliament and the Council: Rebuilding Trust in EU-US Data Flows.* COM (2013) 846 final. Brussels, BE: European Commission.

European Commission. 2005–2006. *Eurobarometer.* Public Opnion Survey. Brussels: European Union.

European Commission. 1973. "The Copenhagen Summit Conference Report." Brussels, BE.

European Data Protection Supervisor. 2016. *2016 Annual Report—The State of Privacy 2017: EDPS Provides a Mid-mandate Report.* Annual Report. Brussels, BE: European Union.

———. 2021. *Prior Checks Register.* Accessed March 30, 2021. https://edps.europa.eu/data-protection/our-role-supervisor/register_en.

European Parliament and of the Council. 2001. *Regulation (EC) No 45/2001 of the European Parliament and of the Council of 18 December 2000 on the Protection of Individuals with Regard to the Processing of Personal Data by the Community Institutions and Bodies and on the Free Movement of Such Data.* Brussels, BE: Official Journal of the European Communities.

Finnemore, Martha, and Kathryn Sikkink. 1998. "International Norm Dynamics and Political Change." *International Organization* 52 (4): 887–917.

Fuster, Gloria González. 2016. *The Emergence of Personal Data Protection as a Fundamental Right of the EU.* Springer.

———. n.d. *GDPR Enforcement Tracker* . Accessed 2021. https://www.enforcementtracker.com.

Grand Chamber. 2015. *Judge of the Court.* Case C-362/14 - Maximillian Schrems v. Data Protection Commissioner. Strasbourg, FR: Court of Justice of the European Union.

Hafner-Burton, Emilie M. 2008. "Sticks and Stones: Naming and Shaming the Human Rights Enforcement Problem." *International Organization* 62: 689–716.

Hermann, Christoph, Simma Bruno, and Rudolf Streinz. 2015. *Trade Policy between Law, Diplomacy and Scholarship.* Springer International.

Hopf, Ted. 1998. "The Promise of Constructivism in International Relations Theory." *International Security* 23 (1): 171–200.

Hyde, Susan D. 2011. "Catch Us If You Can: Election Monitoring and International Norm Diffusion." *American Journal of Political Science* 356–369.

International Trade Association. 2021. *Privacy Shield Framework*. Accessed March 28, 2021. https://www.privacyshield.gov/Program-Overview.
Keck, Margaret E., and Kathryn Sikkink. 1998. *Activists Beyond Borders: Advocacy Networks in Transnational Politics*. Ithaca, NY: Cornell University Press.
Laffan, Brigid. 2004. "The European Union and Its Institutions as 'Identity Builders'." In *Transnational Identities: Becoming European in the EU*, 75–96. Oxford, UK: Rowman & Littlefield.
Laudati, Laraine. 2016. *Summaries of EU Court Decisions Relating to Data Protection 2000–2015*. European Anti-Fraud Office.
Manners, Ian J., and Richard G. Whitman. 1998. "Towards Identifying the International Identity of the European Union: A Framework for Analysis of the EU's Network of Relationships." *Journal of European Integration* 21 (3): 231–249.
Manners, Ian. 2002. "Normative Power Europe: A Contradiction in Terms?" *Journal of Common Market Studies* 40 (2): 235–258.
Meyer, John W., John Boli, George M. Thomas, and Francisco O. Ramirez. 1997. "World Society and the Nation-State." *American Journal of Sociology* 103 (1): 144–181.
Monteleone, Shara, and Laura Puccio. 2017. *Privacy Shield: Advances and Shortcoings of the New EU-US Data Transfer Rules*. In-Depth Analysis, European Parliamentary Research Service.
Newman, Abraham L. 2008. *Protectors of Privacy: Regulating Personal Data in the Global Economy*. Ithaca, NY: Cornell University Press.
Office for Official Publications of the European Communities. 1997. *Treaty of Amsterdam*. Luxembourg: European Communities.
Riddervold, Marianne, and Akasemi Newsome. 2018. "Transatlantic Relations in Times of Uncertainty: Crises and EU-US Relations." *Journal of European Integration* 40 (5): 505–521.
Risse, Thomas, Stephen C. Ropp, and Kathryn Sikkink. 2013. *The Persisten Power of Human Rights: From Compliance to Commitment*. Cambridge: Cambridge Universit Press.
Sandholtz, Wayne, and Kendall Stiles. 2009. *International Noms and Cycles of Change*. Oxford: Oxford University Press.
Smith, Michael E. 2018. "Transatlantic Security Relations Since the European Security Strategy: What Role for the EU in Its Pursuit of Strategic Autonomy?" *Journal of European Integration* 40 (5): 605–620.
Tallberg, Jonas. 2000. "Supranational Influence in EU Enforcement: The ECJ and the Principle of State Liability." *Journal of European Public Policy* 7 (1): 104–121.
The United States Department of Justice. n.d. "Privacy Act of 1974." *The United States Department of Justice*. Accessed April 1, 2021. https://www.justice.gov/opcl/privacy-act-1974.

CHAPTER 9

The Future of Digital Human Rights

In this book, I've shown that human rights now include digital human rights (DHR), which are the extension of fundamental human rights protections for digital data tied to a person's identity and behavior in the physical or virtual realms. Digitized data is a multi-faceted tool, with enormous political and economic power. To the private sector, including ICT firms and data brokers, it's a commodity for profiteering.[1] To state security actors, it is a tool that provides a way to ensure public safety and protect national security interests. To human rights activists, including epistemic norm entrepreneurs, digitized data is inexorably connected to one's personal identity; it should be protected as a fundamental human right by all who generate, store, and use it. The human rights component of data legislation began at the national level in Europe, mainly tied to personal privacy. When the European Union explored regional data legislation, it not only found a point of policy convergence, it created a regime purely based on digital human rights. Let's take one more tour of the things learned in previous chapters.

[1] Zuboff (2015, 2019).

R. Dowd, *The Birth of Digital Human Rights*, Information Technology and Global Governance,
https://doi.org/10.1007/978-3-030-82969-8_9

Lessons from the Digital Human Rights in the European Union

The paradigmatic contribution made by realism, liberalism, and constructivism helps to explain the necessity of legislating data governance via regime creation in the European Union. As individual states computerized data, they faced pressure from three structural groups: the nascent ICT sector, security actors with surveillance needs, and human rights advocates seeking privacy protections during the automatic processing and storage of personal data. In addition to these groups with differing policy preferences, EU states experienced external pressures from the OECD and Council of Europe to harmonize their national policies, and facilitate transborder data mobility to support economic growth among member states.

When uncovering the origins of the norm of digital human rights, Sweden and Germany led the way, by setting early and firm policies on the protection of personal data. In Sweden, government transparency was preserved, as public authorities collected personal and digitized data with oversight from a newly created data protection authority. German officials honored fears of past oppressive government surveillance, and kept a balanced approach to personal data use. Even reluctant states such as the UK adopted data protections during this time, but incorporated digital human rights out of the government's desire to keep their own ICT firms globally competitive through guarantees of data protections. By the end of the 1980s, though motives and measures differed by states, most EU members had passed some form of national data legislation.

Early attempts at opening the EU agenda to data protection legislation focused on regional policy convergence for the purposes of data mobility. With the passing of Directive 95/46/EC, the EU established a comprehensive and stringent digital human rights regime at the international level. Importantly, the Directive set up Working Party 29 (WP 29) as a key advisory body, staffed solely by legal and human rights professionals. WP 29 went on to have a profound influence in expanding the scope of DHR throughout the 1990s and early 2000s. Committee members were epistemic community members, valued for their technical expertise. However, while monitoring data practices and legislation compliance, they also promoted an expanded breadth of digital human rights. Due to their suggestions, EU data legislation grew exponentially, and Directive 95 was replaced in 2016 with the extremely rigorous General Data Protection Regulation (GDPR).

The GDPR addresses ambiguities raised between EU and US as to the content, range, and strength of digital human rights required by outside actors, and offers proof as to the transformation of the EU into a global DHR norm exporter. EU institutions such as the Commission and the Court of Justice in the European Union (CJEU) have willingly held states, firms, and individuals accountable to the standards of Directive 95 and now the GDPR. Public shaming and legal cases yield costs, such as fines and data movement restrictions against data protection violators.

We've learned a lot about past and present digital human rights provision in the European Union. What implications do these findings have for the future of digital human rights in the EU, and indeed, across the international system of states?

In fact, we now know that data governance is a two-level game, and evolved from a national concern into a regional, and potentially, global regime for digital human rights. Understanding this highly interactive process sheds light on other policy-making areas with similar concerns to the DHR environment. Today's private sector and civil societies have become dependent upon the internet and the utilization of internet-based technology. Thanks to swiftly changing technological advances and the involvement of non-state actors, both non-criminal and criminal, governments are faced with complex governance decisions. As seen with the evolution of data policy, security factors, human rights concerns, and economic growth generates diverse policy pressures upon national governments, as well as regional and international organizations. These three structural interests matter to policy-making in multiple areas involving technology use. For now, let's focus on the ongoing interaction between security and human rights.

Government Obligations to Social Order

The social contract obliges a government to ensure a secure and peaceful society, as a primary obligation. Governments and politicians that allow domestic or international actors to infringe upon public security risk losing public trust. Two emerging areas across multiple countries in recent years threaten security in heightened ways: immigration flows and international terrorism. When needed, governments show themselves quite willing to incorporate new means of technology to ensure border controls and reduce terrorism risks.

A few examples from the United States and Europe serve to explain the extent to which digitized data is now essential to state security. In his examination of US border practices, Matt Longo points out that in a post 9/11 world, the idea of border control is not so much one of questioning the idea of borders, but where and how to place them to protect a society. Personal, digitized data is a crucial component of the politics of identification, during which border-protecting officials classify, filter, and identity the riskiest persons seeking entrance into a state. Automated biometric systems and biographic data scrape meta-data collections, but all of this data utility hinges on the ability of various data holders to share their content with one another.[2] Then President François Hollande admitted in 2013, that French authorities triangulate "… human intelligence (HUMINT), electronic intelligence (ELINT), and imagery intelligence (IMINT), which are complementary and indivisible," because, "The full value of intelligence is derived from combining the data gathered from these three channels."[3] As the Edward Snowden leaks reveal, politicians politicize security risks to justify more aggressive uses of surveillance techniques by law enforcement and national security officials. Enormous data caches are deemed as "relevant" to national security, and thereby acceptable to be collected under new more aggressive collection laws, such as the US Patriot Act.[4]

Human Rights and Normative Policymaking: How Many Voices Are Heard?

In addition to expectations to maintain social order, democracies typically imbed human rights into written constitutions, meaning violators are legally punishable by the judicial system. As you've learned, the first mover European states based initial data legislation upon the foundations of human rights, such as the personal integrity and human dignity concepts within the constitutions of Sweden and Germany. The EU Commission opened the legislative agenda to supranational data protection legislation

[2] See Longo (2018, pp. 140–149).

[3] Hollande (2013, p. 68).

[4] McGowan (2014).

for economic reasons, to allow for cross-border data mobility. However, early EU data laws also established personal data privacy as the first of many digital human rights written into the *acquis communautaire*. The process has been long, and quite complicated, but EU citizens enjoy the largest and most complete measure of digital human rights in the world today, when compared against their peers in any other region of the world. Yet even the best of legislation often includes unintended consequences.

Epistemic Advisors and Democratic Deficit

Politicians don't work alone when designing legislation in complex arenas, such as with technology issues. Within the EU, lawmakers rely heavily upon epistemic professionals as information providers over technology governance. These technical advisors can have normative agendas of their own, and in fact evidence from Working Party 29 (WP 29) shows that epistemic actors do act as norm entrepreneurs over digital human rights. This has both positive and negative implications. In the positive sense, ethical concerns about potential human rights violations should be heard when raised by these individuals, due to their recognized levels of topical expertise. However, the negative possibilities include the disproportionately high levels of influence epistemic actors might have, purely based on their professional status and network connections. When policy advisement and oversight is a largely hidden process with only a few voices involved, the opinions of these voices are amplified; they become very powerful.

Keeping a closed policy-discussion and design space will only exacerbate the long-standing criticism about a lack of voice and connection between institutions in Brussels and the citizens in EU states. First, due to the explosive and expanded growth of bureaucracy in the EU, EU citizens complain of a democratic deficit. Heavy use of insular advisory bodies like WP 29 provide fuel to the fire for accusations of the disconnect between people and unelected officials. The EU must work to improve multistakeholder participation and include input by firms and members of civil society to truly reduce any democratic deficit in matters of digitized data policies and technology governance. By disbanding WP 29, and establishing the European Data Protection Supervisor (EDPS), hopefully, more accountability and accessibility will result. The makeup of the EDPS includes not only attorneys, but also IT professionals, offering some improvement on variety of input, especially given the level of autonomy also granted to the agency and its staff. In spite of these improvements, the best planning cannot always prepare governments nor organizations for the challenges they will face.

Exogenous Shocks—Redefining Security Risks and Human Rights

Societies want public security and in Western states, digital human rights. Yet exogenous shocks—those originating from outside a particular industry or even from other countries—have changed the way governments treat national security and human rights, and thereby, the types of data and tech policies they've chosen. The threat landscape has changed to include internet and data-based crimes; the use of digitized personal data is needed to fight not only enemies of the state, but also enemies of the mass public. Let's look at these threats in order: attacks to government and private sector targets and public health threats.

Cyber-attacks by government and non-state actors are on the rise, with accompanying financial and human rights costs. The Center for Strategic & International Studies reports over 750 attacks on technology companies and government entities in countries across the world since 2006, only tabulating entries with financial costs above >$1million.[5] Regarding state-on-state attacks, Russian intelligence purportedly used a group known as Cozy Bear or Apt29 to attack US government agencies and steal vast quantities of government and personal data. Past state targets consist of the Departments of State, Treasury and Commerce, and even the White House.[6] Perpetrators access targets through servers and network management systems.

In addition to intelligence espionage, ransomware attacks that grab personal data have exploded, with new favorite victims being regional state and municipal-level governments and firms. The city of Atlanta spent $2.7 million in 2019 restoring computer networks systems.[7] Lest one think governments are the only targets, think again. High profile corporate victims include the hacking of Sony employees' emails (2014), the

[5] CSIS (2021).

[6] Nakashima and Timberg (2020).

[7] Deere (2019).

credit card data of Home Depot's customers (2014), 143 million individuals' credit histories stolen from the credit-monitoring agency Equifax (2017), data files from multiple Ukrainian banks and energy companies (2018), and a cache of highly sensitive personal insurance information taken from the Israeli company Shirbit (2020).[8] Undoubtedly, personal, digitized data is the new money, to be stolen or used by those with criminal and terrorist intent. Governments and international organizations are adjusting accordingly, to be much more proactive to securitize data.

Yet, data is not just an identity-based or intellectual commodity to protected from theft. Whether a democracy or authoritarian regime, states turn to data as a way to protect populations from previously unknown threats to public safety and welfare. Few could have predicted the incredible impact to use of technology, the internet, and smart phones caused by the Covid-19 pandemic which began in late 2019. During the global pandemic, governments increased data tracking apps to trace the spread of the virus, monitor mandatory quarantines of infected or exposed persons, and record recovery and vaccination rates, causing inquiries into human rights violations in data use. States such as South Korea utilized digital trackers to warn people of exposure to the virus, while the EU issued Digital Green Certificates for citizens and asked for non-citizens to verify vaccinations, in order to free up the movement of people and tourism when exiting the peak of the pandemic.[9] In the United States, Republican lawmakers fought the Biden administration's suggestion of federal adoption of similar measures.[10] Democratic Representative Chriss Rabb worried over personal health data safety, citing, "There's a role for using technology and other means to confirm people's statuses….But we do have concerns around privacy, surveillance and inequitable access."[11]

The Covid-19 crisis exposed the willingness of states, both democratic and non-democratic, to participate in mass digital data collection in the name of "public health." Whether the tracking apps will be de-activated and personal data caches deleted post pandemic remains to be seen. In other words, the provision of DHR may be conditional. Whereas past

[8] CSIS (2021).

[9] Europa (2021) and Kuhn (2020).

[10] Scolford (2021).

[11] Scolford (2021).

security threats were traditional enemies or terrorists, bio-threats give state actors a new reason to collect personal, digitized data.

Like all human rights provisions, a tension remains between the state's role as protector of human rights, and the state's role in protecting the mass public. When fulfilling the latter role requires the state to violate the former role, it will do so.

Outside States' and Digital Human Rights

As we've seen throughout the book, multiple efforts have been made at the international level to generate international instruments for data protection, including the Council of Europe's Convention 108 and the OECD's Guidelines. However, though it began focused on economic growth, the EU regime for digital human rights goes far and beyond the levels of data privacy and protection built into other international efforts. Today, there are stark differences in states' approaches to control over personal, digitized data. The default relationship is often to begin with data commodification, due to the enormous economic contributions gleaned from the presence of ICT industries in the global marketplace. Since the United States, China, and the European Union are the largest producers and participants in the global economy, the future of digital human rights, and indeed human rights related to various forms of computerized and internet-utility technologies, will likely depend on the legal stances taken by these global leaders. Based on the past, the most likely causes of future areas of digital human rights policy diversity include US domestic polarity, China's goals of being the global economic powerhouse, and the commitment the EU has to utilize its own marketplace and institutions to force outside actors to align with EU data legislation. Underneath it all, data brokers are showing a willingness to create a new narrative on safety and privacy controls online. Let's finish up by examining these areas of digitized data governance.

The United States

The decentralized design of the US political system, means that regional states can legislate individual personal data practices and related technology. In the absence of a comprehensive federal law providing human rights protections for data use, individual US states are making their own laws. These laws have and will continue to have global effects. Two states in particular stand out for innovative data laws.

The first case in point is that of the California Consumer Privacy Act (CCPA) of 2018, which embodies some of the same digital human rights as the GDPR. California's "data consumers" are now guaranteed transparency on what data is collected about them, as well as have the rights to be forgotten and to decline data collection altogether. All for-profit firms which amass >$25 million in annual revenue, sell data for profit, and collect data on >50,000 must comply. Estimates call for impact to upwards of 500,000 US businesses.[12] Violators can be punished with fines, and data subjects can file law suits against data controllers.[13] Full data on the effect of the CCPA has yet to be calculated, as it recently came into effect on January 1, 2020.[14] The updated version—CCPA 2.0—in reality, the California Privacy Rights Act of 2020 (CPRA), vastly expands the types of data mandated for protections and protects sensitive personal information such as driver's license numbers, financial account data, as well as ethnicity, religious beliefs, and email/text content.[15]

Other US states are following California's example. On March 2, 2021, Virginia passed the Virginia Consumer Data Protection Act (VCDPA), effective January, 2023. The Virginia law borrows much from the GDPR.[16] It identifies "data controllers," and requires consent of data subjects from companies collecting and/or processing sensitive data such as race, religious beliefs, sexual orientation, and even biometric data, which can be used to identify someone. Like the GDPR, data controllers must offer opt-out options. Unlike the CCPA, private individuals cannot report violations; only the Virginia State Attorney can begin legal proceedings against accused violators. As I write this chapter, New York, Washington, and Florida are considering laws that adopt measures similar to the California and Virginia laws. It seems that if the US federal government won't enact national digital human rights, then individual US states will. The American piecemeal approach will produce international results.

[12] IAPP (2018).

[13] Binnig and Comstock (2019).

[14] The law was updated in 2021, with new changes applicable in 2023.

[15] *The National Law Review* (2020).

[16] *The National Law Review* (2021).

The lack of a national, comprehensive piece of data legislation has direct implications for American-European trade and security relationships. Ongoing data exchanges will likely be conditional upon the majority party in power. Democrats have long supported civil rights and liberties as a mainstay of their party agenda, while Republicans prefer a pro-business, pro-traditional family stance. These keen differences are seen at the policy approaches to control data collection and social media practices taken by Democrats vs. Republicans.

Democrats want less freedom, more government restrictions upon data brokers and media conglomerates. Progressives within the Democratic party are taking aim at anti-monopoly grievances against many of the major American data brokers, threatening to break apart their conglomerate control over the internet and social media spaces. By example, in her 2019 presidential campaign bid, Senator Elizabeth Warren made it a part of her proposed policy platform to target Amazon, Facebook, and Google as overly large tech giants, and warned that their continued dominance of the public space is an existential threat to,

> our economy, our society, and our democracy. They've bulldozed competition, used our private information for profit, and tilted the playing field against everyone else. And in the process, they have hurt small businesses and stifled innovation.[17]

Warren lost her presidential bid, but the Democrats still won the White House with Joe Biden's candidacy. If Democrats gain a unified government—controlling the presidency and both houses of Congress, they may likely push through legislation to accomplish disaggregation of many media firms.

Republicans want less content manipulation and fewer restrictions on innovation and data profiteering. If, on the other hand, a Republican candidate wins future presidential elections, or the executive and legislative branches remain divided between the control of the two parties, this will reduce the likelihood of either an anti-monopoly legislative effort of or an attempt at national digital human rights. It's likely we will continue to see a state-by-state approach unless a major data breach occurs which creates such painful impact to the mass population that they finally demand national digital human rights legislation.

[17] Warren (2019).

Congress has questioned the executives of large tech firms multiple times to explain following the Cambridge Analytica publicity, the 2016 presidential election DNC email fiasco, and the 2021 US capital riot.[18] Congressional representatives dislike the monopolization of internet space and distrust the extent and type of content filtration controls held by decision-makers at Facebook, Twitter, and Google. Either way, both major parties are becoming more skeptical of the self-policing done on content by the social media platforms and search engines. In a 2018 Senate hearing with Facebook's Mark Zuckerberg. Republican Senator John Thune accused Facebook of having ineffective permission seeking parameters, if users' personal data can be farmed out to third-party actors, with identity-based info freely available for sale on the Dark Web.

> One reason that so many people are worried about this incident is what it says about how Facebook works. The idea that for every person who decided to try an app, information about nearly 300 other people was scraped from your service is, to put it mildly, disturbing.
>
> And the fact that those 87 million people may have technically consented to making their data available doesn't make those people feel any better.
>
> The recent revelation that malicious actors were able to utilize Facebook's default privacy settings to match email addresses and phone numbers found on the so-called Dark Web to public Facebook profiles potentially affecting all Facebook users only adds fuel to the fire.
>
> What binds these two incidents is that they don't appear to be caused by the kind of negligence that allows typical data breaches to happen. Instead they both appear to be the result of people exploiting the very tools that you created to manipulate users' information.[19]

On January 6, 2021, the US Congress was attacked by rioters who believed misinformation on the supposed stealing of the presidential election away from incumbent Donald Trump. Democrat Representative Jan Schakowsky noted a bipartisan awareness that existing policies on freedom of speech are faulty, and the various information controls set by online platforms aren't helping matters.

[18] Bond (2021) and *Washington Post* (2018).

[19] *Washington Post* (2018).

> There is a bipartisan agreement that the status quo is just not working…Big tech has failed to respond to these grave challenges time and time again.[20]

While Congress struggles over how to regulate online media, the firms themselves remain divided on which policies they would prefer governments to pass. Zuckerburg wanted Congress to reform Section 230 of the Communications Decency Act, to allow Facebook and others to remove offensive or violent content, as well as material spreading misinformation, and not be held legally liable for content that remains online.

> Sometimes the right thing to do from a safety or security perspective isn't the best for privacy or free expression, so we have to choose what we believe is best for our community and for the world…

As this book is being written, the United State has yet to establish any clear mandates for online content, misinformation removal, or personal digitized data protections when content is being removed for potentially violating the offensive or barred content policies of online media companies.

China

The state of China collects more personal data—through its collective social management governance approach—on a larger population group than any other state or international organization. Data surveillance is primarily motivated by national security and social control measures, not human rights. The social credit score mechanism is but one use for collection of personal behavior online and in person which generates and compares the digitized data of the entire Chinese population. Examining the credit score system is beyond the goal of this chapter.[21] Returning to data legislation specifically, compared to the EU and United States, China presents a nearly opposite approach to data protection in general, with little to no evidence of a digital human rights regime in place. There are many reasons for this, but the primary differences lay in the authoritarian nature of its political system, founded on collective well-being, and

[20] Bond (2021).

[21] Liang et al. (2018).

the absent of individualistic human rights. Chinese laws, therefore, do not designate a space to "data subjects" found within EU legislation and some US laws. China's legal code does contain a right to privacy, based upon the right to dignity. Without basic democratic tenets, and no bill of rights within a judicially enforced constitution, the framework simply doesn't exist upon which to build digital human rights.

Though China has no single law dedicated to data protection, nevertheless, a "cumulative effect" is produced toward some data protections by combining the content of civil and criminal laws, and actions taken by the Ministry of Industry and Information (MIIT), the Standing Committee of its National People's Congress.[22] The latter agency—the MIIT—is the primary regulator of internet and telecom practices. Through a series of regulations passed since 2010, definitions have been set for personal data and legal principles laid out for collection limits, and data breach notifications. To date, such rules only apply to the business sector, and not to the government. In addition, there is no legal recourse for individuals in the event of data violations. Let's look at a few of the actions which have created some data governance outcomes.

A 2012 ruling by the Standing Committee of the National People's Congress (SC-NPC) produced the closest thing to a de facto piece of data protection legislation in China.[23] The reason for its impact is due to the fact that the regulations of other agencies, including the MIIT, are subjugated to the policies set by the SC-NPC. The SC-NPC Decision includes 12 articles in which individual privacy is acknowledged, and some protections seen in the GDPR, such as data processing security are provided for. Individuals may request information deletion, and they have the right to be forgotten (Articles 8,9). While the 2012 Decision may sound encouraging, in that it seems to mimic Western style protection, again, the state is exempt from its requirement. As the CCP relies upon data-driven population surveillance to maintain the desired levels of public control, the effects are better defined as data protection, and not digital human rights.

The legal provisions for data protection continue to be modified, with potential effects to other governments and non-Chinese firms doing business with China. The 2017 PRC Cybersecurity Law requires entities

[22] de Hert and Papakonstantinou (2015).

[23] de Hert and Papakonstantinou (2015) and Pernot-Leplay (2020).

operating as "Key Information Infrastructure Operators ('KIIOs')" to store any personal digitized data collected in China, inside Chinese territory on PRC servers.[24] While the law doesn't expressly forbid export to EU or US locations, it does require KIIOs to inform the data subject of the intended movement of personal data. Furthermore, as Chinese firms continue to expand into Western markets, they may extend their propensity to treat the data of non-Chinese citizens as a security commodity. Of concern to national security and economic actors, Chinese firms working in tandem with the CCP are suspected of using US and EU markets as a source for industrial espionage. Fears over personal data scraping technology and/ or industrial spyware being imbedded in Chinese tech exports have caused the United States to suspect the motives of the world's second largest mobile phone manufacturer Huawei, founded in 1987 by former military officer from the Chinese military, Zen Zhengfei. These fears have already produced foreign policy changes for outside states.

Then President, Donald Trump blocked federal agencies from use of Huawei 5G infrastructure technology, and banned US firms from utilizing their computer chips in 2018.[25] The United States worries that China's 2017 National Intelligence law will compel Huawei to "support, cooperate with and collaborate in national intelligence work."[26] Australia and New Zealand followed suit, while the UK has gone back and forth with commitments to allow Huawei to build out its expanded 5G network capabilities into rural areas. At stake is the level to which China can practice industrial and/or security espionage through the exported products and services of Chinese companies, and whether any of the big three—the United States, EU, or China, can export their philosophy on digital human rights, and their national data regulations through extraterritoriality. The fight over "geo-economic space" is heating up, and the fight over territory goes beyond the Global North.[27]China may yet attempt to shape the global narrative on data protection, seeking to redefine digital human rights using a non-Western perspective. This is one potential challenge that both the EU and the United States may face when

[24] Livingston and Greenleaf (2017).

[25] Maizland and Chatsky (2020).

[26] Bowler (2020).

[27] Cartwright (2020) and Schwartz (2019).

they promote their own data policy preferences within the international system. China's main goals on setting data legislation seem much less motivated by protections, and more about national security and economic gains.

China's neo-mercantilist economic strategies compel growth into newer markets receptive to its technological products and services. To accommodate this goal, China is increasing its trade presence in Latin American and Africa, both spaces that are traditionally important to European states with established trade networks based on colonial legacies. The burgeoning consumer base in developing states in Africa and Latin America offers a lucrative space for Chinese expansion, without the burdens of trade and human rights restrictions imposed by North American and European states.[28] Multiple researchers urge caution as Global South states consider to what extent they allow unfettered access to their markets. Trade dependency and security risks may go hand in hand.[29] Becoming reliant on Chinese technology which is tied to intelligence gathering powers of the CCP is a two-edged sword. As China succeeds in claiming trade space in these countries, it raises security risks for data surveillance within the tech-recipient states. It also threatens to undermine the trade superiority established by European firms in the former colonies of their home states.[30]

Predicting the Future

Even in European Union countries with a high priority for digital human rights, there is a keen awareness of preserving the profits to be made with digitized data, alongside the ever-present security-related uses. The EU has so far walked the tightrope of preserving the flow of ICT-based economic gains, while holding firms, social media giants, and other states accountable to respecting the digital human rights of EU citizens. This is particularly true where ICT industries are concerned. Numerous EU initiatives have been created to encourage economic success, with a focus on tech-based investments and support. Each of these programs had direct effects upon firms reliant upon digitized data in their business

[28] Vila Moreno (2020).

[29] Kaska et al. (2019).

[30] Guzman (2019), Trevisan (2021), and Vila Moreno (2020).

models, and the EU growth programs discussed data in some way. In the mid-2010s, the EU updated the Single Market growth strategy to contain the Digital Single Market. The Digital Single Market sought to improve access to digital goods, encourage innovation in digital networking, and to elicit more of the economic potential in digital technology.[31] In more recent iterations of EU digital growth adjustments, EU Commission President van der Leyen announced two new acts: the Digital Services Act (DSA) and the Digital Markets Act (DMA), designed to marry continued guarantees of fundamental human rights during the use of digital services, with measures to "establish a level playing field to foster innovation, growth, and competitiveness, both in the European Single Market and globally."[32] The practical developments inside the DSA and DSM have yet to be realized, but will be key areas to watch for potential changes to the EU's digital human rights regime.

Data Utility and the Digital Human Rights of Social Media Platforms

Thanks to the Cambridge Analytica scandal, the public and governments are aware of how online behaviors and the data of social media users could be harvested and used during major political campaign targeting.[33] Texas Senator and presidential candidate, Ted Cruz, hired Cambridge Analytica to achieve campaign advantages during his 2016 bid to win the Republican nomination for US presidential candidate. After the accompanying negative media attention broke over the unethically obtained data used for the targeting, Facebook announced plans to incorporate end-to-end encryption on the platforms it owns—Facebook, WhatsApp, and Instagram,[34] and created an "Oversight Board," tasked with evaluating posted content in light of freedom of expression, yet being willing to remove content that violates existing laws.[35]

[31] Europa (2020).

[32] Europa (2021).

[33] Detrow (2018).

[34] Newton (2019).

[35] Facebook (2021).

> The purpose of the board is to promote free expression by making principled, independent decisions regarding content on Facebook and Instagram and by issuing recommendations on the relevant Facebook company content policy.
>
> When fully staffed, the board will consist of 40 members from around the world that represent a diverse set of disciplines and backgrounds. These members will be empowered to select content cases for review and to uphold or reverse Facebook's content decisions.
>
> The board is not designed to be a simple extension of Facebook's existing content review process. Rather, it will review a select number of highly emblematic cases and determine if decisions were made in accordance with Facebook's stated values and policies.[36]

At the heart of the debate is how to define social media companies, and the internet spaces they birth. Is the internet an expanded free speech space, similar to the town square, but online? If the answer is yes, then governments may force content controls designed to forego hate speech and criminal practices. However, what if the internet is not just a public space located online, but is rather a part of the private sector, existing to generate profits as with any other corporate entity? Then Facebook, Twitter, and Instagram may exert their own preferences on leaving content accessible to the public if it is profitable to do so. Most important to the argument in this book—they will keep collecting, collating, and selling personal, digitized data for profit. If they keep such levels of freedom, social media firms and platforms will hold vast quantities of personal data, and continue to use personal data harvesting algorithms based on the goal of data profiteering. This is but one possible way that non-state actors will contribute to diverse types of DHR across the global landscape.

Final Thoughts

The European Union has chosen to cultivate a reputation as a human rights powerhouse. Data protection began as an economically driven endeavor, yet evolved into a regime for digital human rights. Through consistent, and ever-widening legislation, EU institutions formalized

[36] Facebook (2021).

these rights and have consistently supported this legislation with oversight monitoring and legal sanctions against violators, inside and outside the EU. There are no signs that the European Union will backtrack on the regime of digital human rights. What it does face is the challenges posed by ever-changing technology, other states' divergent preferences for data treatment, and perhaps most importantly, a growing intention by tech firms to develop their own norms for digitized data management.

The path taken from economic concerns to human rights to securitization of data will continue to challenges human rights provision in Europe and beyond. Yet, broad-based legislation to address tech-based human rights, be it in national constitutions or EU legislation, is absent in many states outside of the EU. Due to the complexity of technology and uses for digitized, personal data, countries attempting to fill the legislative gap need to design laws that cover a broad-range of tech: AI, internet, social media, biometrics, security surveillance, robotics, and border management. Building broad-based legislation to address these areas is difficult, and requires a multistakeholder approach. Proactive measures, rather than reactive, give governments more control over the content. If states without a comprehensive law for protecting digital human rights continue to rely on reactive policy-making, the private sector will maintain more control over data use, and other tech use as relates to DHR and personal, digitized data. Digital human rights, as with all human rights, is fragile, and are always subject to change, sometimes for the better, sometimes for the worse.

Bibliography

Binnig, Christian E., and Christopher S. Comstock. 2019. *The California Consumer Privacy Act: The First Step Towards an American GDPR?* https://www.americanbar.org/groups/infrastructure-regulated-industries/publications/infrastructure/2018-2019/summer/the-california-consumer-privacy-act-first-step-towards-american-gdpr/.

Bond, Shannon. 2021. *Facebook, Twitter, Google CEOs Testify Before Congress: 4 Things To Know*, March 25. Accessed June 5, 2021. https://www.npr.org/2021/03/25/980510388/facebook-twitter-google-ceos-testify-before-congress-4-things-to-know.

Bowler, Tim. 2020. *Huawei: Why is it being banned from the UK's 5G network?* July 14. Accessed June 3, 2021. https://www.bbc.com/news/newsbeat-47041341.

Cartwright, Madison. 2020. "Internationalising State Power Through the Internet: Google, Huawei and Geopolitical Struggle." *Internet Policy Review* 9 (3): 1–19.

Center for Strategic & International Studies. 2021. *Significant Cyber Incidents.* Washington, DC: Strategic Technologies Program.

de Hert, Paul, and Vagelis Papakonstantinou. 2015. *The Data Protection Regime in China.* LIBE Committee , Policy Department C: Citizens' Rights and Constitutional Affairs, Directorate General for Internal Policies, 1–36. Strasbourg: European Parliament.

Deere, Stephen. 2019. *Cost of City of Atlanta's Cyber Attack: $2.7 Million—And Rising*, October 1. Accessed June 1, 2020. https://www.ajc.com/news/cost-city-atlanta-cyber-attack-million-and-rising/nABZ3K1AXQYvY0vxqfO1FI/.

Detrow, Scott. 2018. *What Did Cambridge Analytica Do During The 2016 Election?*, March 20. Accessed May 30, 2021. https://www.npr.org/2018/03/20/595338116/what-did-cambridge-analytica-do-during-the-2016-election.

Europa. 2020. *Shaping the Digital Single Market.* October 29. Accessed June 1, 2021. https://ec.europa.eu/digital-single-market/en/shaping-digital-single-market.

———. 2021. *Coronavirus: Commission proposes a Digital Green Certificate*, March 17. Accessed June 2, 2021. https://ec.europa.eu/commission/presscorner/detail/en/IP_21_1181.

———. 2021. *The Digital Services Act Package*, April 26. Accessed June 3, 2021. https://digital-strategy.ec.europa.eu/en/policies/digital-services-act-package.

Facebook. 2021. *Ensuring Respect for Free Expression, Through Independent Judgment*, June 1. https://oversightboard.com/.

Guzman, Daniela. 2019. *China's Billions Are Powering Latin America's Tech Boom*, January 8. Accessed June 2, 2021. https://www.bloomberg.com/news/articles/2019-01-08/guess-who-s-behind-latin-america-s-tech-boom-china-of-course.

Hollande, François. 2013. *French White Paper: Defence and National Security.* Paris: République Française.

IAPP. 2018. *New California Privacy Law to Affect 500,000 U.S. Organizations*, July/August. Accessed June 2021. https://iapp.org/news/a/new-california-privacy-law-to-affect-more-than-half-a-million-us-companies/.

Kaska, Kadri, Henrik Beckvard, and Tomáš Minárik. 2019. *Huawei, 5G and China as a Security Threat.* Tallinn: Nato Cooperative Cyber Defence Centre of Excellence (CCDCOE).

Kuhn, Anthony. 2020. *South Korea's Tracking of COVID-19 Patients Raises Privacy Concerns*, May 2. Accessed June 2, 2021. https://www.npr.org/2020/05/02/849535944/south-koreas-tracking-of-covid-19-patients-raises-privacy-concerns.

Liang, Fan, Vishnupriya Das, Nadiya Kostyuk, and Muzammil M. Hussain. 2018. "Constructing a Data-Driven Society: China's Social Credit System as a State Surveillance Infrastructure." *Policy & Internet* 10 (4): 415–453.

Livingston, Scott, and Graham Greenleaf. 2017. "PRC's New Data Export Rules: 'Adequacy with Chinese Characteristics'?" *Privacy Laws & Business International Report*, 9–12.

Longo, Matthew. 2018. *The Politics of Borders: Sovereignty, Security, and the Citizen After 9/11*. Cambridge: Cambridge University Press.

Maizland, Lindsay, and Andrew Chatsky. 2020. *Huawei: China's Controversial Tech Giant*, August 6. Accessed June 3, 2021. https://www.cfr.org/backgrounder/huawei-chinas-controversial-tech-giant.

McGowan, Casey J. 2014. "The Relevance of Relevance: Section 215 of the USA PATRIOT Act and the NSA Metadata Collection Program." *Fordham Law Review* 82 (5): 2399–2442.

Nakashima, Ellen, and Craig Timberg. 2020. *Russian Government Hackers Are Behind a Broad Espionage Campaign That Has Compromised U.S. Agencies, Including Treasury and Commerce*, December 14. Accessed June 1, 2020. https://www.washingtonpost.com/national-security/russian-government-spies-are-behind-a-broad-hacking-campaign-that-has-breached-us-agencies-and-a-top-cyber-firm/2020/12/13/d5a53b88-3d7d-11eb-9453-fc36ba051781_story.html.

Newton, Casey. 2019. *Mark Zuckerberg Says Facebook Will Shift to Emphasize Encrypted Ephemeral Messages*, March 6. Accessed June 1, 2021. https://www.theverge.com/2019/3/6/18253458/mark-zuckerberg-facebook-privacy-encrypted-messaging-whatsapp-messenger-instagram.

Pernot-Leplay. 2020. "China's Approach on Data Privacy Law: A Third Way between the U.S. and E.U.?" *Penn State Journal of Law & International Affairs* 8 (1): 49–117.

Schwartz, Paul M. 2019. "Global Data Privacy: The EU Way." *New York University Law Review* 94 (3): 101–146.

Scolford, Mark. 2021. *Vaccine Passport Efforts Draw Opposition from GOP Lawmakers*, April 4. Accessed June 2, 2021. https://www.latimes.com/world-nation/story/2021-04-04/vaccine-passport-efforts-draw-opposition-from-gop-lawmakers.

The National Law Review. 2020. California Passes Prop 24: Here Comes CCPA 2.0. Vers. Volume XI, Number 152, November 5. Accessed June 1, 2021. https://www.natlawreview.com/article/california-passes-prop-24-here-comes-ccpa-20.

———. 2021. Virginia Passes Second-in-the-Nation Comprehensive Consumer Data Privacy Law. Vers. Volume XI, Number 152, March 13. Accessed June 1 2021. https://www.natlawreview.com/article/virginia-passes-second-nation-comprehensive-consumer-data-privacy-law.

Trevisan, Claudia. 2021. *China's Growing Trade and Investment in Latin America Outpaces Its Influence in the Region's Media and Civil Society*, January 19. Accessed June 3, 2021. https://www.cfr.org/blog/chinas-growing-trade-and-investment-latin-america-outpaces-its-influence-regions-media-and.

Vila Moreno, Miquel. 2020. *China Adapts to a Changing Latin America*, March 13. Accessed June 1, 2021. https://thediplomat.com/2020/03/china-adapts-to-a-changing-latin-america/.

Warren, Elizabeth. 2019. *Here's How We Can Break Up Big Tech*, March 8. Accessed June 2, 2021. https://medium.com/@teamwarren/heres-how-we-can-break-up-big-tech-9ad9e0da324c.

Washington Post. 2018. Transcript of Mark Zuckerberg's Senate Hearing, April 10. Accessed May 30, 2021. https://www.washingtonpost.com/news/the-switch/wp/2018/04/10/transcript-of-mark-zuckerbergs-senate-hearing/.

Zuboff, Shoshana. 2015. "Big Other: Surveillance Capitalism and the Prospects of an Information Civilization." *Journal of Information Technology* 30: 75–89.

———. 2019. *The Age of Surveillance Capitalism: The Fight for the Future at the New Frontier of Power*. London: Profile Books.

Index

R. Dowd, *The Birth of Digital Human Rights*, Information Technology and Global Governance,
https://doi.org/10.1007/978-3-030-82969-8

W

Y

The manufacturer's authorised representative in the EU is Springer Nature Customer Service Centre GmbH, Europaplatz 3, 69115 Heidelberg, Germany. If you have any concerns regarding our products, please contact ProductSafety@springernature.com

Printed and bound by CPI Group (UK) Ltd, Croydon, CR0 4YY
30/09/2026
02225702-0012